Getting
AHEAD
in a Just-Gettin'-By World

BUILDING YOUR RESOURCES
FOR A BETTER LIFE

Philip E. DeVol

Table of Contents

Acknowledgments

Getting Ahead™ graduates constantly push the envelope of learning. Hardly a day goes by that someone isn't lighting up the computer screen with new ideas and deeper, more relevant applications of our work. Bonnie Bazata, director of the Bridges™ initiative in South Bend, IN, called Getting Ahead the "high-octane fuel in the tank" because it drives communities forward.

The explosion of learning in Bridges initiatives and the development of Getting Ahead (GA) can be attributed largely to investigators. Thanks to all of you for sharing your insights and for the wonderful ways you have of expressing your ideas.

GA grads in Syracuse, NY: Nelly Figuera, Diane Miller, Winter Outlaw, Louise Randell, Kathleen Rudy, and Na Tonya Speights

GA grads in South Bend, IN: Rain Adams, Tonjohnique Coppage, Debra Haynes, Dorrine A. Henderson, Valeria Huston, Gloriatine D. Jones, Marilyn K. Lassiter, Daniel J. McLemore, Aholibama Manriquez, Courtney Redmond, Clara Ross, Denise Singh, Michael Singh, Kimberly Smith, Thomas H. Verse, Roy Walker, and Wanda Wheat

In addition, there were a number of GA grads from CPWD (Center for People with Disabilities) in Longmont, CO, who helped with the new community assessment (I hope your ideas are fairly represented!).

GA graduates who have become facilitators play a vital role in delivering and improving Getting Ahead. For all the help they have given me and their communities, I'd like to thank:

Carlos Guajardo and Sonia Holycross in Ohio; Maria Lacey in Idaho; and Debra L. Haynes, A. Baye Sylvester, Leonard Talton, Ana Villareal, Amber Werner, and Lori Whaley in Indiana

Facilitators play a central part in the lives of many investigators. The success of Getting Ahead truly lies in their hands. For your advice and support, thanks go to:

Ruth Andrews, LaTasha Bosse, Nikki Crooks, April English-Palozzola, Venice A. Ervin, Karen Ford, Joe Gerace, Leon Heimberger, Angela Huettl, Kathy Kurosky, Mickie Lewis, Autumn McCully, Nancy Murton, Chris Parsons, Annette Snider, Karen Sommers, Jenny Steinmetz, and Peggy Woods

It was especially helpful to meet with and learn from people who are funders, sponsors, and partners within a Bridges initiative. I appreciate the feedback and support given by:

Chris Nanni from the Community Foundation of St. Joseph County, IN, and Marce Bingham, LaTosha Bosse, Phil Damico, Joan Fischer, Lin Goss, Raquel Harris, Marilyn K. Lassiter, Daniel J. McLemore, Anolibama Mannquez, Jaime Murphy, Courtney Redmond, Denise Singh, Michael Singh, Stacey Toth, Anita Veldman, Lori Whaley, and Luis Zapata, all of whom are business-sector partners in St. Joseph County, IN

Board members take on the responsibility of providing Getting Ahead in their communities and use their heads and their hearts to help improve the economic stability of people and communities. For all of their efforts, I'd like to thank:

Evon M. Ervin, Lindy Glennon, Susanne Merchant, Mary Pagan, Liz Page, Carrie Penner, Ted Finlayson Schueler, and Sheila Sicilia in Syracuse, NY; and Barbara Duncanson, Jenny Dunville, Judith Johns, Nancy King, and David Vanderveen in South Bend, IN

In every community there are catalysts who develop Getting Ahead and Bridges initiatives. In my visits to two Getting Ahead sites I learned from these champions:

Angela Douglas and Marisol Hernandez in Syracuse, NY, and Bonnie Bazata in South Bend, IN

Thanks for all the great things you have done for your communities.

In addition to the United States, Getting Ahead is being used in Australia, Canada, and Slovakia. Thanks to the following for adapting Getting Ahead for their country and for encouraging me to be more inclusive in this edition.

In Australia, Marie McLeod; in Canada, Glenda Clarke, Cheryl Hitchen, Gayle Montgomery, and Mary Jane Murray; and in Slovakia, Marian Baca, Bill Baker, Judita Gogova, Pavel Hansut, Miroslav Pollak, and Judita Varcholova for adapting Getting Ahead principles and Denisa Francanova for translating *Getting Ahead in a Just-Gettin'-By World* and *Bridges Out of Poverty* into Slovak

Getting Ahead wouldn't have been even a dream if it weren't for Ruby Payne, who has been supportive of my efforts from the first day we met in the mid- to late 1990s. Many thanks to her and the team at aha! Process: Ruth Weirich, president and fellow traveler; Peggy Conrad, for her calming and reassuring management of this (and other) publications; and designer Paula Nicolella and marketing specialist Stephanie Burgevin for their help with this book.

An editor can make or break an author. In this case, I think Dan Shenk of CopyProof, Goshen, IN, has been the making of me.

And for the new design and artwork contained in this edition, I want to thank Rajan Kose of Standing Stone Productions, Boulder, CO.

Two special colleagues have figuratively held my hand, responded to hundreds of phone calls and e-mails, and offered support (and sympathy) throughout this effort to whom I'll be forever grateful. They are:

Karla Krodel of Youngstown State University, Youngstown, OH; and Bonnie Bazata, director of the St. Joseph County Bridges Out of Poverty Initiative in South Bend, IN

Finally, I'd like to thank my wife, Susan, for potty training the new puppy (successfully, for the most part) while I worked on the book, cooking great meals to keep my brain cells churning (so, what really was that green stuff you fed me?), keeping our social schedule to a minimum (but allowing me to sleep undisturbed at the concert), and helping out on the editing (so I wasn't quite as embarrassed to hand this over to Dan).

Introduction

The workbook *Getting Ahead in a Just-Gettin'-By World: Building Your Resources for a Better Life* is for people who are living in poverty or unstable situations. It's about building economic stability for ourselves. It's about a better future for our communities.

In Getting Ahead we study poverty and near poverty through the **lens of economic class*** to better understand how our society and the economy work. In groups of 6–12 people, we investigate the impact that poverty and low wages have on us and what it takes to move from a just-getting-by world to a getting-ahead world. The idea of "getting ahead" means action and movement—getting ahead of where we are now, toward a future that we really want.

> * NOTE: All asterisks in this workbook refer to vocabulary words and phrases that will be defined at the end of each section—this introduction and the 10 modules. Some of these words and phrases may already be familiar, but a number of them have special meanings in the context of this work.

The first edition of *Getting Ahead in a Just-Gettin'-By World* was published in 2004 and has been used in many communities in the United States, Canada, Australia, and Slovakia. Thousands of people have already used this learning experience to take charge of their future. Many Getting Ahead (GA) graduates have stabilized their lives and built their financial, educational, and social resources as a result of the investigations sparked by this workbook. They also have begun working with others to deal with poverty at the community level. GA graduates have developed a voice in poverty issues and are now at the decision-making tables in many communities.

Getting Ahead is almost certainly going to be different from any educational experience you've ever had. In Getting Ahead you will be the expert regarding your life, the person with information that others need, and a problem solver in your own life, as well as in the community. No one is going to tell you what to do or think. No one is going to "assess" you, evaluate you, or hand you a plan.

Getting Ahead is about your future story. We're all living out the stories of our lives. Part of each person's story comes from the past, from where and how we live, from the people in our lives, from history, and from world or national events. Just as who we are today was decided by what we did yesterday, who we'll be tomorrow is decided by what we do today. Whether we know it or not, we're all creating our future stories right now. Getting Ahead is one tool you can use to help create your future story.

In 1999 Ruby Payne, Terie Dreussi Smith, and I wrote *Bridges Out of Poverty*. It was for people who work in social services, healthcare, workforce development, criminal justice, and community development. We spent most of our time presenting our ideas to people in those organizations. In 2001 I began meeting with people in poverty to see what they thought of our ideas. It was by listening to them that I developed and wrote *Getting Ahead in a Just-Gettin'-By World*. The people who have gone through Getting Ahead changed our understanding of poverty and showed us what to do about it.

Getting Ahead is going to be hard work. No one will be lecturing or teaching in typical ways, which means the learning has to be done by you and the group. In Getting Ahead you will be an investigator. That defines you as someone who digs for the facts and doesn't settle for the obvious answer. Investigators look for the truth.

The triangle you see below is a symbol that includes, in capsule form, everything we'll be doing. The facilitator will make a large copy of the triangle so the group can refer to it as we move through the workbook. Once you've learned what each section of the triangle means, it will be a quick and easy way to tell where we've been, where we're going, and how it all fits together. To understand what we'll be doing, let's start at the bottom of the triangle and work our way to the top.

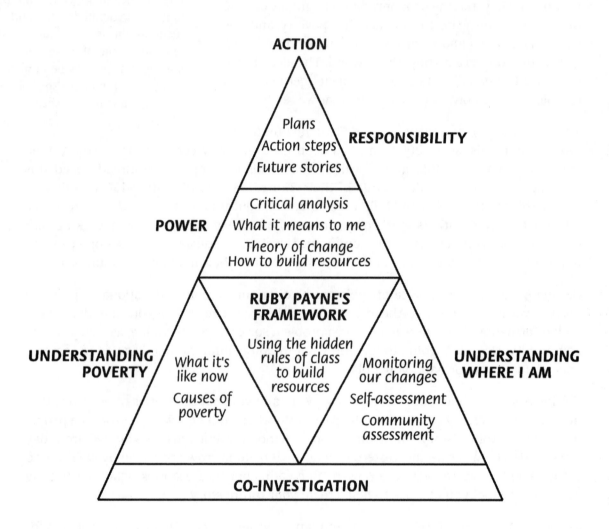

Bottom of Triangle: Co-Investigation

Everyone in Getting Ahead is an investigator. That includes the facilitator, who doesn't have all the answers and will be learning along with everyone else. The facilitator is guiding the group but is also part of the group. Together, the group will co-investigate every part of the Triangle. Sometimes the group will study big issues that affect all people, while at other times we will focus on our own unique experiences.

The idea of co-investigation has been embraced by sponsors (the agencies that organize and host Getting Ahead workgroups) and community groups. Many, like the Bridges

Steering Committees, work closely with GA investigators after they graduate. The GA grads might say, "We are co-investigating the barriers that ex-felons from poverty encounter when trying to find employment." By this they mean that all economic classes are involved in the work.

One of the unique features of Getting Ahead and Bridges initiatives is that the members solve problems by acting as co-investigators. In this way people from all classes have something to offer, and everyone is a problem solver. Co-investigation is the foundation of Getting Ahead work.

Bottom Left of Triangle: Understanding Poverty

We'll spend quite a bit of time investigating what poverty is, what it's like for us personally, and what it's like for our community. The investigations into understanding poverty will be guided by the following modules:

Module 1—My Life Now

We'll define what poverty is like in our community in great detail, and we'll draw a mental model titled "*Mental Model** of Poverty." After investigating our personal situations, we'll each make a mental model called "My Life Now."

Module 3—The Rich/Poor Gap and Research on the Causes of Poverty

To better understand poverty, we have to understand it from different perspectives. This section introduces areas of research that tell part of the story. We'll learn that poverty is about much more than just the choices individuals make. Plans made by individuals, organizations, and communities need to take into account *all* the causes of poverty.

Center of Triangle: Ruby Payne's 'Framework'

This section of the workbook is based on a framework for understanding economic class that was first described by Dr. Ruby K. Payne in the mid-1990s. Her work has been helping teachers do a better job, so that children from poverty do better in school. Payne's hidden rules of economic class can be used to build relationships of mutual respect, help us navigate new environments, and build resources.

Module 4—Hidden Rules of Economic Class

The wealthy, the middle class, and the poor: Every group has its own hidden rules. If we decide to take steps to build economic stability, we have to know and be able to use the hidden rules of middle class. If a person wants to get out of the middle class, he/she has to know and be able to use the hidden rules of wealth. In short, if we want to understand people from different classes, we need to be able to understand and use their hidden rules when the situation calls for it.

Module 5—The Importance of Language

Language is especially important because language can make or break relationships. Language is used for learning and to resolve conflicts. "Formal register" and the language of *negotiation** are powerful tools when dealing with people in the middle class and wealth.

Module 6—Eleven Resources

Poverty is defined as "the extent to which an individual does without resources"; it's not just how much income or wealth we have. A high quality of life includes other resources, such as good physical health, a rich social and emotional life, and more. This definition gives us something to do about poverty: Build resources.

Bottom Right of Triangle: Understanding Where I Am

Having investigated poverty, it's time to apply the information.

Module 2—*Theory of Change**

Building economic stability means making some changes. Whatever plans you make, they should be yours and not someone else's. This module shows us how you can take charge of your changes, and it gives you a way to monitor how you are doing.

Module 7—Self-Assessment of Resources

Most agencies evaluate or assess people in some way. In Getting Ahead, you conduct a self-assessment of your own resources. This self-assessment is even more beneficial because you can include everything, not just one part of your life, and you do it for yourself, rather than having it done for you or to you. This self-assessment is the foundation for the personal plan for economic security that you will soon create.

Module 8—Community Assessment

In this module we complete the work we began in Module 3 by doing an assessment of community resources. This is the foundation for our plan for community prosperity.

Center Section: Power

In this section we reflect back on everything we've learned. When we see the bigger picture, we can do a critical analysis and figure out what it means to us and what we want to do about our particular personal situations. With the information we have, we can gain power—both in our own lives and in our communities.

Module 2—Theory of Change

Here we revisit Module 2. The Getting Ahead Theory of Change helps free us from being in the cycle of solving the same problems again and again. When we are in a safe place, have time to think, and can come up with new ideas, we're able to take charge of our lives.

Module 9—Building Resources

Building resources is virtually the only way to establish economic stability, but it's hard to do. If it were easy, we wouldn't be getting together like this. The thinking we do here will be used when you make your individual plan.

Top Section of Triangle: Responsibility

Module 10—Personal and Community Plan

This is when you develop a detailed plan that will move you toward your future story. This plan develops naturally from everything you've done so far. You will create a "Mental Model of My Future Story," and the group will create a "Mental Model of Community Prosperity."

As you work through the modules, you will develop a "Future Story Portfolio." This is basically a folder of all your work (mental models, worksheets, reflections, and, of course, your plans).

Top of Triangle: Action (Getting Started on Your Future Story)

Information about how GA graduates have supported each other is found in the websites mentioned in Appendix J of the *Getting Ahead* workbook. It also describes some of the support strategies developed by sponsors, communities, and other organizations. Your sponsor will let you know about the supports in place in your community. Those plans may have been developed with the help of GA graduates from the first classes. Or, it could be that your group will need to help design the supports for those in the group—and those who follow you.

Taking Part in Getting Ahead

We know that everyone has experiences, skills, and talents that can be used to help others and the community, so we need you to share your ideas, thoughts, and feelings with the group. About half of the learning that you get out of Getting Ahead comes from the content of the workbook. The other half will result from the discussions you have around the table.

For the best possible learning experience, the group members need to be accountable to each other. Your input and the input of the others are crucial to the success of Getting Ahead. You want to be accountable to yourself first, then to the group for attending every session, being on time, doing your share of the investigations, and participating in the discussions.

You are the reason Getting Ahead works. As always, it's going to be an adventure!

Best wishes.

Phil DeVol

---

*Vocabulary List for the Introduction

Lens of economic class: examining poverty and prosperity by focusing primarily on economic information and class issues instead of age, gender, race, ethnicity, disability, sexual orientation, all of which are valid lenses

Mental models: pictures in the mind that help us learn quickly and remember longer

Negotiation: ways to reach an agreement

Theory of change: a system of ideas intended to explain how something happens

My Life Now

Poverty is experienced differently in every city, county, and country. We begin Getting Ahead by describing and defining what poverty is like in our community.

WHAT'S COVERED

We will:

Learn what a mental model is

Investigate what poverty is like in your community

Make a Mental Model of Poverty

Make a "Mental Model of Floor Plan of My Apartment/House"

Investigate income and wage information

Figure personal financial indicators

Make a "Mental Model of My Life Now"

Investigate "Where Does the Time Go?"

WHY IT'S IMPORTANT

It's important that we start with what is real. To do that we have to listen to each other and ask tough questions. Everything you do in Getting Ahead is based on having a true and accurate picture of what life is like.

It's also important that we investigate community issues that relate to poverty (like wages and the cost of housing) because poverty isn't just about the choices an individual makes.

Almost every agency you go to will have a plan for you. Going through this workbook is the first step in creating your own plan.

HOW IT'S CONNECTED TO YOU

These are the first mental models you will create. We will use mental models throughout the workbook.

You will use the Mental Model of My Life Now to show where you are now. This marks the beginning of your journey to a future story.

You'll first investigate your community and personal situation. You'll also learn some indicators of financial stability.

Mental Models—Background

We need to begin by explaining what we mean by mental models because we'll be using mental models from here on out. Mental models are pictures in the mind that help us learn quickly and remember longer. They are usually in the form of a story, video, cartoon, *analogy**, *metaphor**, diagram, chart, or drawing. They help us see the whole picture with all of its parts. In this way we can understand complex issues without a lot of lectures or reading.

Think, for example, of weather reports on TV. It would take a long time to talk about everything that we can see in seconds just by looking at the symbols on the map.

Mental Model of Poverty

If we're going to do something about poverty, we had better know what we're talking about. In other words, we need an accurate, specific, and complete picture of poverty and instability in our community.

This is the first time we are going to act as *investigators*. Getting Ahead (GA) investigators are like police detectives or private investigators (PIs). GA investigators are curious. They don't settle for the obvious answer. They dig for information and the real story. As GA investigators, you will do the work of learning. You won't be waiting to have it handed to you. The facilitator is an investigator too and is sometimes referred to as a co-investigator.

See "Tips for Getting Ahead Investigators" in Appendix B. These tips may apply more to later activities than to the first one (below).

This activity is your first investigation. You are the experts who hold the information we seek, so you will be investigating your own knowledge. You are the experts on your community. Your knowledge about the realities of poverty is vital information. It needs to be examined and organized so that we can use the information throughout the Getting Ahead workshop.

We use mental models to learn quickly and remember longer.

As a group, you are going to describe what life is like for people who are living in poverty in your community. There are different levels of poverty and different levels of instability. Many people who are living just above the **Federal Poverty Guidelines*** are experiencing instability and stress. Include them in your thinking when you create the mental model.

Activity: Mental Model of Poverty

Time: 30 minutes
Materials: Chart paper, colored markers

Procedure:

1. At the top of the paper have a volunteer write: "Mental Model of Poverty"

2. Draw a circle on the page, leaving room all around the circle to add stuff later.

3. Discuss what it's like to live in or near poverty. Here are some questions that will help get you started:

   a. What are some of the problems a person in or near poverty has to solve?

   b. What do people in or near poverty worry about?

   c. Where does the most time and energy go?

   d. What happens in a typical week?

4. As you discuss life in poverty, have someone write in key words on the paper. You may want to make a copy for yourself in your Future Story Portfolio.

5. After discussing the questions below, come back to the mental model and add words and phrases around the outside of the circle that summarize your thinking about poverty.

6. When you are done, hang your mental model on the wall next to the Group Rules.

Discussion

1. What are the biggest problems for people in poverty? What problems take up the most time and energy? Does that make them the most important problems—or the most urgent and demanding?

2. How do people solve problems when living in very unstable situations or poverty? What strengths and skills are needed?

3. How is instability or poverty pretty much the same for everyone? How is it different?

4. Is poverty different in other communities in the state or nation? If so, what are some of the differences?

5. What are some of the things middle-class and wealthy people know about living in poverty? What are some things they don't know?

6. What is it about poverty that makes it hard to get out? What happens to someone who lives in poverty a long time?

7. Do you think the leaders in your community have seen mental models like this? What would be the value of having people like the mayor, police chief, or school superintendent have this information? List other community leaders, organizations, and associations that could use the information from these mental models.

8. Now that you have investigated the concrete experience of poverty, how would you summarize the environment of poverty? What observations can you make that describe or summarize your thinking about poverty?

Housing

The Mental Model of Poverty in the community is a general picture representing people in the community.

Now we're going to look into our own situations. Every investigator has his/her own story. Some of us may have been on public assistance a long time. Others may be in situational poverty and have only started using public assistance. Still others may be in near poverty and might be using only free and reduced lunch benefits for our children. In one way or another, all of us are probably struggling to get by.

If you want to do something about your situation, you'll need to examine it carefully so you can create a mental model of your life as it is now.

When we did the Mental Model of Poverty, we talked about housing and jobs in a general way. Now we're going to dig into the details of housing and wages.

The lack of affordable housing is one of the engines that drive chaos and insecurity. Some people have subsidized housing, while others are on their own to find housing they can afford. With the collapse of the housing bubble in recent years, many people are returning to live with relatives or crowding into apartments, houses, and trailers with friends. People are living in campgrounds, long-term motels, shelters, cars, and on the street.

Activity: Mental Model of Floor Plan of My Apartment/House

Time: 15 minutes
Materials: Paper and pen or pencil

Procedure: Draw the floor plan of the house or apartment where you are staying now (see an example below). Put the initials of everyone who sleeps in the house in the room where he/she sleeps.

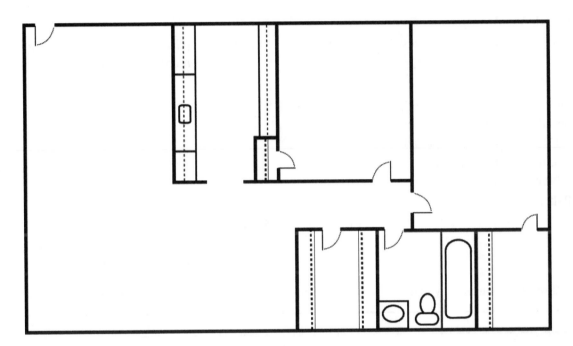

Discussion

1. What are the conditions of the house or apartment in terms of lighting, bathrooms, kitchen fixtures, furniture, and entertainment centers?

2. How many people are staying where you live? How many are related to you—and how many aren't?

3. Are people doubling up or "couch surfing"? If so, how many?

4. How does the living arrangement affect children?

Activity: Affordable Housing Payment Threshold Calculator

Time: 10 Minutes
Materials: Calculator

Procedure: Review the example, then enter your information in the "Actual" worksheet.

Example: Affordable Housing Payment Threshold

Calculation A		$4,000		
Monthly income (before taxes)	x 30%	$1,200	A.	Payment threshold is 30% of monthly income
Calculation B				
Monthly income (before taxes)		$4,000		
Monthly loan payments (car loans, school loans, other loans)	–	$500		
Monthly utility payments (phone, electric, water, etc.)	–	$300		
Balance	=	$3,200		
	x 35%	$1,120	B.	Payment threshold is 35% of monthly income minus loan and utility payments.

Affordable Housing Payment Threshold (enter the amount in A. or B., whichever is less): $1,120

Actual

Calculation A		$		
Monthly income (before taxes)	x 30%	$	A.	Payment threshold is 30% of monthly income
Calculation B				
Monthly income (before taxes)		$		
Monthly loan payments (car loans, school loans, other loans)	–	$		
Monthly utility payments (phone, electric, water, etc.)	–	$		
Balance	=	$		
	x 35%	$	B.	Payment threshold is 35% of monthly income minus loan and utility payments.

Affordable Housing Payment Threshold (enter the amount in A. or B., whichever is less): $ _____

Note. Worksheet provided courtesy of Paul J. Pfeiffer, MBA, CFP®.

Discussion

1. How much are you paying for housing now? How does that compare with the calculation you just did?

2. How does the housing payment recommended by the Affordable Housing Payment Threshold calculator compare with what the other GA investigators are paying?

3. How does this information relate to the recent housing crisis where you live?

If your cost of housing is more than 35% of your income, the next activity will help you figure how much you need to earn.

Wages

How much does your current job (or your last one, if you aren't working now) pay? How many hours a week do (or did) you work? What kind of job can you do that would earn enough to make the rent payment? What is the relationship between housing costs and wages?

The key questions are: "How much do we have to make an hour to afford the rent?" and "How much is left over for the rest of the expenses?"

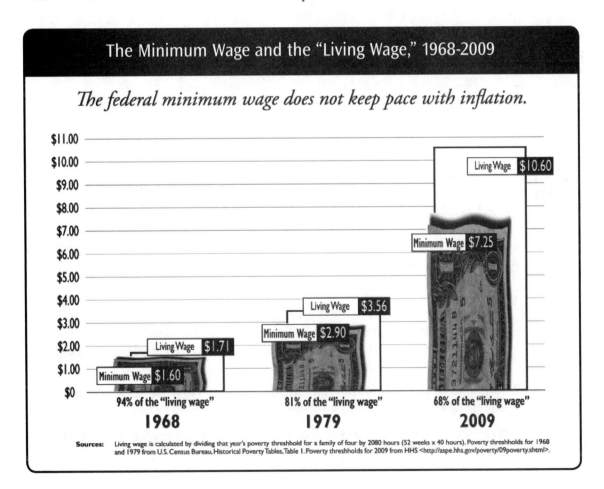

The Minimum Wage and the "Living Wage," 1968-2009

The federal minimum wage does not keep pace with inflation.

1968 — 94% of the "living wage" — Minimum Wage $1.60, Living Wage $1.71

1979 — 81% of the "living wage" — Minimum Wage $2.90, Living Wage $3.56

2009 — 68% of the "living wage" — Minimum Wage $7.25, Living Wage $10.60

Sources: Living wage is calculated by dividing that year's poverty threshhold for a family of four by 2080 hours (52 weeks x 40 hours). Poverty thresholds for 1968 and 1979 from U.S. Census Bureau, Historical Poverty Tables, Table 1. Poverty threshholds for 2009 from HHS <http://aspe.hhs.gov/poverty/09poverty.shtml>.

This graph looks at the federal minimum wage in 1968, 1979, and 2009 and compares it to the "living wage" in each of those years. A *living wage* is the hourly pay a full-time worker needs to lift his/her family of four up to the Federal Poverty Line. That is *only* up to the Federal Poverty Line. It could be called a "poverty wage."

The minimum wage is worth much less now than in 1968. The chart shows that in 1968 a minimum-wage worker was making only 11 cents less an hour below a living wage. By 2009 the gap had widened to $3.35 an hour!

Federal Poverty Guidelines: Family Size and Monthly Income, 2012								
Family Size	1	2	3	4	5	6	7	8
Poverty Line	$10,890	$14,710	$18,530	$22,350	$26,170	$29,990	$33,810	$37,630

Note. National Center for Appropriate Technology, www.ncat.org

We use life itself as the source of learning.

Activity: Getting Ahead or Just Getting By?

Time: 15 minutes
Materials: None

Calculate the hourly wage needed to pay the rent and have enough money left over to meet your other expenses.

Procedure:

1. How much do you earn? In the chart below find the full-time hourly wage (in Column 1) or the monthly income (in Column 3) that is closest to what you are earning now—or at your last job—or in a job you might be qualified for today (check the newspaper). *Circle that dollar amount.*

2. How much do you pay for housing? Next, in Column 5 find the dollar amount closest to what your rent or mortgage is now *in the 35% rows only.*

3. Now you can see what hourly or monthly wage you would need to be making to afford the rent.

Income Related to Cost of Housing

1 Hourly wage	2 Hours worked per month full time	3 Monthly income	4 Percentage of income for rent	5 Cost of rent	6 Money available for other expenses	7 How much more money is left over for other expenses when you pay 35% instead of 50% of your income for rent
$6	173	1,038	35%	363	675	156
			50%	519	519	
$7	173	1,211	35%	424	787	181
			50%	606	606	
$8	173	1,384	35%	484	900	208
			50%	692	692	
$9	173	1,557	35%	545	1,012	233
			50%	779	779	
$10	173	1,730	35%	606	1,125	260
			50%	865	865	
$11	173	1,903	35%	666	1,237	285
			50%	952	952	
$12	173	2,076	35%	727	1,349	311
			50%	1,038	1,038	

Note. Adapted from work of Glenn Corliss, Columbiana County (Ohio) One Stop.

Example of how to read the chart: If John worked eight hours a day, five days a week, he would be working an average of 173 hours a month. If he earned $7 an hour and his rent was 35% of his income, he would be paying $424 for rent and would have $787 left over for other expenses. If John paid 50% of his income on rent, he would be paying $606 for rent and have only $606 left over for other expenses. When paying rent at 35%, John would have an extra $181 to use for other expenses.

Discussion

1. What are the "other" expenses mentioned in Columns 6 and 7 that people have?

2. Discuss some ways that people can balance the wage/rent issue in the short term. How do people solve this problem?

3. Discuss some ways that people can solve the wage/rent problem in the long term.

4. What's the minimum wage in your state? How does it compare with the Federal Poverty Guidelines shown earlier?

5. How many people in your GA group are working more than one job? Or ever did?

6. How many hours do you have to work to fill the gas tank of your car?

7. How many of the employers of investigators in your GA group provide health insurance? Has that changed in recent years? If so, how?

Investigate This!

1. What is a living wage in your state or country? What is the self-sufficiency standard?

2. How much income does a single mom with an infant and a toddler need to cover housing, transportation, taxes, utilities, food, childcare, clothing, and healthcare costs without using any governmental support at all?

3. How many cities and counties have passed a living-wage ordinance? How many states have worked out the self-sufficiency standard for every county? Is there a self-sufficiency standard for your nation?

4. Where might you go to learn more about this?

Rules of Money

Very few people in the U.S. learn the rules of money in high school. In fact, many people never learn the rules of money.

The rules of money change with our age and stage of life. However, there are some basic measures of financial health that everyone should know, such as *debt-to-income (DTI) ratio**. There are two types of DTIs: The first is the percentage of income that goes to housing, which we've already investigated. The second covers all income and all debts and is called a *debt load**. A debt load of more than 37% is generally regarded as a sign of trouble.

In the housing bust that started in 2007, many people had a DTI of more than 37% and suffered for it. Most of them knew very little about mortgages, and many were taken advantage of because of their ignorance. But even Edmund L. Andrews, an economics reporter for the New York Times, got into trouble. On the strength of his credit rating he bought a home he couldn't afford. Despite the help of (or maybe because of) a loan officer from a mortgage corporation, Andrews plunged into a series of *go-go mortgages*, liar loans*, piggyback loans*,* and a *no-ratio mortgage** and ended up in foreclosure (Andrews, 2009).

Getting Ahead is not a course in *financial literacy**. It is designed to give you an idea of where you stand. Figuring your own DTI will open another window into your financial situation.

Activity: Calculating Your Debt-to-Income Ratio

Time: 20 minutes
Materials: Calculator

Procedure: Review the example, then fill in the worksheet with your information—and do the calculations.

Debt-to-Income Ratio: Example	
1. How much is your monthly rent or house payment?	$400
2. How much do you owe in car payments per month?	$100
3. How much do you pay on credit cards per month?	$50
4. How much do you pay for loans, payday lenders, lease/purchase per month?	$50
5. How much do you pay for renters/home insurance per month?	0
TOTAL DEBT: ITEMS 1–5	$600
6. How much gross income (before taxes and deductions) do you have per month?	$800
7. How much do you get in food stamps per month?	$50
8. How much child support do you get each month?	$200
TOTAL INCOME: ITEMS 6–8	$1,050
Divide your DEBT by your INCOME. This is your DEBT-TO-INCOME RATIO.	57.14 57%

Debt-to-Income Ratio	
1. How much is your monthly rent or house payment?	
2. How much do you owe in car payments per month?	
3. How much do you pay on credit cards per month?	
4. How much do you pay for loans, payday lenders, lease/purchase per month?	
5. How much do you pay for renters/home insurance per month?	
TOTAL DEBT: ITEMS 1–5	
6. How much gross income (before taxes and deductions) do you have per month?	
7. How much do you get in food stamps per month?	
8. How much child support do you get each month?	
TOTAL INCOME: ITEMS 6–8	
Divide your DEBT by your INCOME. This is your DEBT-TO-INCOME RATIO.	

Discussion

1. What DTI ratios do members of the group have?

2. What are some of the largest debts that people have?

3. To what extent are the rules of money taught in the schools in your state or country?

4. Do you think you need to learn more about the rules of money? Where could you go to learn more?

5. How does this information apply to you?

We use four words to show respect:
"What do you think?"

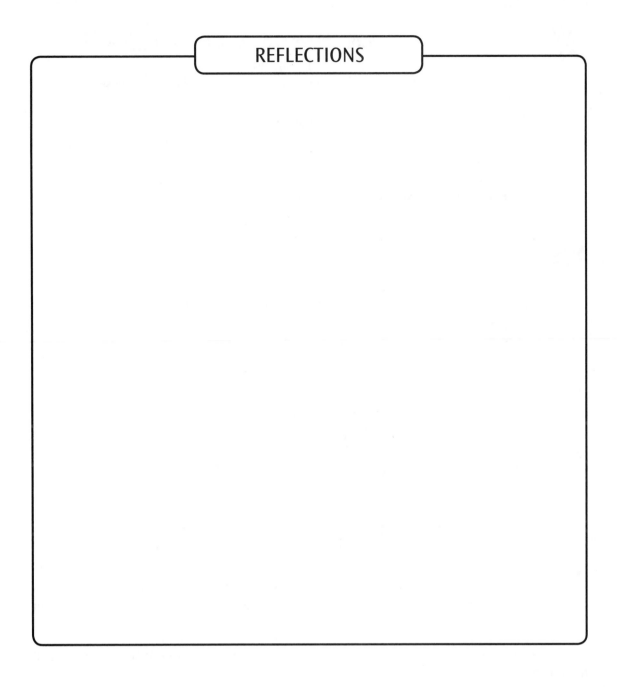

Mental Model of My Life Now

We began this module by investigating the impact poverty has on our community. Then we examined housing, wages, and financial aspects of our lives. These activities helped us focus on our individual situations—our lives as they are now.

In Getting Ahead we look at instability and poverty through the lens of economic class. But there are other lenses that are part of our experience. These include gender, race, ethnicity, disability, sexual identity, religion, and immigrant status. For example, how is poverty different for women than men? How does poverty impact children or the elderly? How is it different for people of color or people with disabilities? When you create your own mental model, include all the lenses that apply to you.

Activity: Personal Mental Model of My Life Now

Time: 30 minutes
Materials: Notebook paper and any other materials you choose

Procedure:

1. On a separate paper create the Mental Model of My Life Now.

2. Use any method and materials you like (drawings, charts, diagrams, stories, or poems) to illustrate what your life is like now. This mental model will go into your Future Story Project Portfolio, and you will be referring to it from time to time throughout the GA workshop experience.

Discussion

1. Share your mental models with one or two others (or the entire group, if you feel comfortable).

2. What was difficult or easy about making your mental model?

3. What stood out for you?

4. How was making these mental models useful to you?

5. What did you learn from your mental model?

Exploring How to Plan

Willem de Kooning, a Dutch American artist (1904–97) who also experienced extreme poverty, said, "The trouble with being poor is that it takes up all your time." Going back to the Mental Model of Poverty and the Mental Model of My Life Now, to what extent would you say that he was right?

The following investigation will help us see how we spend our time. What we learn will help us when we begin making plans.

For the next seven days, you will investigate exactly what you do with a week of your time (even if it isn't a completely typical week) by monitoring how you spend your time. This information is personal: Share with others only what feels comfortable.

Activity: Time Management—Where Does the Time Go?

Time: Five minutes, three times a day—morning, noon, and night for seven days
Materials: One Estimated Time vs. Actual Time chart (below)
and one weekly Time Monitor sheet

Procedure:

1. First, estimate how many hours a week you spend in the following activities, and record that in the second column.

2. Beginning today, fill in the Time Monitor sheets (see next two pages) with all your activities since you got out of bed in the morning.

Next to the time you got out of bed, write what you did first (for example, showering, shaving, and dressing could be shortened to "grooming").

Round off to the nearest 15-minute block. If you got up at 6:55 a.m., record that as 7 a.m.

Continue to record how you spend your time in 15-minute blocks.

3. Keep the Time Monitor with you and fill it in every few hours—or at least three times a day so you don't forget anything significant.

After seven days, add up the categories of time to see how much time you actually were in class, studying, with friends, and so on. Then record that in the third column of the *Estimated Time vs. Actual Time* table below.

Estimated Time vs. Actual Time

Activity	Estimated time spent in a week	Actual time spent in a week
Grooming		
Eating		
Classroom		
Studying		
Working		
On the Internet		
Traveling/commuting		
Watching TV		
With friends		
Childcare		
With family		
Church		
Clubs		
Sleeping		
Other		

Weekly Time Monitor

Monday ___ / ___ / ___		Tuesday ___ / ___ / ___		Wednesday ___ / ___ / ___	
7:00 7:15 7:30 7:45	7:00	7:00 7:15 7:30 7:45	7:00	7:00 7:15 7:30 7:45	7:00
8:00 8:15 8:30 8:45	8:00	8:00 8:15 8:30 8:45	8:00	8:00 8:15 8:30 8:45	8:00
9:00 9:15 9:30 9:45	9:00	9:00 9:15 9:30 9:45	9:00	9:00 9:15 9:30 9:45	9:00
10:00 10:15 10:30 10:45	10:00	10:00 10:15 10:30 10:45	10:00	10:00 10:15 10:30 10:45	10:00
11:00 11:15 11:30 11:45	11:00	11:00 11:15 11:30 11:45	11:00	11:00 11:15 11:30 11:45	11:00
12:00 12:15 12:30 12:45	12:00	12:00 12:15 12:30 12:45	12:00	12:00 12:15 12:30 12:45	12:00
1:00 1:15 1:30 1:45	1:00	1:00 1:15 1:30 1:45	1:00	1:00 1:15 1:30 1:45	1:00
2:00 2:15 2:30 2:45	2:00	2:00 2:15 2:30 2:45	2:00	2:00 2:15 2:30 2:45	2:00
3:00 3:15 3:30 3:45	3:00	3:00 3:15 3:30 3:45	3:00	3:00 3:15 3:30 3:45	3:00
4:00 4:15 4:30 4:45	4:00	4:00 4:15 4:30 4:45	4:00	4:00 4:15 4:30 4:45	4:00
5:00 5:15 5:30 5:45	5:00	5:00 5:15 5:30 5:45	5:00	5:00 5:15 5:30 5:45	5:00
6:00 6:15 6:30 6:45	6:00	6:00 6:15 6:30 6:45	6:00	6:00 6:15 6:30 6:45	6:00
7:00 7:15 7:30 7:45	7:00	7:00 7:15 7:30 7:45	7:00	7:00 7:15 7:30 7:45	7:00
8:00 8:15 8:30 8:45	8:00	8:00 8:15 8:30 8:45	8:00	8:00 8:15 8:30 8:45	8:00
9:00 9:15 9:30 9:45	9:00	9:00 9:15 9:30 9:45	9:00	9:00 9:15 9:30 9:45	9:00

Weekly Time Monitor

Thursday __/__/__		Friday __/__/__		Saturday __/__/__	
7:00 7:15 7:30 7:45	7:00	7:00 7:15 7:30 7:45	7:00		
8:00 8:15 8:30 8:45	8:00	8:00 8:15 8:30 8:45	8:00		
9:00 9:15 9:30 9:45	9:00	9:00 9:15 9:30 9:45	9:00		
10:00 10:15 10:30 10:45	10:00	10:00 10:15 10:30 10:45	10:00		
11:00 11:15 11:30 11:45	11:00	11:00 11:15 11:30 11:45	11:00		
12:00 12:15 12:30 12:45	12:00	12:00 12:15 12:30 12:45	12:00		
1:00 1:15 1:30 1:45	1:00	1:00 1:15 1:30 1:45	1:00		
2:00 2:15 2:30 2:45	2:00	2:00 2:15 2:30 2:45	2:00	**Sunday __/__/__**	
3:00 3:15 3:30 3:45	3:00	3:00 3:15 3:30 3:45	3:00		
4:00 4:15 4:30 4:45	4:00	4:00 4:15 4:30 4:45	4:00		
5:00 5:15 5:30 5:45	5:00	5:00 5:15 5:30 5:45	5:00		
6:00 6:15 6:30 6:45	6:00	6:00 6:15 6:30 6:45	6:00		
7:00 7:15 7:30 7:45	7:00	7:00 7:15 7:30 7:45	7:00		
8:00 8:15 8:30 8:45	8:00	8:00 8:15 8:30 8:45	8:00		
9:00 9:15 9:30 9:45	9:00	9:00 9:15 9:30 9:45	9:00		

*Vocabulary List for Module 1

Analogy (example): "Think of the heart as a very regular pump"

Debt-to-income (DTI) ratio: the percentage of income that goes to housing

Debt load: the second kind of DTI ratio that indicates the percentage of income that goes toward paying all recurring debt payments, including those covered by the first DTI, as well as other debts, such as credit-card payments, car-loan payments, student-loan payments, child-support payments, alimony payments, and legal judgments

Federal Poverty Guidelines: a series of dollar amounts, determined by the federal government, which are used as the basis for determining whether an individual or a family is in poverty

Financial literacy: knowing the rules of money as needed at all stages of life

Go-go mortgages, liar loans, piggyback loans, and no-ratio mortgages: In the go-go years of the U.S. housing boom, virtually anybody could get a few hundred thousand dollars to buy a home, and private lenders flooded the market, aggressively pursuing borrowers no matter their means or financial history; there are differences between *liar loans, piggyback loans, and no-ratio mortgages,* but they are in the same category

Metaphor (example): "I'm going to be toast when I get home"

Readings

Alexie, Sherman (2007). *The absolutely true diary of a part-time Indian.* New York, NY: Little, Brown and Company.

Childers, Mary. (2005). *Welfare brat: A memoir.* New York, NY: Bloomsbury Publishing.

Kiyosaki, Robert T., & Lechter, Sharon L. (1998). *Rich dad, poor dad.* Paradise Valley, AZ: TechPress.

Shipler, David K. (2004). *The working poor: Invisible in America.* New York, NY: Alfred A. Knopf.

Upchurch, Carl. (1996). *Convicted in the womb.* New York, NY: Bantam Books.

Wilkinson, Richard, & Pickett, Kate. (2009). *The spirit level: Why more equal societies almost always do better.* London, England: Penguin Group.

Theory of Change

When daily life is unpredictable and unstable, people can get caught up in solving problems all day long. Breaking out of that trap can lead to a new future story.

WHAT'S COVERED

We will:

Examine how we make changes

Understand the "righting reflex"

Investigate how organizations try to get people to change their behavior

Fill out the Stability Scale

Learn the Theory of Change for Getting Ahead

Learn the "Stages of Change"

WHY IT'S IMPORTANT

To move toward your future story and build resources will mean making some changes.

The Theory of Change in Getting Ahead can help free you from the *tyranny of the moment**.

Learning the Stages of Change will make it easier to make changes.

HOW IT'S CONNECTED TO YOU

Changes are harder to make when a person is living in an unstable environment.

Agencies have some of the resources that you may need. So you'll probably have to work with them—at least for a while.

It's important that you are in charge of the changes you make. This information helps you make changes and monitor yourself.

What About Change?

You just made the Mental Model of My Life Now. When you were doing that, did you think about making any changes? You might be happy with the way things are or you might want to do some things differently.

This module is necessary because making changes can be hard to make. Change can be hard even when we know that we need to, even when we want to. It's harder yet when someone else is pressuring us to change.

Some people say they hate change. They never want to change, they don't want things to change, and they don't want others to change. But even those who hate change ... change. There is truth in the saying: "The only thing that stays the same is change."

In Getting Ahead we will create a future story for ourselves. To make the future story come true, we need to be in charge of the changes we make.

Let's begin by investigating how changes and plans are handled by the agencies we use.

Activity: Examining Agency Approaches to Change

Time: 30 minutes

Materials: Chart paper, markers, Mental Model of Poverty from Module 1

Procedure:

1. Review the Mental Model of Poverty.

2. Identify agencies and programs in the community that work with people in poverty and near poverty. Examples might include schools, substance abuse treatment programs, mental health clinics, homeless shelters, food pantries, welfare-to-work agencies, probation/parole offices, and employment agencies.

3. Make a list on chart paper of the agencies and programs used by your family, neighbors, and the members of the group.

4. Now mark an "X" beside the name of any agency that requires you to make changes.

5. Mark a second "X" by any agency that helps you create plans for how to change (sometimes these plans are called treatment plans, agreements, contracts, or commitments).

Discussion

1. Are there any parts of the Mental Model of Poverty where there is no agency or organization available to assist people?

2. About what percentage of the agencies require people to make a plan for change?

3. How many organizations did you go to last year? How many of them made you work on a plan?

4. How do you feel when you look at the agencies surrounding the Mental Model of Poverty?

5. What have your "change" experiences been like with agencies? How much has your life changed as a result of being involved with these agencies?

Change Is Hard

Change is hard for everyone. But for those in low-wage jobs and poverty, it can be even harder. In unstable situations there are many barriers to change. Some barriers have to do with individual choices, while some come from family members and friends. Others come from the very agencies that people go to for help, and still others come from the community or society as a whole.

In this module we'll look at individual responsibility for change. In later modules we'll look at *systemic barriers**.

Here are some things to consider about change:

1. *The righting reflex*:* The righting reflex is when you see something that is wrong and you can see what it would take to "fix" it. In other words, "That's wrong, and I know how to fix it … and I'm going to tell you how to fix it!" There are two sides to the righting reflex: the helpful side and the annoying side.

Getting Ahead is agenda-free*.

The problem is that it's easier to see what's wrong in others than to see what's wrong in you. An example is if you see that the guy your niece is dating is not good for her. You think she should dump him and … you tell her so. You may see this as helpful, but she just sees it as annoying.

People who work at agencies can have a righting reflex too. The idea is that "you should" or "you ought" to get busy, get a job, go to school, quit smoking, and so on. Again, they see it as helpful, but you just see their advice as annoying, even irritating.

The righting reflex (even when someone is trying to be helpful) is often met with *psychological reactance**, which goes something like this: "I'm sick and tired of everyone telling me to quit drinking! If I want to kill myself by drinking, I will" (Miller & Rollnick, 2002, p. 18). "Psychological reactance" sometimes is expressed with a simple gesture: giving "the finger."

Happily the righting reflex also works in deeper ways. Inside all of us is that place where we know the difference between right and wrong. It's a powerful, internal guide or compass. People who live in unstable and stressful environments may not always be doing what others think is right. But usually they are doing the best they can with what they have. In Getting Ahead we trust that our internal compass will steer us toward our own best future story. We don't try to "fix" anyone.

People in the helping role would be wise to avoid the righting reflex. And individuals who are making a change would be wise to overcome their psychological reactance. After all, when people come together to solve problems, it's better if they're on the same team.

2. **Paying for change:** Many agencies and organizations that serve people in distress or in poverty want and/or require them to change. Their funding sources want to see results from their investments. The agencies are paid for the changes they achieve. That means that clients are expected to change the way they think and behave.

Exceptions to this would be funding and programming for people who need support for a long time or for the rest of their lives. These are people who cannot support themselves because of age, illness, or disability.

3. **Theories of change:** Behind the plans agencies and programs create is a theory of change. A theory of change basically describes what a program does and why agency staff members think it's going to make a difference.

Following are just a few of the approaches—or models—that agencies use to help clients change. Some models are very sophisticated and are based on research.

Others are based on best practices. Some are based on good *intentions** or common sense without much evidence that they work. Most of these models have value, but they also have some shortcomings.

a. *Education model:* If we're given accurate information (an education), then we'll change.

b. *Support model:* If we're given support that removes barriers to participating (like transportation, childcare, etc.), then we'll change.

c. *Access model:* If a program is designed so we can participate, then we should be able to change.

d. *Incentive model:* If we're aware of the benefits of change, then we'll be motivated to try new behaviors.

e. *Sanctions model:* If it's painful or we feel personally threatened by a problem, then we'll be willing to change.

f. *Skilled self-interest model:* If we have the skills or abilities to change and the benefits outweigh the costs, then we'll change.

g. *Accountability model:* If we're held accountable for our choices and behaviors, then we'll change.

h. *Redemption model:* If we believe in _____ and pray, _____ will provide what we need or want.

Discussion

1. Do you have experience with any of the change models described above?

2. Which experiences were positive? Which experiences were negative? What made the difference?

3. Can you picture yourself going to an organization and asking, "What is your theory of change?" To what extent will knowing an agency's theory of change make a difference?

Stability and Change

Getting Ahead is for people in poverty and those living in unstable situations. The following activity will help us determine where we are on the Stability Scale.

Activity: Stability Scale

Time: 20 Minutes
Materials: Pen or pencil

Procedure:

1. Read through the Stability Scale Indicators below.

2. For each indicator (time, housing, etc.) circle one of the five descriptions that best describes your situation.

3. Count the circled items in each column. Determine which column has the most circled items.

4. Mark an "X" on the following Getting Ahead continuum that represents the stability factor in your life now.

Stability Scale Indicators					
	Extremely Unstable 1	Unstable 2	Fairly Stable 3	Stable/Secure 4	Very Stable 5
Time horizon	I can't see past today	I can plan and complete goals 2 to 8 weeks into the future	I can plan and meet goals 2 to 24 months into the future	I can plan and meet goals 2 to 4 years into the future	I can plan and meet goals 5 to 50 years into the future
Housing	I have no housing or rely on others for temporary housing solutions	I have uncertain housing and spend more than 35% of my income on housing	I have secure housing and spend about 35% of my income on housing	I have assured housing and spend 30% or less of my income on housing	I am buying my house and my mortgage payment is 30% or less of my income
Bills	I live day to day and help pay bills some of the time	Most of my bills are overdue	I rarely have overdue bills	None of my bills are overdue	I live within my budget comfortably and I have a good credit rating

	Extremely Unstable 1	Unstable 2	Fairly Stable 3	Stable/Secure 4	Very Stable 5
Emotional	I can rarely choose and control my emotional responses; I often behave in ways that are harmful to me or others.	I can sometimes choose and control my emotional responses; I sometimes behave in ways that are harmful to me or others	I almost always choose and control my emotional responses; I almost never behave in ways that are harmful to me or others	I am good at choosing and controlling my responses; I almost always engage in positive behaviors toward others	I am able to work through major differences and emotional issues with others.
Income	Less than 50% of my income is from wages and/or child support	Fifty to 80% of my income is from wages and/or child support	Eighty to 100% of my income is from wages and child support	One hundred percent of my income is from wages and investments.	One hundred percent of my income is from wages, investments, bonuses, stock options and/or trust funds
Employment	I am not employed and have not had a job in some years	I work day labor and/or odd jobs; I sometimes work for people who operate 'under the table'	I work full time with few benefits but worry about layoffs and reduction in hours. Sometimes I have to work part-time or take a second job.	I work contractually but without benefits, paid vacation, or the possibility of upward mobility, or employee status.	I have full time employment with benefits, paid vacation, learning opportunities, and the possibility of moving up in the company.

Stability Scale Indicators

Stability Scale Indicators

	Extremely Unstable 1	Unstable 2	Fairly Stable 3	Stable/Secure 4	Very Stable 5
Wages	I have no regular pay and earn cash as I can; I rely on public assistance	I'm paid a minimum wage that is subsidized by public assistance	I'm paid a living wage.	I'm paid above a self-sufficient wage.	I'm paid above a self-sufficient wage with contributions in stock options, bonuses, and/ or matching pension contributions.
Stress	My stress comes from having almost no control over the important things in my life	My stress comes from having some but not enough control over the important things in my life	My stress comes from working hard to stay in control of the important things in my life	My stress comes from not being able to maintain the control and security I have achieved in my life	I am able to control almost all of the important things in my life
Physical and mental health	Problems almost constantly interfere with my work or school	Problems often interfere with my work or school	Problems sometimes interfere with my work and school	Problems rarely interfere with my work or school	Problems almost never interfere with my work or school
Legal issues	Legal problems almost daily interfere with my work and school	Legal problems often interfere with my work and school	Legal problems rarely interfere with my work and school	I haven't had any legal problems in a very long time	I've never had legal problems
Safety	People are rarely safe in my house or neighborhood	People are often unsafe in my house or neighborhood	People are safe in my house and neighborhood much of the time	People are safe in my house and neighborhood almost all of the time	People are always safe in my house and neighborhood

Stability Scale Indicators					
	Extremely Unstable 1	Unstable 2	Fairly Stable 3	Stable/Secure 4	Very Stable 5
Destructive behaviors of others	Destructive behaviors of others often have a great deal of influence on me	Destructive behaviors of others occasionally have some influence on me	Destructive behaviors of others rarely have any influence on me	Destructive behaviors of others have almost no influence on me	Destructive behaviors of others have no influence on me
Behavior of children	My children are pretty much out of control and often interfere with my work or school	My children are out of control sometimes and occasionally interfere with my work or school	My children behave most of the time and rarely interfere with my work or school	My children behave almost all of the time almost never interfere with my work and school	My children's behavior never interferes with my work or school
Transportation	The transportation I use is not reliable	The transportation I use is often unreliable	The transportation I use is generally dependable	The transportation I use is almost always dependable	The transportation I use is always dependable
Social Connections	I spend a lot of time with people who are often in trouble at work, school, or with the law.	I spend some time with people who are often in trouble at work, school, or with the law.	I spend time with people who are in recovery and those who are on a positive path.	I spend time with people who are making positive life choices	I spend time with people who are part of a positive community

Continuum of Those Who Use Getting Ahead

1   2   3   4   5

Extremely Unstable Environments

Daily life disrupted by violence, illness, addiction, disabilities, and/or unstable community conditions. Highly affected by generational poverty. Stabilizing the environment and building resources may take a very long time.

Unstable Environments

Daily life can be stabilized enough with supports to attend weekly or bi-weekly workshops. People in generational and situational poverty. Building resources may take a long time.

Fairly Stable Environments

Daily life can be organized fairly easily. May be able to build resources rather quickly. Some people in situational poverty.

Discussion

1. How much does stability/instability affect the ability to change?

2. What is causing the most instability for investigators in the group?

3. What can we learn from people who experience different levels of instability and stability?

4. What will it take to build a stable environment? What supports are needed?

5. How does this information apply to you?

"The Theory of Change Mental Model changed my outlook on life. Those things I thought were unattainable are attainable*, and I didn't see them because I was so focused on the here and now."

—Getting Ahead Graduate and Facilitator, Josh Howard, Monroe, MI

The Getting Ahead
Theory of Change

Now that we've examined the change theories of the organizations that you have gone to, it's only right that we ask, "What is Getting Ahead's Theory of Change? To what extent do you think Getting Ahead's Theory of Change will make a difference?"

Activity: Facilitator Draws the Getting Ahead Theory of Change

Time: 20 minutes
Materials: Chart paper, markers

Procedure:

1. The facilitator draws the "Mental Model of Getting Ahead's Theory of Change."

2. In the space below, copy the drawing for your own use.

3. Review the description below for an explanation of Getting Ahead's Theory of Change.

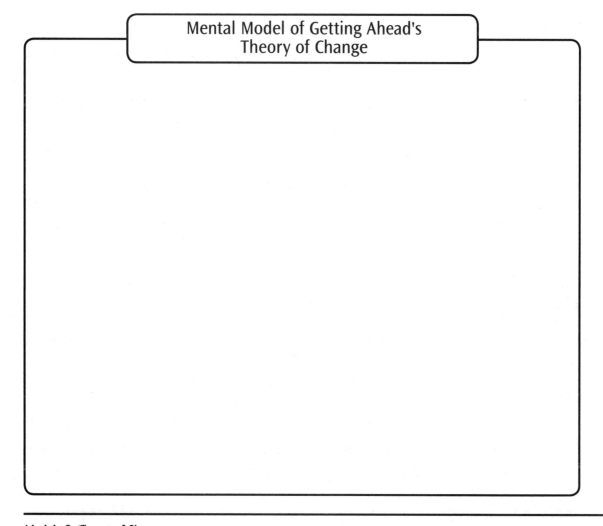

Mental Model of Getting Ahead's
Theory of Change

- Living in chronically unstable conditions or in persistent poverty can make it hard for people to change. Poverty traps people in the tyranny of the moment where concrete problems demand immediate attention.

- People in poverty are problem solvers. They frequently use the people they know (their relationships) to solve problems. Because they often have to solve problems that pop up during the day, they become masters of *reactive problem-solving** skills.

- The choice to do *abstract thinking** can free GA investigators from the tyranny of the moment and allow them to separate themselves from their problems, to *detach** and become objective, to analyze their situations, learn new information, make their own arguments for change, and do *proactive planning**.

- There are multiple causes of poverty; it isn't caused by choices of the individual alone.

- It's important to learn how poverty impacts individuals. Information about the environments of class, the causes of poverty, the hidden rules of class, language issues, and resources will help GA investigators do a critical analysis of the situation.

- Doing a Self-Assessment of Resources, along with an Assessment of Community Resources, will help individuals make plans for economic stability for themselves and their communities.

- The information in Getting Ahead, the discussions around the table, and the Theory of Change will help GA investigators break out of the tyranny of the moment and develop new future stories for themselves.

- Using the investigations conducted by the group, individuals will be able to make plans to build resources.

- Partnerships with people in middle class and those in wealth will build social capital.

- The impact of poverty on institutions and communities is similar to its impact on individuals. Developing strategies that address poverty at the individual, institutional, and community levels will provide a more comprehensive approach to "community" and everything it involves.

Discussion

1. Does Getting Ahead's Philosophy accurately describe the problem-solving strategies needed to survive in near poverty and poverty?

2. What do you most want to remember about the Theory of Change?

3. Is it possible to live in an unstable situation and choose to think in the abstract? In other words, can the Theory of Change free a person from the tyranny of the moment?

4. Have you ever seen an organization in the tyranny of the moment? Or a city or county?

5. How might the Theory of Change benefit you?

Stages of Change

The way people make changes fall into patterns. Carlo DiClemente and Mary Velasquez at the University of Rhode Island call these the "Stages of Change." They conducted a study on how smokers gave up the habit, but their work applies to other changes as well.

Knowing the stages can help us identify problems, become more motivated, and make plans. The examples in the table below relate to smokers, but they also could pertain to people who are thinking of going to college, getting a job, or creating their future stories.

Stages of Change	
1. Pre-Contemplation	Ignorance is bliss. We aren't even thinking about changing. We may not know how, so we don't concern ourselves with it. We may not have suffered much (yet), so we don't see the need. We aren't willing.
	Example: Take someone (let's say a woman) who has been smoking a while. She knows it's bad for her health, but she's annoyed by everyone harping about it. The more others push for her to quit, the more it feels like her rights and freedoms are being challenged. She doesn't ever expect to change and, what's more, she doesn't want to.
2. Contemplation	Sitting on the fence. We're concerned and worried, and we begin considering a change, but we're not sold on it yet.
	This stage is all about thinking. We can be in this stage for a long time. Knowing this, we might be able to move through it more quickly. There are two important things that have to be dealt with in this stage: ambivalence and identity.
	Ambivalence: This is when we want to change but are weighing the pros and cons. We are worried about how hard it will be to make the change. We think about family and friends and how they might react to the changes we make.
	Identity: We worry that we won't be the same person if we change. Will the people who are in our lives now reject us if we change? Fear of failure becomes a part of this, and so does fear of success. We wonder what will happen if we do or don't change. Most of all we think, When in doubt, put it off!
	Example: Something happens that makes the woman in our story start thinking. Someone she knows dies of cancer, a child asks her to quit, or she gets disgusted with the way her clothes smell. She stays on the fence for a long time, thinking, "I'm a smoker. Always have been, always will be." That identity is hard to change.

Stages of Change

3. Preparation	Testing the waters. For the first time, we begin to make the argument for change, not the others who always seem to know what's best for us. That is a sign that we're motivated. We think, "I'm going to change, and I'm figuring out what to do." We intend to change in the near future. We're in transition, so we make small behavior changes and play the "yes/but" game.
	Example: Our smoker has decided to stop smoking—but only sort of. She switches to low-tar/nicotine cigarettes, tries to smoke less, might try patches, or even quits for a few days, but she doesn't tell her friends or even family (in some cases) what she's trying to do.
4. Action	We're doing it, but it's shaky. We make a public commitment to the change, we've made a plan, and we're trying to stick to it. When we have some success we begin to think we can do it. Our identity may not have changed yet, but we're thinking differently.
	Example: Our smoker still thinks of herself as a smoker, and she promises never to be like others who quit and become crusading anti-smokers. Her plan develops out of the preparation phase, and she now takes a behavioral class and uses patches. She even has a plan to prevent relapse, and she tries to keep the *back door** of her commitment closed so she won't run out that back door the first time she gets into trouble.
5. Maintenance and Relapse Prevention	"I've done it; now I'm working at keeping it going." But it's not a sure thing. Many things can trigger a relapse, so strategies have to be put into practice for some time. Efforts have to be made to prevent relapse—and to recover from relapse quickly if/when it occurs.
	Example: Our non-smoker works hard to stay smoke-free and begins to gain real confidence in herself as time passes. Her sense of self slowly changes, and she increasingly becomes at ease with her new identity and lifestyle.

Note. Adapted from "Motivational Interviewing and the Stages of Change," by C. C. DiClemente and M. M. Velasquez. *In Motivational Interviewing: Preparing People for Change* (2nd ed., pp. 201–216), by W. R. Miller and S. Rollnick, 2002, New York, NY: Guilford Press. Copyright 2002 by Guilford Press.

Discussion

1. What changes have you made in the past? To what degree did you go through these five stages?

2. Are you making a change in your life now? If so, what stage of change are you in?

3. Have you begun to think of changes you want to make about stability and poverty issues?

4. Making a change can alter how you see yourself and how others see you. Does making a change mean that your identity changes too? What would it mean to your identity to work on poverty issues in your own life?

> *"We can use the Theory of Change to overcome the tyranny of the moment."*

*Vocabulary List for Module 2

Abstract thinking: having thoughts outside of concrete realities

Agenda-free: when no one is trying to tell you what to do, where they don't want something from you

Attainable: something that can be reached, done

Back door: a way to avoid doing something, an escape hatch

Bridging social capital: connecting with people who are different from you but with whom you have relationships of mutual respect

Detach: to slightly separate from the things we worry about the most, let go, step away to better see the problem

Intentions: something that somebody plans to do

Philosophy: a set of underlying concepts about an area of knowledge, a system of thought

Proactive planning: looking ahead and starting to deal with problems you know you will face in the future

Psychological reactance: responding negatively when being told what to do or when being ordered around

Reactive problem solving: dealing with issues by using quick reactions and solutions, not planning

Righting reflex: seeing something wrong and trying to quickly fix it; there are two sides to the righting reflex—the helpful side and the annoying side

Systemic barriers: things that get in the way of change that are caused, not by individuals, but by how organizations or institutions operate—or how policies and rules are written

Time horizon: how far into the future a person can see and plan for

Tyranny of the moment: being stuck in the immediate moment, the now—not being able to see past today

Readings

Farson, Richard. (1997). *Management of the absurd: Paradoxes in leadership.* New York, NY: Touchstone.

Klein, Naomi. (2007). *The shock doctrine: The rise of disaster capitalism.* New York, NY: Metropolitan Books.

Miller, Matt. (2009). *The tyranny of dead ideas: Letting go of the old ways of thinking to unleash a new prosperity.* New York, NY: Times Books.

Pransky, Jack. (1998). *Modello: A story of hope for the inner city and beyond.* Cabot, VT: NEHRI Publications.

The Rich/Poor Gap and Research on Causes of Poverty

Until we explore and understand all the causes of poverty, we won't be able to build communities where everyone can live well.

WHAT'S COVERED

We will:

Understand the range of causes of poverty—from personal to systemic

Establish a strategy to protect us from *predators**

Learn how the middle class was created

Learn about *disparity** in income and wealth

Make mental models for what life is like in middle class and wealth

Complete a Personal Chart on Economic Class and write "My Economic Class Story"

Establish that it is necessary to address all the causes of poverty across the four areas of research

Learn how to use the *Community Sustainability Grid**

WHY IT'S IMPORTANT

We experience the causes of instability and poverty every day. Going to the abstract puts words to our experience.

Studying the research on poverty will help free us from the tyranny of the moment so we can see the big picture and build a different future story.

It's important to know how the economic system works so we can see what hurts and helps people who are near the bottom of the economic ladder.

Poverty isn't just about the choices of the individual: Communities and *political/ economic structures** also must be addressed.

It's important that we have a voice in how poverty is addressed in our communities.

Learning how to manage time well gives us the long view for making plans.

HOW IT'S CONNECTED TO YOU

We described the reality of life in poverty when we made the Mental Model of Poverty. Now we're investigating additional information about income and wealth creation.

Having mental models of poverty, middle class, and wealth helps us understand other people's experiences, motivation, and behavior—and how they think and reason.

We need to have a plan for ourselves and our community's political/economic structures if we're going to build economic stability and sustainability.

We need to prepare to be at the planning and decision-making tables in our community.

Research on the Causes of Poverty

To people who are living paycheck to paycheck (or without paychecks), learning about poverty research may seem like a waste of time. But in the Getting Ahead Theory of Change, we talked about the value of thinking in the abstract—how it can free us from living in tyranny of the moment.

This statement from N. Smith makes the case for why we should study the causes of poverty: "When you live in reaction, you give your power away. Then you get to experience what you gave your power to." –N. Smith, Universe of HeartMath, http://images.heartmath. com/heartquotes/hq320.html

There's a huge debate going on in the U.S. about the growing number of people in poverty and why there is a widening gap between the rich and poor. David Shipler says in his book *The Working Poor* (p. 5), "As a culture, the United States is not quite sure about the causes of poverty and is therefore uncertain about the solutions." But we do know that some people will be making decisions that will impact GA investigators and others who are at or near the bottom of the economic ladder.

The goal of this module is for GA graduates to understand the causes of poverty and to be certain about what they'll do about poverty in their own lives.

Activity: Identifying Our Own Thoughts About the Causes of Poverty

Time: 10 minutes
Materials: Notepaper, chart paper, markers

Procedure:

1. Without talking to others, make a list of what you think causes poverty. Put your list aside to look at later.

2. Have a volunteer write a list of the group's answers to the following question: "What do most people say causes poverty?" Put this aside too while we investigate the material in the module.

Introducing the 'Causes of Poverty— Research Continuum'

Poverty has been in the news a lot since much of the economy collapsed in 2008. The last time poverty was a lead story was 1996 when the Welfare Reform Act was passed.

But there has always been a research industry made up of universities, governmental organizations, foundations, institutes, and think tanks that study poverty.

The **Research Continuum*** below organizes the research and reporting into four categories: individual behaviors and circumstances, community conditions, exploitation, and political/economic structures.

It's not important that you understand every phrase or topic in the table below. But it is important to know that there are many causes of poverty. We'll examine some of these topics in detail.

Causes of Poverty—Research Continuum

INDIVIDUAL BEHAVIORS AND CIRCUMSTANCES	COMMUNITY CONDITIONS	EXPLOITATION	POLITICAL/ECONOMIC STRUCTURES
Definition: Research on the choices, behaviors, and circumstances of people in poverty	*Definition:* Research on resources and human and social capital in the city or county	*Definition:* Research on the impact of exploitation on individuals and communities	*Definition:* Research on political, economic, and social policies and systems at the organizational, city/county, state, national, and international levels
Sample topics: ~ Racism ~ Discrimination by age, gender, disability, race, sexual identity ~ Bad loans ~ Credit-card debt ~ Lack of savings ~ Skill sets ~ Dropping out ~ Lack of education ~ Alcoholism ~ Disabilities ~ Job loss ~ Teen pregnancies ~ Early language experience ~ Child-rearing strategies ~ Bankruptcy due to health problems ~ Street crime ~ White-collar crime ~ Dependency ~ Work ethic ~ Lack of organizational skills ~ Lack of amenities	*Sample topics:* ~ Racism ~ Discrimination by age, gender, disability, race, sexual identity ~ Layoffs ~ Middle-class flight ~ Plant closings ~ Underfunded schools ~ Weak safety net ~ Criminalizing poverty ~ Employer insurance premiums rising in order to drop companies with record of poor health ~ Charity that leads to dependency ~ High rates of illness leading to high absenteeism and low productivity ~ *Brain drain** ~ City and regional planning ~ Mix of employment/wage opportunities ~ Loss of access to high-quality schools, childcare, and preschool ~ Downward pressure on wages	*Sample topics:* ~ Racism ~ Discrimination by age, gender, disability, race, sexual identity ~ Payday lenders ~ Lease/purchase outlets ~ Subprime mortgages ~ Sweatshops ~ *Human trafficking** ~ Employment and labor law *violations** ~ Wage and benefits theft ~ Some landlords ~ Sex trade ~ Internet scams ~ Drug trade ~ Poverty premium (the poor pay more for goods and services) ~ Day labor	*Sample topics:* ~ Racism ~ Discrimination by age, gender, disability, race, sexual identity ~ Financial oligarchy—the military, industrial, congressional complex ~ *Return on political investment** (ROPI) ~ Corporate lobbyists ~ *Bursting "bubbles"** ~ Free Trade Agreements ~ *Recessions** ~ Lack of wealth-creating mechanisms ~ *Stagnant wages** ~ Insecure pensions ~ Healthcare costs ~ Lack of insurance ~ De-industrialization ~ Globalization ~ Increased productivity ~ Minimum wage, living wage, self-sufficient wage ~ Declining middle class ~ Decline in unions ~ Taxation patterns ~ Wealth-creating mechanisms

A Closer Look at the Research Continuum

Individual Behaviors and Circumstances

People make choices that can lead to instability and poverty. For example, the choice to drop out of high school often leads to low-wage jobs and sometimes to poverty. Having a disability or a chronic disease can lead to poverty also.

Most of the work in Getting Ahead is focused on individual behaviors and choices. In other words, most of the work is about you—your situation, your investigations, your self-assessment, and your future story: those things that are under your control, those things you can do something about.

This module, however, will not focus on the individual category. Instead it will investigate the other areas of research. Instability and poverty are not caused only by the choices an individual makes.

Community Conditions

Getting out of poverty is hard to do. For one thing there are many more people at the bottom of the ladder who are looking for work than there are jobs. And the jobs that are available don't pay as well as before the *Great Recession** (2008–09).

In the chart below you'll see that in the Great Recession, 40% of the jobs *lost* in the private sector were in higher wage industries. However, 49% of the job *growth* during the early stage of recovery was in lower wage industries. Many entry-level jobs pay less than $9 an hour. This trend makes it harder to move up to better paying jobs, and it's an example of how the "downward pressure on wages" contributes to the growing number of people in poverty and near poverty.

Tracking emerging recovery in private sector			
The private sector saw a net gain of 1.26 million jobs between February 2010 and 2011. During the same period the public sector lost almost a quarter of a million jobs.			
	Wages	Percentage of job loss	Percentage of recent job growth
Lower-wage industries	$9.03–$12.91	23%	**49%**
Mid-wage industries	$12.92–$19.04	36%	37%
Higher-wage industries	$19.05–$31.40	**40%**	14%

Note. NELP National Employment Law Project, Data Brief, February 2011
www.nelp.org/page/./Justice/2011/UnbalancedGrowthFeb2011.pdf?nocdn=1

Where you live matters. Some communities have deeper problems and fewer opportunities than others. The Great Recession hit some communities very hard, while others were barely touched.

Some communities don't have a good mix of employment opportunities. In communities where you have a fair shot at a well-paying job, a good education, good healthcare, and fair credit, you'd have an easier time getting out of poverty. A "fair shot" means access to those four things. It also means support along the way in the form of transportation, affordable childcare, and affordable housing. All of that would add up to true opportunity.

Some regions of the country have deep and persistent poverty. People living in the states bordering Mexico, the Appalachian region, Native American reservations, and old manufacturing cities will find it harder to get out of poverty.

Many cities and counties are in deep financial trouble. Their leaders may be as much caught up in the tyranny of the moment as are most people in poverty.

In some communities the leadership is taking the long view and seeking new solutions. A growing number of communities are using Bridges concepts to address poverty in a comprehensive way.

Discussion

1. How hard was your community or country hit by the Great Recession?

2. What would be a "good mix" of employment opportunities? To what extent is there a good mix of employment opportunities in your area?

3. Are people leaving the community or country to find jobs?

4. Does your community or country offer the four fair shots described above?

"My investigations showed me people's differences–not the stereotypes* about rich and poor and black and white, but what the differences mean and what they don't mean. Everyone in class learned from the struggles each other had. Before, I'd take risks that could have gotten me in trouble. Now I take risks that make me stretch–that help me get ahead. I even see my family differently."

–Janae Brooks, College Student, Investigations Co-Facilitator, Youngstown (OH) State University
Bridges Out of Poverty Student Union

Exploitation

The following activity will help you understand how predators are a significant cause of poverty.

Activity: Identifying Predators

Time: 30 minutes
Materials: Worksheet, Mental Model of My Life Now
from Module 2, pen or pencil

Procedure:

1. Read the following case study.

2. Interview people in the neighborhood who have used the "services" of the predators. Predators are businesses that provide services or goods to people but charge them more than the services or goods may be worth—in other words, they "prey" on people.

   a. Ask how many times they have been to the business.

   b. Find out what interest rate they are paying and what the average annual interest rate is.

   c. Find out how the predator gets the person's "business."

3. List all the illegal and legal predatory businesses you learn about on the chart below.

4. *Brainstorm** how to get out from under the control of a predator. What might a person have to do?

5. Privately, not as a group, mark an "X" in the middle column for every predator you have gone to. If you have any connections with a predator, go back to your Mental Model of My Life Now and add the information.

Case Study: The Meat Man

(This example was provided by a GA investigator in Indianapolis.)

Your family is eating cereal. That's all you have left to eat, and you hope there's enough for everyone. A meat man knocks on the door. He comes in with pre-seasoned, vacuum-packed chicken, pork, and beef. He says he's overstocked and needs to sell it soon. You and your family would love to buy it, but your food stamp card is empty. The meat man says, "No problem. I understand. Keep the meat, cook it up right now. I'll come back next week and swipe your card."

Discussion

Review the Theory of Change from Module 2. Analyze the strategy used by the meat man.

1. What did he offer the family?

2. How did he treat the family?

3. What do you think the chicken cost per pound?

4. What do you think the GA investigator (the mother) did?

5. What makes it possible for this kind of business to be successful?

Predators		
List the predators in your community	Are you involved with this predator? If so, how?	How can someone get out from under a predator's control? How long might it take?

Investigate This!

Learn more about predatory lending by going to www.responsiblelending.org

Discussion

1. What did you need that caused you to become associated with a predator?

2. What alternatives to using the "services" of the predator existed in the community at that time?

3. Was there ever a time when you didn't have to deal with predators? When was that? What were your circumstances at that time?

Political/Economic Structures

Systemic causes are the most complex and hardest to address. It's much easier to focus on individual behaviors and blame the person in poverty than it is to address all the causes of poverty, including political/economic structures.

In order to understand systemic causes, we're going to investigate:

- How the middle class was built in the U.S.
- How the rich/poor gap causes poverty

Creation of the Middle Class

When people in poverty build their resources and stabilize their situations, they move toward a middle-class environment. However, recent political and economic conditions have contributed to the decline of the middle class and an increase in poverty.

How much harder will it be for people in poverty to achieve stability if the middle class is losing its stability?

It's important that we know how the middle class was created. Did it come from individual effort alone? Did it come from earning paychecks and saving money? What's it going to take to rebuild the middle class in a shaky economy?

In his 2004 article "Are We Still a Middle-Class Nation?" Michael Lind lists seven factors in describing how the middle class in the U.S. was created:

1. The U.S. was able to create middle-class farmers. The farms they passed on to their children did not come from their labor alone. They also came from government policies, such as the 1862 Homestead Act, which gave most farmers 160 acres from which to make a start.

Slave labor created wealth for many of the owners. In 1850 the average income of a slave owner in South Carolina was 10 times that of the average income of other whites in the state.

In 1848 Mexico lost half its territory in the war with the United States, and in 1851 the Sioux tribe had to give up the entire state of Iowa to the U.S. All these policies and governmental actions created wealth for the agricultural middle class.

2. The industrial middle class did not earn its stability, prosperity, and wealth through its paycheck alone. Government policies protected workers by cutting off "Oriental" immigration and, after World War I, immigration from Europe.

   Children were removed from the workplace by child-labor laws, and the "family wage" increased income for married men. Henry Ford raised wages because he wanted employees to be able to own the cars they made.

   Later, unionization helped introduce the 40-hour work week, higher wages, and job security. With government support, employers provided employer-based health insurance.

3. Building on these gains, the white-collar middle class benefited from tax codes that encouraged employers to provide employer-based health insurance and employer-based pensions.

   After World War II, the GI Bill provided education, student loans, and home mortgages.

   Government policies also created Social Security and Medicare—and paid for the roads, highways, and infrastructure that supported manufacturing, home ownership, and the growth of the suburbs.

4. The wealth created by these policies and passed down through the generations did not extend to everyone. In fact, these wealth-creating mechanisms were achieved at the expense and exclusion of people of color.

   In *The Color of Wealth*, published by United for a Fair Economy in 2006, the authors explain the wealth divide in the United States.

   During the 1850s the land made available to whites was taken from Native Americans and Mexico in a series of battles, appropriations, and treaties. In many instances people of color were not allowed to buy land.

We recognize the impact that income and wealth disparity has on individuals and communities.

And while whites became wealthy on slave labor, Mexicans lost their land to the U.S. Only whites were eligible for California land claims during the Gold Rush. Additionally, the "Foreign Miner's Tax" of 1850 stopped Mexicans from participating in the Gold Rush. In 1852 this policy was extended to exclude the Chinese as well.

5. Industrial and white-collar, middle-class opportunities also were largely limited to white workers.

There were not enough black colleges for the returning black veterans of World War II wanting to use the GI Bill. Most colleges were still segregated, which left most of the African American veterans with no place to go.

From 1930 to 1960 only 1% of all mortgages were issued to African Americans, who made up about 10% of the U.S. population. Japanese Americans, who lost property while interned during World War II, received just 10 cents on the reparation dollar.

In Puerto Rico (a territory of the U.S.) most locally owned businesses were crowded out by U.S. companies when Operation Bootstrap gave the companies tax incentives in 1947.

During World War II, Mexicans were brought to the U.S. to fill labor shortages, then later deported in Operation Wetback. In the 1950s Congress terminated recognition of certain Native American tribes, thus throwing the prosperous Menominee and Klamath tribes, among others, into poverty.

6. Despite the civil rights laws of the 1960s, discrimination still exists in the United States. Individual and institutional racism may not seem obvious, but there's still a huge economic benefit to being white and a comparable cost to being people of color.

   Those who think we don't need to talk about color, race, and diversity are expressing a color-blindness not supported by the facts. For example, the *racial wealth gap* continues to grow. According to the U.S. Federal Reserve Bank, the median net worth (assets minus debts) of families of color has dropped dramatically in recent years.

7. Finally, it should be noted that the middle class is shrinking for the first time in U.S. history. The very policies and structures that made the middle class are disappearing, including employer-based healthcare, employer-based pensions, the full-time 40-hour work week, wages, student loans, and mortgage assistance.

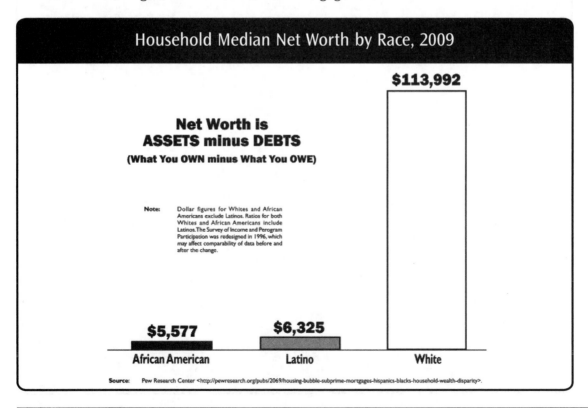

Household Median Net Worth by Race, 2009

Net Worth is ASSETS minus DEBTS
(What You OWN minus What You OWE)

$113,992

Note: Dollar figures for Whites and African Americans exclude Latinos. Ratios for both Whites and African Americans include Latinos. The Survey of Income and Program Participation was redesigned in 1996, which may affect comparability of data before and after the change.

$5,577
African American

$6,325
Latino

White

Source: Pew Research Center <http://pewresearch.org/pubs/2069/housing-bubble-subprime-mortgages-hispanics-blacks-household-wealth-disparity>.

Discussion

1. Have any assets or wealth been passed on to you from your family?

2. How does this information apply to your situation?

3. How are assets developed if none were passed on from previous generations?

REFLECTIONS

Disparity in Income and Wealth

In Module 1 we created the Mental Model of Poverty. Now we are investigating the growing disparity or divide between the rich and poor in the U.S. The widening gap results in very different living environments. Later in this module we'll create a Mental Model of Middle Class and a Mental Model of Wealth.

For the past 30–40 years in the United States, the rich (top 10%) have been getting richer while the bottom 90% have been getting poorer. This is the fourth time in U.S. history that the gap has widened in a statistically significant way. The first was in the Gilded Age (the 1870s); the second was during the Roaring Twenties (1920s); the third was the Nifty Fifties (1950s); and the most recent growing divide has been fueled by the "bull markets" of the 1980s, 1990s, and the "bursting bubbles" of the first two decades of the 21st century.

The CIA World Factbook presents information on *inequality** or disparity in family income for 140 nations. The country with the highest income inequality is Namibia (1); the country with the least inequality is Sweden (140). The United States is No. 40. There is more inequality in the U.S. than in Russia, China, India, Egypt, Iran, Venezuela, and many others. The table below shows the ranking of countries where there are Getting Ahead groups.

Countries where Bridges Out of Poverty and Getting Ahead in a Just-Gettin'-By World are used	Inequality in family income ranking
Australia	115
Canada	105
Czech Republic	137
Ireland	121
Slovakia	133
United States	40

Note. https://www.cia.gov/library/publications/the-world-factbook/rankorder/2172rank.html

A Note on Statistics and Sources

The following material (up to and including the chart titled "Ownership of Household Wealth in the U.S., 2007") is provided by United for a Fair Economy (*The Growing Divide*, 2011).

Whenever possible, we use government sources—such as the U.S. Census Bureau (for things like family income), the Federal Reserve Bank (for household wealth), and the U.S. Bureau of Labor Statistics (for unionization rates)—for the statistics we provide. Even with their well-documented flaws, government statistics are generally the most comprehensive, frequently updated, and widely cited (*The Growing Divide*, 2009, p. 4).

Activity: Real Family Income Growth by Quintile & for Top 5% & Top 1%, 1979–2009

Time: 15 minutes
Materials: Five income placards

Procedure:

1. Review the charts on the next three pages. The charts display information about family income separated into five economic groups (*quintiles**), then they break out the top 5%.

2. Investigate, as a group, the information presented by the facilitator and five volunteers.

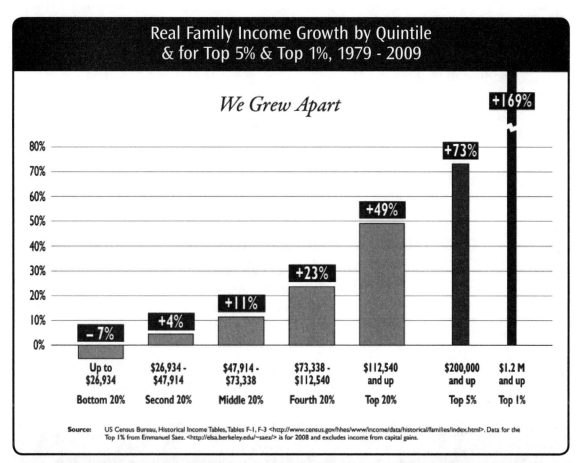

Real Family Income Growth by Quintile & for Top 5% & Top 1%, 1979 - 2009

We Grew Apart

	Up to $26,934	$26,934 - $47,914	$47,914 - $73,338	$73,338 - $112,540	$112,540 and up	$200,000 and up	$1.2 M and up
	−7%	+4%	+11%	+23%	+49%	+73%	+169%
	Bottom 20%	Second 20%	Middle 20%	Fourth 20%	Top 20%	Top 5%	Top 1%

Source: US Census Bureau, Historical Income Tables, Tables F-1, F-3 <http://www.census.gov/hhes/www/income/data/historical/families/index.html>. Data for the Top 1% from Emmanuel Saez. <http://elsa.berkeley.edu/~saez/> is for 2008 and excludes income from capital gains.

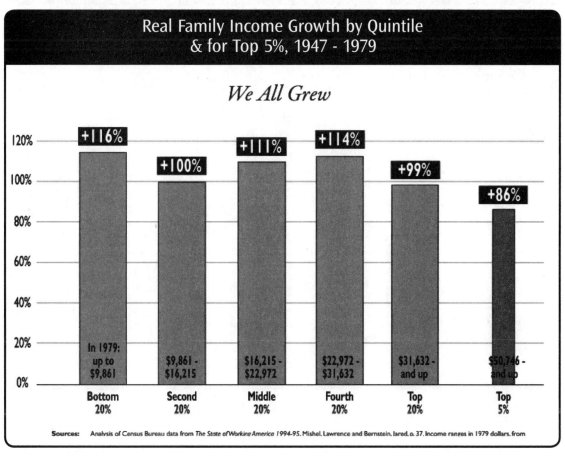

Real Family Income Growth by Quintile & for Top 5%, 1947 - 1979

We All Grew

Bottom 20%	Second 20%	Middle 20%	Fourth 20%	Top 20%	Top 5%
+116%	+100%	+111%	+114%	+99%	+86%
In 1979: up to $9,861	$9,861 - $16,215	$16,215 - $22,972	$22,972 - $31,632	$31,632 - and up	$50,746 - and up

Sources: Analysis of Census Bureau data from *The State of Working America* 1994-95. Mishel, Lawrence and Bernstein, Jared, p. 37. Income ranges in 1979 dollars, from

Discussion

1. What stood out for you in this information about the growing divide between the rich and the poor?

2. What was helpful to you from these activities?

3. Does this information change your thinking about your own situation?

4. Does this information relate to the conditions in your community? If so, how?

Activity: CEO Pay as a Multiple of Average Worker Pay, 1960–2008

Time: 15 minutes
Materials: Six placards

Procedure:

1. Review the table.

2. Investigate the information presented by the facilitator and six volunteers.

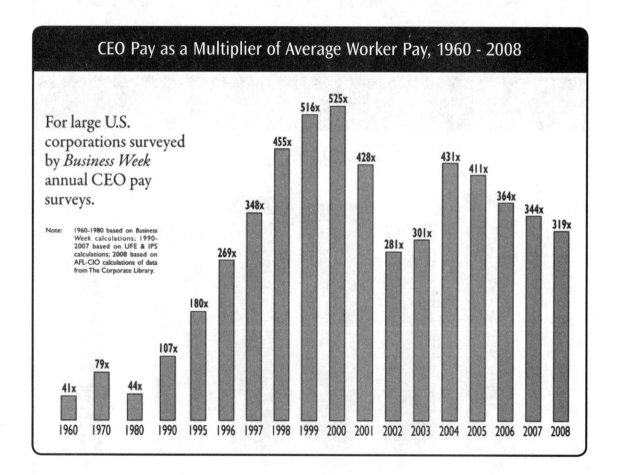

CEO Pay as a Multiplier of Average Worker Pay, 1960 - 2008

For large U.S. corporations surveyed by *Business Week* annual CEO pay surveys.

Note: 1960-1980 based on *Business Week* calculations; 1990-2007 based on UFE & IPS calculations; 2008 based on AFL-CIO calculations of data from The Corporate Library.

Year	Multiplier
1960	41x
1970	79x
1980	44x
1990	107x
1995	180x
1996	269x
1997	348x
1998	455x
1999	516x
2000	525x
2001	428x
2002	281x
2003	301x
2004	431x
2005	411x
2006	364x
2007	344x
2008	319x

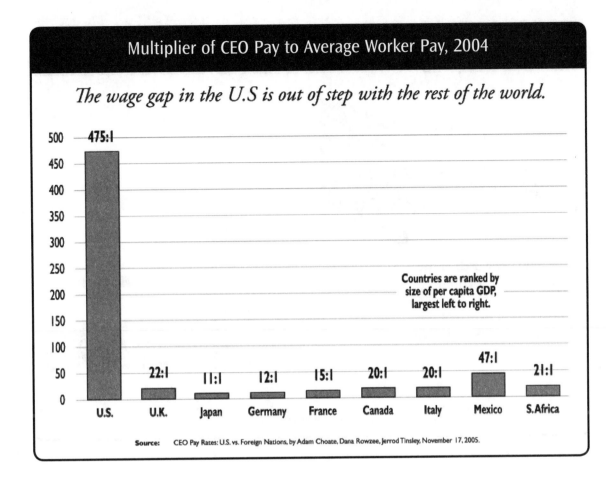

Multiplier of CEO Pay to Average Worker Pay, 2004

The wage gap in the U.S is out of step with the rest of the world.

475:1 (U.S.)

Countries are ranked by size of per capita GDP, largest left to right.

U.S.	U.K.	Japan	Germany	France	Canada	Italy	Mexico	S.Africa
475:1	22:1	11:1	12:1	15:1	20:1	20:1	47:1	21:1

Source: CEO Pay Rates: U.S. vs. Foreign Nations, by Adam Choate, Dana Rowzee, Jerrod Tinsley, November 17, 2005.

Discussion

1. What strikes you about the income comparison between CEO pay and average worker pay?

2. How might the difference in pay affect the relationship of a CEO with employees?

3. How might it help to know how the U.S. compares with other nations?

Activity: Ownership of Household Wealth in the U.S., 2007—'The Ten Chairs: the Difference Between Wealth and Income'

Time: 10 minutes
Materials: 10 chairs

Procedure:

1. Review the chart.

2. Investigate the information presented by the facilitator and 10 volunteers.

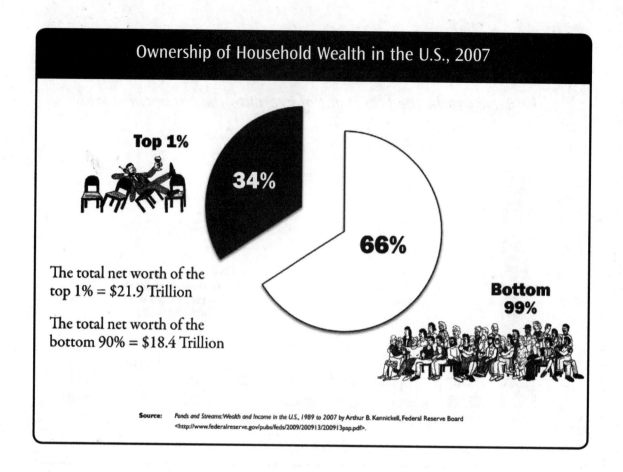

Ownership of Household Wealth in the U.S., 2007

Top 1%

34%

66%

Bottom 99%

The total net worth of the top 1% = $21.9 Trillion

The total net worth of the bottom 90% = $18.4 Trillion

Source: *Ponds and Streams: Wealth and Income in the U.S., 1989 to 2007* by Arthur B. Kennickell, Federal Reserve Board
<http://www.federalreserve.gov/pubs/feds/2009/200913/200913pap.pdf>.

Discussion

1. Notice the circumstances you are in and your own feelings about this. How are you feeling about the top 10%? How about the bottom 90%?

2. Who in North American society usually gets pushed off the chairs? How does that work?

3. What conclusions do you draw regarding the focus of public policy discussions—looking up the chairs (at the top 1%) or looking down the chairs (at the disadvantaged 99%)?

4. What caused the drop in median net worth for all races?

5. Why do you think the drop in net worth has been so dramatic for African Americans and Latinos?

6. Does this information change your thinking about your own situation? If so, how?

Wealth and Access to Power—Disparity in Wealth as a Cause of Poverty

Those with extreme wealth have greater access to power. That power can be used to support the political and economic policies that lead to more wealth and power. Here are some of the ways this works:

Campaign contributions: Individuals may support and help elect candidates who share their interests. Corporations influence politicians by using lobbyists, think tanks, campaign contributions, and the media to advertise their messages and to establish laws that favor them.

On January 21, 2010, the U.S. Supreme Court ruled in favor of Citizens United. This allowed individuals, organizations, and corporations to pour *unlimited* amounts of money into Super PACs (political action committees). Super PACs that are set up as "educational" or "charitable" do not have to disclose the names of contributors. The only limitation is that Super PACs cannot directly coordinate their efforts with a candidate's campaign. This ruling increases the power of those who have the most money to significantly influence elections.

Return on political investment (ROPI): In February 2006 *Fortune* magazine reported that since 1999 Lockheed Martin spent $55 million lobbying Congress. During that time it won roughly $90 billion in defense contracts. This was a ROPI of 163,536% (Miller, 2006, p. 36).

Meanwhile, average citizens investing in the stock market in 2012 consider investment returns of 8–10% to be extremely good by any standard. By comparison, certificates of deposit (CDs) at local banks in late 2009 would yield 1% for a 21-month deposit, 1.98% for 42 months, and 2.71% for 59 months.

> *"Income changes on a dime; wealth is created over time."*
>
> –Phil DeVol

Revolving door*: In this scenario, high-level executives get jobs with the government regulating the industry he/she came from. Corporate leaders then have the opportunity to make decisions and regulate the very sectors they used to work in. When they leave the government job, many of them go back to work in the very industry they had been regulating. Meanwhile, many elected officials whose term expires or who lose an election join corporations that contributed to their campaigns and whose work they supported while in the government.

This sort of power can give voice to some people and make others invisible. It supports its own system and people as it becomes more embedded in the larger power structure.

Discussion

1. When we began the module, you made a list of the causes of poverty. Looking at that now, what was your personal "favorite" category: individual choices, community conditions, exploitation, or political/economic structures?

2. Which ideas from this module's four investigations into the causes of poverty stand out for you?

3. How might having a bias about the cause or causes of poverty affect your relationships with others?

4. Given that many programs are based largely on the bias that poverty is caused by the choices of the poor, what does this mean to people who are on the receiving end of the programs?

5. What, if anything, does your community do that helps people get out of poverty?

Investigate This!

There is a paper titled "Who Pays the Most Taxes? What Does It Mean to the Community?" It can be found in Appendix C.

Mental Models of Middle Class and Wealth

We need mental models of middle class and wealth so we can better understand those environments. In this module we've seen that inequality in income and wealth tends to separate us from each other. Good things can come from understanding how other people live. We can:

- Be less judgmental and more understanding

- Have relationships of mutual respect with people from other classes

- Build social connections, social capital

- Resolve conflicts and solve problems more readily

- Work together more effectively to solve community problems

Activity: Mental Models of Middle Class and Wealth

Time: 1 hour and 15 minutes
Materials: Chart paper, markers

Procedure:

1. Read the following case studies of a family from middle class and a family from wealth.

2. Discuss what life is like in middle class, then create a Mental Model of Middle Class.

3. Discuss what life is like in wealth and create a Mental Model of Wealth.

4. Review the Mental Model of Poverty that was created in Module 2.

5. Compare and contrast the three environments for:

   a. The types of businesses in the neighborhood that people go to

   b. People's relationships with institutions (schools, courts, agencies)

   c. The level of stability in daily life

   d. The degree of vulnerability and fear

   e. The time horizon (how far ahead people think and make plans)

   f. How much time there is for living in the abstract

   g. How much access to power people have

   h. What types of problem-solving skills people have

   i. What resources people have in different classes

6. Reminder: Put these mental models on the wall at the beginning of each session, along with all the other mental models the group creates. Add information to them as it arises in group discussions.

Middle Class

Mark and Donna were both raised in middle-class families. Mark's father worked in an insurance company. His mother ran the house and was active in the community. Donna's father was an accountant, her mother a teacher. Donna has a bachelor's degree and is a certified respiratory therapist (CRT). She works for a company that provides in-home health services. Mark has a bachelor's degree and is a mid-level manager in a food distribution company. He was in the military for four years. They are in their early 40s and recently bought a house in a new development in order to have their children in a better school system. This is the second marriage for Donna. They have three children: a 15-year-old daughter from Donna's first marriage and two sons they had together; the boys are 13 and 11 years of age.

Mark's salary of $50,000 and Donna's salary of $33,000 were sufficient when they lived in the older section of the city. But when they moved to the new development, the mortgage payments and the longer commutes to work became a burden. They have excellent healthcare benefits, but their employers are increasingly shifting the cost of premiums to the employees. Mark was just diagnosed with Type II diabetes, and their eldest son has asthma. Donna's first husband hasn't been able to keep jobs because of a drinking problem, and he rarely pays child support. Mark and Donna bought their cars new. Donna drives a minivan; Mark drives an SUV.

Everyone in the family has a cell phone, and there are three computers in the home. They have a family tradition of visiting different states and Major League Baseball stadiums in the summer. These sports/camping trips are not working out so well now the children are older and involved in more summer activities. Mark is a member of Kiwanis. Donna and her friends go shopping together and like home decorating. She goes to the YWCA to exercise and is active in the PTA.

The children are very busy. The girl has been in dance and singing classes from the time she was little, and now she's on the volleyball and swimming teams. Mark coaches baseball for his sons' teams, and they enjoy playing golf together. The younger boy is in his school's chess club, and the older boy is in Boy Scouts. Moving to the new school district has given the children more to do, which is becoming increasingly expensive. In order maintain their active lifestyle, Mark and Donna have stopped saving money for emergencies and for college. Their credit-card debt has grown to $30,000.

Mark and Donna are worried about the future because their financial situation is worsening, and Mark's diabetes is progressing. They realize they won't be able to help their children much with the cost of college. They have had a number of arguments about money but haven't made any significant changes in spending or saving habits.

Thanksgiving, Christmas, and other holidays have to be scheduled very carefully because their daughter goes to her father's house. Mark's parents live close by, so the family sees them regularly. About the only time they see aunts, uncles, and cousins are at Thanksgiving and a summer picnic.

Old Money

Olen is 24 years old and in generational wealth, also known as old money. The original fortune was made 150 years ago. A trust fund was established at his birth, but Olen also was named in other funds as "future progeny," so he has several trust funds. He was registered for private boarding school at birth and went there at age 6. He graduated from Yale University, as did his father and grandfather. At 21 he began receiving a monthly check from the interest his trust funds generate, but he won't control the principal until he's 35. Twice a year Olen meets with his trust adviser to be updated on his trust funds.

Olen's allowance is $10,000 a month. He doesn't have bills, because he lives in one of the many staffed and furnished houses his family owns around the world. He doesn't pay for the utilities, upkeep, or staff. He has no debt. Additionally, two houses were given to him as gifts. His club memberships are paid for by his mother, and one of his cars was a gift at college graduation. In the garage Olen has several cars and vehicles, all of which have been fitted to one key so a last-minute choice of cars can be made.

Olen divides his year among Palm Springs, CA; Aspen and Vail, CO; Europe; and New York City. He flies first class or, more often, in either the corporate or the family jet. There is domestic help at all the houses who take care of everything, including his clothing, cleaning, and meals. A tailor makes his clothes and often selects both fabric and style, as he knows Olen's personal tastes. At one of the family estates, one person is hired full time to take care of the pool area and another to polish the brass. Because there is always staff around, privacy becomes a huge issue. Staff members have been fired for talking about Olen or his family.

Olen's hobbies are sailing, golf, ballooning, flying, skiing, and the theater. He spends a great deal of time in social activities but, in part, Olen uses his social and financial connections to further his career as a playwright. Olen is a bit unusual for his social group in that he wants to be a famous writer. He is welcome in theater, film, and television circles because of his name and wealth; creative people are welcome in his circles because of their achievements. He knows he can be published—he has enough connections to do that—but he wants to be respected and renowned "in his own right."

It is expected that by age 30 Olen will participate in one of the family businesses. Besides social functions he is expected to take part in business meetings, foundation board meetings, and political fund-raising events. He spends considerable time with the family's law firm on a complex lawsuit he filed to protect his property rights. Most of his time is spent with family members, old-money friends, or friends from the theater. Olen doesn't need to worry that the theater people will make fun of him for his tastes in clothes or art—or that they will want to use him for his money. He has learned to guard his privacy by picking his friends carefully.

> *We engage people from all classes, races, sectors, and political points of view.*

Discussion

1. What do you most want to remember from this activity?

2. What made this information hard/easy for you?

3. Discuss whether this information on economic class changed your thinking or feelings about people from other classes.

4. How might this new information change how you see your future—or what you think you might do in the future?

5. What, if anything, do the associations, agencies, institutions, and businesses in the community do well to help people out of poverty? What might they do more of? What things might they do differently?

6. What kinds of things might people in middle class and poverty do together if they decided to work with one another? What might happen if wealthy people also came to the table?

7. What are some things that people from all three classes can do to make a more stable community where everyone can live well?

My Economic Class Story

The investigation into economic class and the causes of poverty has given us lots to think about. Now it is time to personalize the learning we've done (although you might have been doing that all along). The following exercise will give you a way to look at your personal economic class situations over two generations.

Activity: Personal Chart on Economic Class and My Economic Class Story

Time: 30 minutes
Materials: Notepaper, pen or pencil

Procedure:

1. Review the information, activities, and mental models that we have created so far.

2. Think about your own journey and the journey of your family.

3. Now identify the economic class that fits the closest to your own and your family experience. Then circle the dot within that class that fits your situation. There are three dots for each group because we know economic class is a continuum with many variations. For example, within the middle class there are three levels: lower middle class, middle class, and upper middle class.

    a. When you think about the difference between *poverty and middle class,* think about whether you had enough resources to be stable and plan for and predict the future.

    b. When you think about the difference between *middle class and wealth* consider whether you (or your family) was in a position to manage income or manage wealth.

4. Answer the questions that follow the chart and review all that you have investigated in Getting Ahead so far. Consider that on average, more than 80% of all personal wealth comes from intergenerational transfers. What is your story?

    a. What did you inherit from your grandparents and parents?

    b. Did it help you build your stability and self-sufficiency?

    c. Did it help you build your resilience and creativity?

    d. How did it shape who you are today?

5. Write a short paper titled: My Economic Class Story

For a comprehensive approach to poverty, we must address all causes of poverty.

Personal Chart on Economic Class

	Poverty	Middle Class	Wealth
Father's parents	• • •	• • •	• • •
Mother's parents	• • •	• • •	• • •
Father	• • •	• • •	• • •
Mother	• • •	• • •	• • •
My birth to 3	• • •	• • •	• • •
4 to 10	• • •	• • •	• • •
11 to 15	• • •	• • •	• • •
16 to 20	• • •	• • •	• • •
21 to 30	• • •	• • •	• • •
31 to 45	• • •	• • •	• • •
46 to 60	• • •	• • •	• • •
61 to 80	• • •	• • •	• • •
My spouse/partner	• • •	• • •	• • •
Most of my siblings	• • •	• • •	• • •
Most of my friends	• • •	• • •	• • •
Most of my colleagues	• • •	• • •	• • •
Other	• • •	• • •	• • •

Note. Provided by the St. Joseph County Bridges Out of Poverty Initiative, South Bend, IN.

The Community Sustainability Grid: A Planning Tool for Addressing All Causes of Poverty

Getting Ahead investigators from Burlington, VT, helped create the Community Sustainability Grid. It is a mental model that presents four ideas:

1. All the causes of poverty must be addressed; see the top row (individual, community, exploitation, and political/economic structures). It is too simplistic to hold either the individuals in poverty or the political/economic structures accountable for poverty. That is either/or thinking. In Getting Ahead we use both/and thinking. Poverty is caused both by the choices people make and by political/economic structures—and everything in between.

2. A sustainable community where everyone can live well must be created. The sustainability grid is a tool that can be used to engage people from all classes, organizations (agencies, schools, healthcare providers, courts, etc.), sectors (elected leaders, business sector, faith-based entities, and cultural groups), and political positions (liberals, conservatives, and independents). The grid includes the thinking of all groups.

3. Everyone can take action. The first column calls for action by individuals, organizations, and communities, as well as changes in policy.

4. GA graduates play an important part when using this tool. They need to be at the table with other community leaders.

Community Sustainability Grid				
	Individual Choices, Behaviors, and Circumstances	Community Conditions	Exploitation	Political/ Economic Structures
Individual Action				
Organizational Action				
Community Action				
Policy Changes				

Investigate This!

Community Approach to Poverty

Most GA graduates are busy stabilizing their situations and building resources—and don't have time to become deeply involved in working on policy issues right away.

Those who are interested can investigate what their own communities are doing to address poverty in a comprehensive way. You might start by asking the sponsor of the Getting Ahead classes for information.

In Appendix D you can learn how the Community Sustainability Grid is being used in other communities.

*Vocabulary List for Module 3

Brain drain: when educated people leave a community to find work and opportunities

Brainstorm/brainstorming: thinking quickly and creatively in a group discussion with little time for reflection

Bursting "bubbles": overinflated financial growth like the dot.com balloon of the late 1990s and the housing crash of 2008; the overexpansion draws investors (like homebuyers) into making financial decisions that often lead to ruin

Community Sustainability Grid: chart used to help community members address all the causes of poverty

Disparity: lack of equality between people, not being the same

Great Recession: what the U.S. economic downturn that started in the fall of 2008 is often called; it was generally regarded as the worst economic slump in the U.S. since the Great Depression in the 1930s

Human trafficking: illegal trade of human beings for the purposes of reproductive slavery, commercial sexual exploitation, or forced labor

Inequality (in income and wealth): the gap between the rich and poor, income and wealth being distributed in an uneven manner

Political/economic structures: the balance of power between government and business creates conditions that determine both benefits and barriers for people in different classes

Predator: someone who plunders or destroys; a person, group, company, or state that steals from others or destroys others for gain—providing services or goods but charging more than the services or goods are worth; in other words, predators "prey" on people

Quintile: one-fifth of a group, or 20% of a group; it takes five quintiles to make 100%

Recession: an extended decline in general business activity—typically at least two consecutive quarters of economic decline

Research Continuum: studies that cover a range of topics from a focus on individual behavior at one end to a focus on political/economic structures at the other

Return on political investment (ROPI): the payoff for investing money in lobbyists, campaign contributions, and other forms of influence on legislators

Revolving door: consultants and lobbyists who move back and forth through the "doors" of special-interest groups, along with governmental offices and agencies often working for the benefit of the special-interest groups

Stagnant wages: a pay scale that "stands still" or stays the same—and doesn't keep up with inflation

Stereotypes/stereotyping: categorizing individuals or groups according to an oversimplified standardized image or idea

Violations: broken or disregarded laws or promises

Readings

Individual Behaviors and Circumstances

Lareau, Annette. (2003). *Unequal childhoods: Class, race, and family life.* Berkeley, CA: University of California Press.

Warren, Elizabeth, & Warren Tyagi, Amelia. (2003). *The two-income trap: Why middle-class mothers and fathers are going broke.* New York, NY: Basic Books.

Community Conditions

Putnam, Robert D. (2000). *Bowling alone: The collapse and revival of American community.* New York, NY: Simon & Schuster.

Sered, Susan Starr, & Fernandopulle, Rushika. (2005). *Uninsured in America: Life and death in the land of opportunity.* Berkeley, CA: University of California Press.

Exploitation

Lui, Meizhu, Robles, Barbara, Leondar-Wright, Betsy, Brewer, Rose, & Adamson, Rebecca. (2006). *The color of wealth: The story behind the U.S. racial wealth divide.* New York, NY: The New Press.

Rivlin, Gary. (2010). Broke, USA: *From pawnshops to poverty, Inc.—How the working poor became big business.* New York, NY: HarperCollins Publishers.

Political/Economic Structures

Correspondents of the *New York Times.* (2005). *Class matters.* New York, NY: Times Books.

Galeano, Eduardo. (1998). *Upside down: A primer for the looking-glass world.* New York, NY: Metropolitan Books.

Kelly, Marjorie. (2001). *The divine right of capital: Dethroning the corporate aristocracy.* San Francisco, CA: Berrett-Koehler Publishers.

Lind, Michael. (2004, January-February). Are we still a middle-class nation? *The Atlantic.* 293(1), 120–128.

Hidden Rules of Economic Class

Learning about the hidden rules of class can increase understanding, reduce judgmental attitudes, and help people come together across class lines to solve problems.

WHAT'S COVERED

We will:

Define the hidden rules of class

Understand the Key Points about this approach to economic class

Investigate the hidden rules

Analyze power and public policy

Study how poverty affects families and children

Create a "Mental Model of My Family Structure"

Create a Time-Management Matrix

WHY IT'S IMPORTANT

This information is abstract. It provides new ideas on how to solve problems. It will help us navigate new situations more skillfully.

Knowing this information will help develop economic security.

In communities where Bridges and Getting Ahead are being used, everyone is expected to know and use the hidden rules to build relationships of mutual respect and to solve problems.

HOW IT'S CONNECTED TO YOU

Earlier we found that instability and poverty can trap us in the tyranny of the moment.

In the "Theory of Change" module, we learned that we need abstract information to give us options.

Ruby Payne's approach provides a way to understand our personal experiences and the environments and behaviors of others. When we detach emotionally, we can make decisions that are more helpful to our long-term goals.

Defining Hidden Rules

In this module we will investigate Ruby Payne's ideas on poverty, beginning with the hidden rules of economic class that she has identified. In later modules, we'll look at language issues and Dr. Payne's definition of poverty. These three modules provide co-investigators with new information about common experiences, a new way to look at those experiences.

What are hidden rules? Hidden rules are the unspoken cues and habits of a group. If you know the rules, you belong; if you don't, you don't. When you belong, you seldom have to explain what you say or do to the people around you; they automatically understand you. If you know the rules, you can get along in the group more easily than someone who is new to the group.

How do you know when you *don't* belong? It's when you *break* a hidden rule. There's that moment of silence, or people laugh, or you get "the look." By the way, it's pretty easy to break a rule when it's hidden.

Rules get broken when we go to new places or meet new groups of people. All groups of people and all cultures have their own rules. So, wherever we go we're surrounded by hidden rules. We have hidden rules for nationality, neighborhoods, clubs, gangs, churches, race, age, gender, ethnicity, the workplace, and, of course, economic class.

Where do hidden rules of economic class come from? They come from the environments we were raised in. The mental models of poverty, middle class, and wealth that we created in the last module describe those environments. Those environments in turn were created by the great divide between the rich and the poor. As we saw in the last module, there were times in American history when there wasn't much of a divide between the rich and poor, but now there is.

We grow up learning how to survive in our environment by watching how our parents survive the environment. We didn't have to be taught the hidden rules directly. All we had to do was breathe, and we got it.

Discussion

1. What groups do you and the others in this workshop belong to?

2. Name a group you belong to and explain one hidden rule a new person would need to know in order to fit in.

3. Have you ever seen a person who was at a disadvantage because he/she didn't know the hidden rules of school, college, or the workplace? How did the person handle it? How did the "insiders" handle it?

Key Points That Underlie This Work

The Key Points below are definitions and ideas the will help us understand the Getting Ahead approach to poverty.

Key Points About the Bridges and Getting Ahead Approaches

1. There are many lenses through which poverty can be studied, such as race, ethnicity, gender, age, sexual orientation, and disability. In Getting Ahead we use the lens of economic class to address poverty because it encompasses all the other lenses. We need a clear understanding of how income and wealth affect the environment we live in. Otherwise, it will be difficult to address poverty effectively.

2. This work is based on patterns in the ways poverty impacts individuals, institutions, and communities. All patterns have exceptions, so it would be inaccurate to apply patterns across the board to particular individuals, institutions, and community; that would be stereotyping. Where Bridges and Getting Ahead are used, the patterns are defined locally to a large degree by GA investigators. In this way, patterns are tested and defined.

Key Points That Refine How We Think About Poverty and Economic Class

3. Economic class is a continuous line, not a clear-cut distinction. Some people have experienced a mix of two (or even three) of the mental models of class that we created. The Personal Chart on Economic Class we did in Module 3 might have shown that you experienced more than one economic class environment in your lifetime.

4. Poverty is relative. It's determined by comparing income levels or standards of living with others in society. It also can be determined by comparing the level of instability experienced by different groups. Many people in Asia and Africa in particular live in *absolute poverty** where they are struggling to survive. In poverty like that, it isn't a matter of comparison, it's life and death every day.

5. Generational poverty and situational poverty are different. In Getting Ahead, generational poverty is considered to be two or more generations on public assistance. Situational poverty, on the other hand, is when only one generation has been on public assistance. There are a number of ways that people can get into situational poverty: divorce, debt, drugs, depression, downsizing, disease, disability, death, and disasters, to name just several causes (all of which all just happen to start with the letter "d"!).

Key Points About the Application of Bridges and Getting Ahead

6. You take with you the hidden rules of the class in which you were raised.

7. Schools and businesses generally operate from middle-class norms and almost always use the hidden rules of middle class.

8. In order to build relationships of mutual respect between people in different economic classes, we need to be familiar with more than our own set of hidden rules.

9. The more we understand how economic class affects us and the more open we can be to hear how it affects others, the more effective we can be.

10. In order to achieve anything an individual may have to give up relationships (at least for a time). This is true for people of all classes and applies to all sorts of achievements.

Discussion

1. Which Key Points stood out for you?

2. What ideas are new to you?

3. What will be helpful to you from the Key Points?

Suggestions on How to Study the Hidden Rules

Activity: Studying the Hidden Rules

Time: 1 hour
Materials: Chart below, pencil

Procedure:

We suggest that you use the following pattern for studying each of the 16 hidden rules.

1. First, make sure you understand the hidden rules. Investigate why the hidden rules make sense for each class.

2. Find examples of the hidden rules being used or broken by others; look at films, songs, and books that deal with hidden rules. See Appendix H for a list of films, literature, and poetry about economic class. Using the forms provided, give examples of how you have seen the hidden rules used.

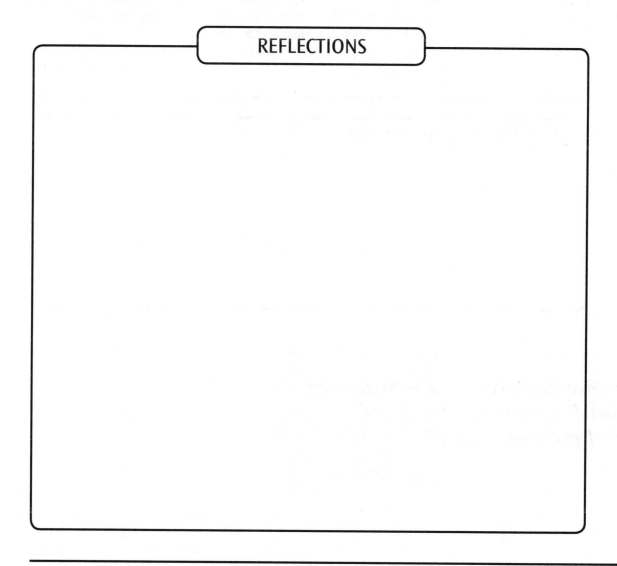

REFLECTIONS

Hidden Rules of Economic Class			
	POVERTY	MIDDLE CLASS	WEALTH
Driving Forces	Survival, relationships, entertainment	Work, achievement	Financial, political, social connections
Power	Power is linked to respect; must have the ability to fight; people respond to personal power; there is power in numbers; people in poverty can't stop bad things from happening	Power is separated out from respect; must have the ability to negotiate; power is linked to taking responsibility for solutions; people respond to positional power; power is in institutions; people in middle class run most of the institutions of the country	Power is linked to stability; must have influence, connections; people respond to expertise; power is information; people in wealth set most of the policies that direct business, corporations, and society
Time	Present most important; decisions made for the moment based on feelings, emotions, or personality	Future most important; decisions made against future ramifications	Traditions and history most important; decisions made partially on basis of tradition and decorum

HIDDEN RULE	YOUR EXAMPLES

People from different classes begin to overcome their own judgmental attitudes and build relationships of mutual respect.

	POVERTY	MIDDLE CLASS	WEALTH
Destiny	Believes in fate; cannot do much to mitigate chance	Believes in choice; can change future with good choices now	*Noblesse oblige**
World View	Sees world in terms of local setting	Sees world in terms of national setting	Sees world in terms of international setting
Language	Casual register; language is about survival	Consultative and formal register; language is for negotiation	Formal register; language is about networking

HIDDEN RULE	YOUR EXAMPLES

	POVERTY	MIDDLE CLASS	WEALTH
Education	Valued and revered as abstract but not as reality	Crucial for climbing success ladder and making money	Necessary tradition for making and maintaining connections
Money	To be used, spent	To be managed	To be conserved, invested
Family Structure	Tends to be matriarchal	Tends to be patriarchal	Depends on who has the money
Possessions	People	Things	One-of-a-kind objects, legacies, pedigrees

HIDDEN RULE	YOUR EXAMPLES

	POVERTY	MIDDLE CLASS	WEALTH
Personality	Is for entertainment; sense of humor is highly valued	Is for acquisition and stability; achievement is highly valued	Is for connections; financial, political, and social networks are highly valued
Social Emphasis	Social inclusion for personally likable people	Emphasis is on self-governance and self-sufficiency	Emphasis is on social exclusion
Love	Love and acceptance conditional, based upon whether individual is liked	Love and acceptance conditional, based largely upon achievement	Love and acceptance conditional, related to social standing and connections

HIDDEN RULE	YOUR EXAMPLES

	POVERTY	MIDDLE CLASS	WEALTH
Humor	About people and sex	About situations	About *social faux pas**
Food	Key question—did you have enough? quantity important	Key question—did you like it? quality important	Key question—was it presented well? presentation important
Clothing	Clothing valued for its individual style and expression of personality	Clothing valued for its quality and acceptance into norm of middle class; label important	Clothing valued for its artistic sense and expression; designer important

HIDDEN RULE	YOUR EXAMPLES

Note. Adapted from *A Framework for Understanding Poverty* (pp. 42–43), by R. K. Payne, 2005, Highlands, TX: aha! Process. Copyright 1996 by aha! Process.

Discussion

1. How comfortable were you with the hidden rules?

2. Did they click with your experience?

3. Are there hidden rules of class in your country? Are the hidden rules similar to these? If not, how are they different?

4. Did you relate more to one class than another?

5. Did you have hidden rules from more than one class? How did that come about?

6. Is one set of rules better than another?

7. Which hidden rules captured your interest? Why?

8. Is there an advantage in knowing more than one set of rules? If so, give examples.

9. How can knowledge of the hidden rules be used to improve relationships between people of different classes?

10. Are the hidden rules of the economic class you are in part of your identity? If so, to what degree?

11. When you begin to build your future story, do you think the way you see yourself will change? Do you think others will see you differently?

12. A GA graduate said, "You can't play poker if you don't know the rules." Do you think it would be helpful to think of the hidden rules of class as the rules of a game?

13. How can knowledge of the hidden rules be helpful to agencies and other organizations?

Hidden Rules of Power at the Organizational Level

Most of the United States' institutions (schools, business, courts, and service providers) operate according to middle-class rules and norms. This gives middle-class individuals power that they may not be fully aware of. As noted earlier in this module, power that is **normalized*** is often invisible to the dominant group that enjoys the benefits. It's those who don't have power who are most sensitive to power issues, to their own powerlessness, and to their invisibility. In addition, information is power, and the institutions generally hold the information (this is changing somewhat in the era of the Internet, but middle-class institutions still hold "most of the cards"). Those looking for resources or services from the institutions must usually access them through the middle-class people working there.

Most middle-class employees know how to steer their way through institutions and systems. Members of the middle class who are familiar with power structures within the organization and wish to maintain their careers—and a stable environment for their families—will show respect for the position a person holds, even when they don't respect the person. This makes it possible for the middle-class employee to separate respect from power, and so keep his/her job even when there's a disagreement with a superior.

According to Jodi Pfarr (2009):

> In poverty, power and respect are directly linked. If a worker in poverty does not respect a supervisor, then that worker may find it extremely difficult to take direction from that supervisor. In poverty, because your survival depends upon other people, it is hard to grant power to those for whom you have no respect. (pp. 29–30)

Disputes with supervisors often arise from the power/respect interaction. The supervisory role—with all of its money and perks—doesn't always command respect. People in poverty generally hold low-wage, entry-level positions and are the first to be laid off. Low-status jobs can be hard on an individual's sense of self-worth. Any show of disrespect from the supervisor can be seen as a huge insult. One way to maintain personal dignity is to walk off the job (think of the song "Take This Job and Shove It"). Many people have given up good jobs because they felt disrespected.

When people in poverty join the middle class and the wealthy at the decision-making table, there's a shift in power. The dominant classes are required to make physical space at the table, to share time with other speakers. They have to listen to the information that is provided by people in poverty. They might even have to take direction from people who once were not at the table—who were previously invisible to them. Getting Ahead is designed to prepare investigators to take a seat at the table, ready to interact, by providing valuable information, new insights, and the tools to analyze problems and propose solutions.

Getting Ahead uses the hidden rules of class to bring people together across class lines to solve community problems.

Power and Policy

Let's explore how our knowledge of the hidden rules can help us figure out what is happening at the national policy level. We can use this information to understand, analyze, and predict decisions and actions of wealthy and middle-class people.

People in poverty normally have very little power, influence, or voice at any level in our society. In the module on the rich/poor gap, we investigated ways in which those with wealth and power have been using the revolving door, lobbyists, and campaign contributions to create more wealth and power for themselves.

Activity: Studying the Hidden Rules

Time: 5 minutes
Materials: Chart below, pencil

Procedure:

1. In the boxes below, draw an arrow from the economic class that creates national policies regarding poverty and social services to the economic class that runs the social service institutions. Label this arrow "A."

2. Draw an arrow from the economic class that runs the social service institutions to the economic class that most often uses the institutions. Label this arrow "B."

POVERTY	MIDDLE CLASS	WEALTH

Discussion

1. How much influence to shape policies and program designs do people in poverty have? How much influence do people of the middle class have to shape policies and program designs?

2. To what extent does economic stability influence the time and resources needed to solve problems and pursue personal interests?

Hidden Rules of Family Structures

The hidden rules indicate that families in poverty tend to be matriarchal (headed by the mother), those in middle class tend to be patriarchal (headed by the father), and those in wealth are usually run by the person who has the money. The word "tend" is important here because we don't want to assume that all families in poverty or middle class would be headed by a mother or a father.

Most people have strong opinions about families. There are disagreements about what a family is and what a family "should" be. We want to be very careful when discussing this topic so we don't become judgmental. After all, we don't want to get sidetracked from what we're really wanting to investigate. What's important here is exploring the impact that poverty has on children and families.

We'll look at families, using what we learned in previous modules. We'll look at individual choices, community conditions, and policies that impact children and families.

Individual Choices, Behaviors, and Circumstances

The number of births to unmarried women has been going up since the 1970s, according to data from the National Vital Statistics System (NVSS) and as described in Stephanie Ventura's May 2009 paper "Changing Patterns of **Nonmarital*** Childbearing in the United States" (Ventura, 2009). The same trend is occurring in most developed countries.

Some of the key findings from the study are:

- In 2007 nearly four in 10 births in the U.S. were to unmarried women

- Birth rates for unmarried women:

  Have risen considerably for women who were in their 20s and older
  —60% of births to women ages 20–24 are nonmarital
  —Nearly one-third of births to women ages 25–29 are nonmarital

  Have been declining or changing little for unmarried teenagers
  —86% of births to teenagers are nonmarital

  Are highest for Hispanic women, followed by African American women
  —Rates for non-Hispanic white and Asian or Pacific Islander women are much lower

What does this mean to children? Babies born to unmarried women are:

- At a greater risk of low birth weight

- At a greater risk of premature birth

- At a greater risk of dying in infancy

- More likely to live in poverty than babies born to married women

In 2010 there were 17 million poor children. The U.S. Center for Budget and Policy Priorities found that "… just over half of those children lived in households that reported at least one of four major hardships: hunger, overcrowding, failure to pay the rent or mortgage on time, or failure to seek needed medical care" (*New York Times* editorial, November 23, 2011).

Discussion

1. What stood out to you as you read this information?

2. Is there anything from this information that you think should be added to the Mental Model of Poverty?

3. Look at the Mental Model of the Floor Plan of My Apartment/House and the Mental Model of My Life Now. How does poverty impact the economic stability and well-being of the children?

Community Conditions

Individual choices and behaviors that impact children in poverty are only part of the story. Where you live—by neighborhood, county, region, and state—has a huge impact on children too.

High child poverty and persistent child poverty are a growing problem in the United States. A Carsey Institute study found that between 1980 and 2009 twenty-three percent of U.S. counties (706) had persistently high poverty.

Other findings from the Carsey Institute study showed:

- 81% of counties with persistent child poverty are in rural areas

- 26% of rural children reside in counties whose poverty rates have stayed persistently high

- 12% of urban children live in counties with persistently high poverty rates

- Counties with persistent child poverty are found largely in Appalachia, the Mississippi Delta, some parts of the Southeast and Southwest, and in the Great Plains

- Between 2005 and 2007, a total of 484 counties averaged greater than 30% of children in poverty

- Between 2008 and 2009, the number of counties with 30% of children in poverty rose to 556

Note. University of New Hampshire, Carsey Institute, Fall 2011, Issue Brief 38, "More Poor Kids in More Poor Places: Children Increasingly Live Where Poverty Persists." Marybeth J. Mattingly, Kenneth M. Johnson, and Andrew Schaefer.

Discussion

1. What information from this study is important to you?

2. Do you or members of your extended family live in one of the high child-poverty areas?

3. What would it take in a community where the child poverty rate is 30% for a child to get out of poverty?

4. What would a single mother have to think about and deal with if she planned to help her children develop high resources?

Policies That Impact Children and Families; Segregation by Income

Another study throws light on the negative impact that the rich/poor gap has on community life and child poverty. Income inequality determines what families can afford to pay for housing. That leads to increased *"residential sorting"** by income or *"income segregation"** (when economic classes live separately).

The 2010 study on "Residential Segregation of Families by Income" reported the following facts:

- From 2000 to 2007 in the U.S., family income segregation grew in 89% of the large and moderate-size metropolitan areas

- In 1970 only 15% of families were in neighborhoods that were affluent or poor. By 2007, thirty-one percent of the families lived in affluent or poor neighborhoods

- The affluent are more segregated from other Americans than the poor are

- Income segregation among African American and Hispanic families increased much more than it did among white families from 1970 to 2007; now income segregation among African American and Latino families is much higher than white families

Income segregation has a negative impact on children:

- Children living in poor neighborhoods have less access to:
    - —Educational opportunities and high-quality schools
    - —A secure tax base
    - —High-quality social services
    - —Green space (parks)
    - —Diverse social connections

- Among African American children living in poor neighborhoods, there is a loss in learning equal to a full year of school—and lower graduation rates by as much as 20%

- Where violent crime is high and where there are few neighborhood associations, there are lower birth weights

Income segregation limits the opportunity for children in poverty to move up economically. The lack of money and other resources, as well as the lack of power, creates more poverty, inequality, and powerlessness, just as wealth and power create, yes, more wealth and power.

Note. "Growth in the Residential Segregation of Families by Income, 1970–2009." US2010: Discover America in a New Century. Sponsors: Russell Sage Foundation, American Communities Project of Brown University.

Discussion

1. What is the child poverty rate in your community?

2. What is the rate of nonmarital births (births to parents who are not married to each other) in your community?

3. To what extent is income segregation a factor in your community?

4. What is your immediate neighborhood like? How much economic diversity is there in your neighborhood?

5. What do you want to remember most about this information?

> *"I'm not going to get ahead and leave my children behind."*
>
> —James Williams Jr., GA Graduate

Activity: Create a Mental Model of My Family Structure

Time: 20 minutes
Materials: Worksheet, pen or pencil

Procedure:

1. Review these two examples of family structures.

   a. The first is an example of a multi-relational, matriarchal structure. You can see that Jane had relationships with three men whom she never married.

      i. Joe is not in the home, and their relationship is over.

      ii. Roger is out of the home too. He and Jane had a son named Willie. Willie is married to Shea. They have a son, Bill. They live with Jane.

      iii. Roger is now married to Ann, and they have a child. Roger also had a child, Jill, with another woman, and Jill is living with Jane.

      iv. Jane is currently with Scott. Their son, John, had a child (Pris) with Pat. Pris is Jane's second grandchild.

   b. The second is an example of a multi-relational, patriarchal structure. It shows a married couple, Larry and Becky.

      i. They have three children: Phil, age 15; Mary, 11; and Todd, 9.

      ii. Larry is divorced from Peg. Their 17-year-old son, Grant, lives with Larry and Becky during the school year.

2. Look over the following mental models that were created to represent the two examples.

Matriarchal Structure

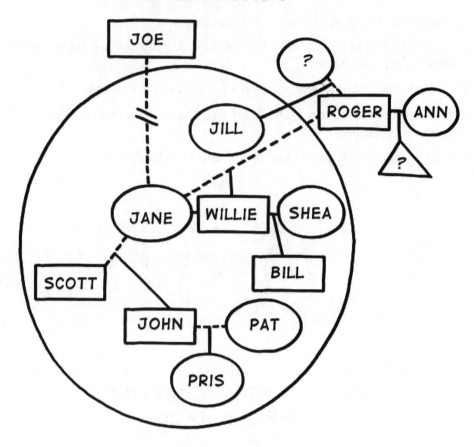

Patriarchal Structure

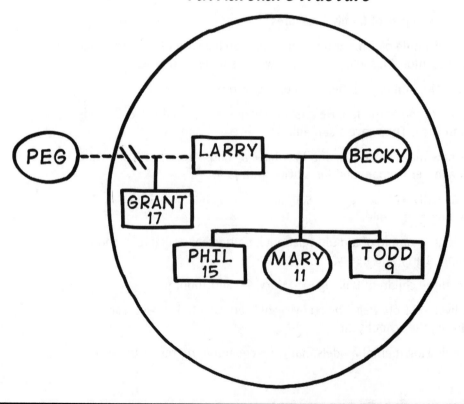

3. Create a Mental Model of My Family Structure.

   a. On a separate paper draw a circle in the middle of the page. Inside the circle, draw the members of your household. Use squares for males and circles for females.

   b. Connect the parents in the household with lines that represent the status of their relationship by using:

      i. A solid line if they are married and living together.

         1) Add a single diagonal slash (/) across the sold line if they are no longer together but still talk to each other.

         2) Add two diagonal slashes (//) across the sold line if they are no longer together and are not talking to each other.

      ii. Dashes if they are living together but not married.

         1) Add a single diagonal slash (/) across the dashes if they are no longer together but still talk to each other

         2) Add a two diagonal slashes (//) across the dashes if they are no longer together and are not talking to each other

   c. Draw the children beneath the parents with vertical lines linking the children to their parents. Children are placed from left to right, with the oldest to the left. Twins are connected to each other with a solid line. To indicate a child has moved out, draw a short horizontal line through the vertical line.

   d. Write in names, ages, and other information that you think is important.

   e. Add people who are not related but living in the house. Then add others you think are important outside the household. Add notes to explain their connection to the family.

4. When you have completed the Mental Model of My Family Structure, place it in your Future Story Portfolio.

Discussion

1. How comfortable were you doing this exercise?

2. Which of the people in the household contribute to paying the bills?

3. How do the different people contribute to solving problems?

4. What positive roles do men and women play to help family members manage their situations?

5. Who heads the household?

6. If that person is not you, how much support do family members give you for the changes you are considering?

Exploring How to Plan

Once free of the tyranny of the moment, we can learn to really manage our time. The challenge is how to fit everything we have to do into our day. Stephen Covey's book, *The 7 Habits of Highly Effective People* (1989), offers a way to think about how we spend time. Covey suggests that all activities can be put into four categories, depending on how important they are and how urgent they are. Look at the following Time-Management Matrix, which gives an example of a GA graduate who is going to college.

Time-Management Matrix		
	Urgent	**Not Urgent**
Important	**Quadrant I—Emergencies and Crises** *Examples:* Death, illness, accidents Spending the entire weekend in the library finishing a term paper Completing add/drop procedures on the last allowable day	**Quadrant II—Takes Planning: You, Relationships, School, Work, Maintenance of Material Things** *Examples:* Filling in all test dates, assignment due dates, academic deadlines, breaks, holidays and special days on a semester planner Keeping a file of all the financial information needed for FAFSA (Free Application for Federal Student Aid) and other grant/scholarship applications
Not Important	**Quadrant III—Other People's Problems** *Examples:* Rushing to a last-minute meeting with your roommate about a project that has nothing to do with you Getting to the student center for free pizza before the party ends Giving your little brother your last $20 for a haircut and driving him to the barber shop	**Quadrant IV—Time Wasters** *Examples:* Surfing the Internet for travel deals when you don't have the time or money to travel Reviewing course material that you are already knowledgeable about Watching reruns on TV

Note. Adapted from *The 7 Habits of Highly Effective People* (p. 151), by S. R. Covey, 1989, New York, NY: Simon & Schuster. Copyright 1989 by Simon & Schuster.

Covey tells us that the best place for us to be most of the time is Quadrant II. In Quadrant II the activity is important but not under the pressure of time. There is time to think and plan and create and organize.

Quadrant I activity is important too, but it's under the stress of a deadline or consequence. If you don't take care of things that belong in Quadrant II, they usually end up being emergencies in Quadrant I. An example of this is in Quadrant I above.

In Quadrant III the activities are usually about someone else's stuff that you got pulled into. Quadrant III activities need to be done now, but they aren't necessarily going to help you.

Quadrant IV is full of activities that don't get us very far. We all do them: watching TV, doing stuff on the computer/Internet, sitting around, playing with the dog. The unimportant and non-urgent activities are time wasters unless you intentionally plan for them because they're important to you. If you plan for these activities, they go into Quadrant II. In that case, the activities have a place in your life and are called such things as relaxation, fun, entertainment, or down time. But if you're watching TV five hours a night most nights, it's probably going to put most class work into Quadrant I—last-minute, high-pressure, and high-stakes.

Activity: Effective Time Management

Time: 20 minutes

Materials: Time-Management Matrix Worksheet on next page and your completed Time Monitor sheets from previous week

Procedure:

1. Refer to the following open chart.

2. Analyze your Time Monitor sheets:

   a. Where does each activity fall in relation to the four quadrants?

   b. Assign each activity to a quadrant. If the activity occurs often (for example, talking on the phone) just put ditto marks (") after the first time you write it.

   c. Might some activities appear in more than one quadrant?

3. Finally, make a new plan for how you'll spend your time in the week to come. Set aside certain blocks of time to study certain courses. Look for blocks of time you spent in Quadrant III and IV. Can you redirect that time? Are there "natural" spaces in your schedule, such as between classes, when you can find a quiet spot to study?

Time-Management Matrix

	Urgent	Not Urgent
Important	**Quadrant I—Emergencies and Crises**	**Quadrant II—Takes Planning: You, Relationships, School, Work, Maintenance of Material Things**
Not Important	**Quadrant III—Other People's Problems**	**Quadrant IV—Time Wasters**

Note. Adapted from *The 7 Habits of Highly Effective People* (p. 151), by S. R. Covey, 1989, New York, NY: Simon & Schuster. Copyright 1989 by Simon & Schuster.

Getting Ahead in a Just-Gettin'-By World

Discussion/Journal

1. What did you discover that you didn't realize the first time you looked at your Time Monitor sheets?

2. Think of one or two people you know who have achieved great things, changed their life, "succeeded." Think about how they spent time while they were making their changes. Where (in what quadrant) do you think they spent the most time?

3. Look at your chart and at the activities you wrote in the four quadrants. Put a check mark (✓) by the ones that, a year from now, will have made a positive difference in your life.

4. Look at your chart again and make a different mark beside any activity that involved another person or persons. Write their name(s) outside the chart and draw a line from their name to the activity they are involved in with you. What conclusions can you draw from this exercise?

5. Go to http://www.literacynet.org/icans/chapter06/time1.html and take two quizzes on saving time and wasting time. What does your score tell you?

6. What are some specific steps you can take today to use your time more effectively? Make a list.

*Vocabulary List for Module 4

Absolute poverty: about survival, about not having enough physical, human necessities like food, clean water, and shelter

Noblesse oblige: with wealth, power, and prestige comes a responsibility to act nobly

Nonmarital: not married

Normalized: social norms and patterns that are made "normal" by the dominant group and the pressure to get others to conform to the standard—being right-handed, using Standard American English, using middle-class rules and norms

Residential sorting/income segregation: people of different classes living apart from each other because higher incomes allow people to buy houses in areas that people with less income cannot afford

Social faux pas: an embarrassing social blunder, a blooper, a bungle, a boo-boo

Readings

Bragg, Rick. (1998). *All over but the shoutin'.* New York, NY: Vintage Books.

Fuller, Robert W. (2004). *Somebodies and nobodies: Overcoming the abuse of rank.* Gabriola Island, BC: New Society Publishers.

Fussell, Paul. (1983). *Class: A guide through the American status system.* New York, NY: Touchstone.

hooks, bell. (2000). *Where we stand: Class matters.* New York, NY: Routledge.

Oshry, Barry. (1996). *Seeing systems: Unlocking the mysteries of organizational life.* San Francisco, CA: Berrett-Koehler Publishers.

Robinson, Eugene. (2010). *Disintegration: The splintering of black America.* New York, NY: Doubleday.

The Importance of Language

Language skills can help us learn, solve problems, and create relationships of mutual respect.

WHAT'S COVERED

We will:

Learn about the registers of language and *discourse patterns**

Learn about *code switching** between Standard American English and community language patterns

Examine the "voices" and body language

Explore the connection between story structure and a child's readiness for school

Investigate the importance of *language experience** in the first three years of life

Learn *mediation** strategies to help prepare children for school

Use language to resolve conflicts

Learn the language of negotiation

Do a self-assessment of negotiation skills

WHY IT'S IMPORTANT

We use language to make relationships, to prepare children for school, to negotiate, and to express ourselves when we're at the decision-making tables in our communities.

Being able to use language in different settings with people from different classes will empower us.

HOW IT'S CONNECTED TO YOU

We can begin to use some of this information *right away*.

We can use this information at all levels: in the Getting Ahead workshops, with family, friends and neighbors—and at work, school, and in community work.

We can use it to build social capital.

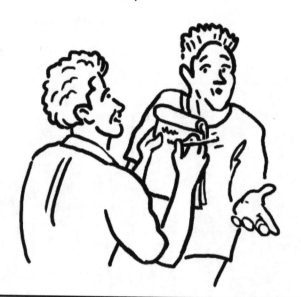

Nine Language Concepts

In this module we will investigate the following nine language concepts:

1. Registers of Language

2. Discourse Patterns

3. Code Switching

4. 'Voices': Parent, Child, Adult

5. Story Structure

6. Language Experience

7. Mediation: the What, the Why, the How

8. Using Language to Resolve Differences

9. The Basics of Negotiation

Registers of Language

The hidden rule of language registers was touched on in Module 4. Now language deserves a chapter of its own and needs to be investigated fully—so that we can work with people across class lines to solve problems. Why? Well, here's an example: One of the very first GA investigators said she went to an agency and ... "As soon as I started talking they looked at me like I was stupid." With one look the person behind the desk managed to disrespect the client. In those few seconds the possibility of developing a relationship of mutual respect was lost.

The GA investigators in her group decided that language issues were so important that language was not just a hidden rule. In addition, knowledge of language registers and discourse patterns was necessary for most people who were trying to get out of poverty. In that example, it would've been very helpful if the person behind the desk understood the language issues that we're going to cover in this module. The investigator recognized that she needed to build her language resources too.

In this module we're going to cover a lot more than the registers of language. At the end you're going to decide what you want and need in your life. It could be you need to know more than what we cover here. Think of this module (and all the others) as introductions to topics. They aren't designed to be everything you'll ever need to know. You might decide you need to do more with language after you graduate from Getting Ahead.

As we work through the module, keep a running list of any ideas you want to follow up on.

Martin Joos defined language registers in The Five Clocks: A Linguistic Excursion into the Five Styles of English Usage (1967). As you read through the list, you'll probably come up with examples of each register.

Registers of Language	
REGISTER	**EXPLANATION**
Frozen	Language that is always the same. For example: Lord's Prayer, wedding vows, etc.
Formal	The standard sentence syntax and word choice of work and school. Has complete sentences and specific word choice.
Consultative	Formal register when used in conversation. Discourse pattern not quite as direct as formal register.
Casual	Language between friends and is characterized by a 400- to 800-word vocabulary. Word choice general and not specific. Conversation dependent on nonverbal assists. Sentence syntax often incomplete.
Intimate	Language between lovers or twins. Language of sexual harassment.

Note. From *Under-Resourced Learners* (p. 40), by R. K. Payne, 2008, Highlands, TX: aha! Process. Copyright 2008 by aha! Process.

Discussion

1. Can you identify people in your life who use one register more often than any other?

2. When have you seen people get into conflicts over the way they use these registers?

3. Which register are you most comfortable using?

4. Do you know people who are *bilingual**, meaning they can "code switch" and move back and forth between registers easily?

5. Which register is better for understanding intentions, feelings, and daily life?

6. Which register is best for ideas, logic, negotiation, and things far removed from daily life?

7. Which register is needed for construction jobs? Manufacturing jobs? *Service sector** (fast food, discount stores, gas stations, convenience stores, hotels) jobs? *Knowledge sector** (nurse, lab technician, teacher, accounting, technology, finance) jobs?

8. Which of the employment sectors mentioned above requires the ability to write in the formal register?

9. How far can a child or young person go in school and be successful with only the casual register?

10. Which hidden rules of economic class are behind the fact that most people in middle-class institutions (like schools, agencies, and many work settings) use formal register?

11. What registers are used much of the time in e-mails, instant messages, and social-networking sites?

12. What are the implications of those personal web pages being accessible to future employers?

13. Discuss who holds the power in frozen-, formal-, and casual-register settings.

Discourse Patterns

Another aspect of language is called *discourse patterns**. This refers to the way people carry on a conversation. For example, in some groups it's OK—even expected—for people to "talk over" each other. In other words, before one person is done speaking another begins talking. In other societies and cultures, the rule is to wait at least one or two seconds after a person has finished talking to begin speaking. It would be considered rude to "step on" someone's sentences, to "interrupt."

The discourse pattern when we use formal register tends to be quite direct. We usually present the story or information in chronological order—the way it happened from beginning to end. We would use abstract terms to present ideas and information. We might go directly to the point and say things like, "Let's get down to business." Listeners are not expected to add information, but they might ask questions to clarify something that has been said.

Direct Discourse Pattern

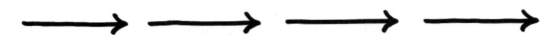

The discourse pattern when we use the casual register, on the other hand, tends to be in a *circular story pattern**. We go around and around before coming to the point. We may jump into the story just about anywhere, not necessarily at the "beginning." Instead, we may start where the story is most interesting or funny or has the greatest emotional impact.

The casual-register pattern relies on the use of common words and an ability to tell what people mean by the way they move their eyes, hands, and body (nonverbal communication) or by tone of voice. Hosts of late-night talk shows often speak in casual register, using body language and "reading" the social situation while conversing with their guests.

Circular story patterns take much longer to tell than stories in the formal-discourse pattern. In the casual register, listeners often contribute information and side remarks to the story as it is told.

Circular Discourse Pattern

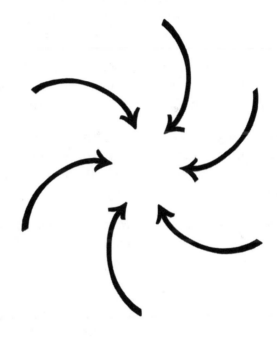

Discussion

1. Which hidden rules are behind the circular story pattern?

2. How do discourse patterns—casual and formal—lead to misunderstandings? Give examples.

3. How might it help someone to use both circular and direct discourse patterns?

4. Does the information about registers and discourse patterns apply differently in different regions and in other countries?

5. How can you use this information?

Code Switching

People who are "bilingual," who can use the formal register and casual register of the community, are able to code switch. People in the dominant culture (the middle class) are not likely to have this skill. But people who aren't in the dominant culture are familiar with frequently having to code switch in order to maintain positive relationships and be successful at work and school.

The lack of formal register or Standard American English (SAE) can work against you and your children at work and school. Negative assumptions are often being made about the intelligence and learning capacities of people who have only the casual register (consider the story of the investigator at the beginning of this module).

Rebecca Wheeler (2008) writes about how the traditional language lens used by many teachers misdiagnoses students as needing special education for learning disabilities because the students use the patterns of speech in casual register.

Her research shows that the students usually aren't learning disabled, but rather the teachers don't understand casual register. Wheeler explains that the students' use of casual register is not wrong; it is simply different from SAE.

Students using casual register are "not making errors, but instead are speaking or writing correctly using the language patterns of their community." She also recognizes that to be successful in school—and eventually work—students do need to master SAE in formal register.

Wheeler and Swords' (2010) work addresses the most common informal English grammar patterns that crop up in students' work. In each chart, there are examples both in casual or informal English and in formal or SAE—and then the pattern is spelled out, so you can see the difference.

Showing Possession	
INFORMAL	**FORMAL**
We went to my <u>aunt house</u>.	We went to my <u>aunt's house</u>.
A <u>giraffe neck</u> is very long.	A <u>giraffe's neck</u> is very long.
My <u>dog name</u> is Princess.	My <u>dog's name</u> is Princess.
I made <u>people beds</u>.	I made <u>people's beds</u>.
Be good for <u>Annie mom</u>.	Be good for <u>Annie's mom</u>.
THE PATTERN	**THE PATTERN**
owner + what is owned	owner + 's + what is owned

Note. From *Code-Switching Lessons: Grammar Strategies for Linguistically Diverse Writers* by R. S. Wheeler and R. Swords, 2010, Portsmouth, NH: Heinemann. Copyright 2010 by Heinemann.

Past Time Patterns

INFORMAL	FORMAL
<u>Yesterday</u> I trade my MP3 player.	Yesterday I trad<u>ed</u> my MP3 player.
We walk all around the school <u>last night</u>.	We walk<u>ed</u> all around the school last night.
<u>Last Saturday</u> we watch that movie.	Last Saturday we watch<u>ed</u> that movie.
I call my grandma <u>two days ago</u>.	I call<u>ed</u> my grandma two days ago.
Martin Luther King talk to the people.	Martin Luther King talk<u>ed</u> to the people.
THE PATTERN time words and phrases common knowledge	**THE PATTERN** verb + -ed

Note. From *Code-Switching Lessons: Grammar Strategies for Linguistically Diverse Writers* by R. S. Wheeler and R. Swords, 2010, Portsmouth, NH: Heinemann. Copyright 2010 by Heinemann.

Plural Patterns

INFORMAL	FORMAL
I have <u>two</u> dog and <u>two</u> cat.	I have two dog<u>s</u> and two cat<u>s</u>.
Three <u>ship</u> sailed across the ocean.	Three ship<u>s</u> sailed across the ocean.
<u>All</u> of the boy are here today.	All of the boy<u>s</u> are here today.
Tay<u>l</u>or loves cat.	Taylor loves cat<u>s</u>.
THE PATTERN number words other signal words common knowledge	**THE PATTERN** noun + -s

Note. From *Code-Switching Lessons: Grammar Strategies for Linguistically Diverse Writers* by R. S. Wheeler and R. Swords, 2010, Portsmouth, NH: Heinemann. Copyright 2010 by Heinemann.

Instructors who teach code switching will use a lot less red ink on the papers of children who are learning SAE. Wheeler tells a story about a fourth-grade boy who wrote a story about a mouse that was a detective. His teacher commented on his story saying, "This was a very sweet and interesting story. I noticed that you used Standard English very well, except for one character." The boy replied, "Oh, that mouse, he didn't know Standard English."

Discussion

1. How comfortable are you with the idea of code switching between casual and formal register?
2. How does the ability to code switch affect relationships?
3. Can this information help you or your children?
4. How might organizations in your community benefit from this information?

'Voices': Parent, Child, Adult

How people talk to each other makes all the difference in getting along and not getting along—and in respect and disrespect. When we learn about the registers of language and discourse patterns, we have a way to understand where other people are coming from and what they expect to hear.

Another helpful tool is to understand the "voices" that we use: the parent voice, the child voice, and the adult voice. Eric Berne, a therapist who developed Transactional Analysis, says all three voices exist (to a greater or lesser degree) in every person's mind. They are what is sometimes called "self-talk," like recorded messages that play back from our childhood—sometimes put there by others, sometimes what we have created. These inner voices reflect our concept of what we were taught, of relationships, of how life feels, and of how we see the world.

Parent Voice

The "internal parent" is ingrained in us by our real parents, teachers, and caregivers. It is the *taught* concept of life. The parent voice is made up of many messages that come out in phrases like these:

• You shouldn't (should) do that …
• That's the wrong (right) to do.
• That's stupid, immature, out of line …
• Do as I say.
• Don't lie, cheat, steal …
• Life isn't fair; get busy.
• You are worthless …
• If you weren't so _____, this wouldn't happen to you.
• Why can't you be like _____?
• You must never …

Note. Adapted from *A Framework for Understanding Poverty* (p. 84), by R. K. Payne, 2005, Highlands, TX: aha! Process. Copyright 2005 by aha! Process.

Getting Ahead in a Just-Gettin'-By World

The body language that goes with the parent voice is often angry, with impatient gestures, finger pointing, and a loud voice. These phrases tend to be orders, demands, criticisms, and threats.

These are things we say to ourselves and to others. When we use the parent voice in our self-talk, sometimes it "keeps us in line." But often it reinforces feelings that we aren't good enough. When we use the parent voice on others, it frequently causes conflict because people usually don't like being told what to do or being talked down to. It isn't easy to change the way we talk to ourselves or others, but it is possible.

Child Voice

Our "internal child" is how we react to what we see, feel, and hear from the world around us. It is the felt concept of life. When our internal child is angry or afraid, it can dominate our thinking; the child is in control. Our child voice expresses itself in phrases like these:

• If you liked (loved) me …	• I don't care.
• If you respected me, you would …	• This is the worst day of my life.
• Things never go right for me.	• Don't blame me.
• You don't trust me.	• I don't trust you.
• You make me sick.	• You make me mad.
• It's your fault.	• You made me do it.

Note. Adapted from *A Framework for Understanding Poverty* (p. 83), by R. K. Payne, 2005, Highlands, TX: aha! Process. Copyright 2005 by aha! Process.

These phrases tend to be defensive, victimized, emotional, and exaggerated. The body language that often accompanies the child voice is rolling eyes, shrugging shoulders, temper tantrums, and a whining voice.

Even as adults, the child voice still comes out in how we communicate with ourselves and others. When we use the child voice in our self-talk, we are usually avoiding responsibility for our own situation. When we use the child voice on others, it can invite the parent voice from them in response. The child voice can be very manipulative and thus powerful. But it becomes annoying and tiring to others—and thus harmful to relationships.

Adult Voice

Our "internal adult" begins to form around 10 months of age, according to Berne. We develop the ability to think and determine our behaviors and actions. The adult is the thinking part of who we are, which gives us a way to control our child and parent. This is the voice that is needed for learning. We use it to discover how other people think and feel. We use this voice to resolve conflicts. The adult voice is heard in phrases like these:

• What are the options in this situation?	• What factors will be used to determine the quality of _____ ?
• When you _____ I feel _____.	• These are the consequences of that choice or action.
• What did you mean by _____ ?	• In what ways could this be resolved?
• I realize, I see, I think, in my opinion …	• We agree to disagree.
• I would like to recommend …	

Note. Adapted from *A Framework for Understanding Poverty* (p. 84), by R. K. Payne, 2005, Highlands, TX: aha! Process. Copyright 2005 by aha! Process.

The body language that goes with the adult voice is attentive, leaning forward, not threatened or threatening—and the voice is calm. The phrases tend to be respectful, comparative, informative, and reasoned. Questions might include: What, when, where, who, how?

> *We identify and address language issues that cause conflicts and misunderstandings between people from different economic classes.*

There are no hard-and-fast rules about the use of the three voices. In some situations the parent voice might be the most effective. For example, if there is a fire, and you want people to leave the room quickly and calmly, you'd use the parent voice. Being directive would be necessary. "Quiet, everyone! Use the doors at the back of the room, and do not push!"

But the parent voice (and/or body language) can be insulting and disrespectful. The parent voice pushes the listener into the child role. It can break relationships and is not effective when trying to teach. One way to deal with a situation could be responding to the parent voice with the adult voice.

The child voice, when teasing playfully, can defuse angry and potentially dangerous situations. But some people use it to manipulate and get what they want. Again, the adult voice in response might help.

As noted, Berne would suggest that we use the adult voice to control our internal child and parent, as well as in relating to others. Speaking adult to adult can be used for building relationships, learning, resolving conflicts, and negotiating. In short, the adult voice is respectful, which enhances the chances that real communication and connection will happen.

Discussion

1. What "recorded messages" do you have in your mind, and where did they come from (yourself or other people or both)? How do you react to the voices that you carry within you?

2. Share examples of the voices—when they worked and when they didn't.

3. How do you tend to react when you hear the child voice or parent voice in others? How about the adult voice? Is there anything about the adult voice that also can be annoying or disconnected from reality? Why?

4. What happens to voices when we write? Examine some e-mail messages and discuss how the voices might be misunderstood.

5. How does this information apply to you?

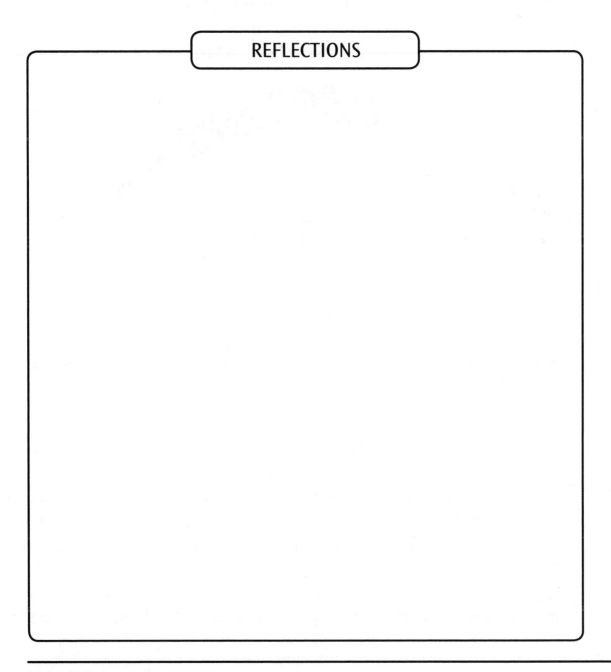

REFLECTIONS

Story Structure

Most children learn to talk by the time they are 3 years old. Their experience with language depends almost entirely on their immediate family. The register and discourse pattern of their family will become their register and discourse pattern. All families have their own "culture of talk." Some families talk more than others. Some encourage children to join in the conversation, while others don't, saying explicitly or in effect that children should be "seen but not heard."

During the first three years of life, the brain is building neural pathways for thinking. The more words a child hears from family members and others, the more pathways are created. The more stories a child hears, the more a family explains how things work, the more pathways are created. Research tells us that children need to hear stories and fairy tales several times a week in order to build thinking pathways.

The typical story pattern in books for children looks like this:

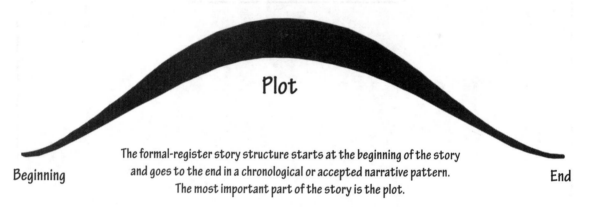

Plot

Beginning

The formal-register story structure starts at the beginning of the story and goes to the end in a chronological or accepted narrative pattern. The most important part of the story is the plot.

End

Goldilocks and the Three Bears

Remember the story of Goldilocks and the Three Bears? Take a minute to talk about the story in the group, then answer these questions:

1. What happened first?

2. When Goldilocks got to the house, she did three things. What were they, and in what order did they happen?

3. Each time she tried something in the bears' home she tried them in a certain order. What was that order?

4. Have you ever noticed what happens when you read a fairy tale to a child but skip a page or try to change the story?

The above story pattern is much more than just a story. It is a storage/retrieval system that children use for remembering the information in the story. In their brain they put the porridge first on the "plot curve," the chair second, and the bed last. Putting these items into the thinking pattern of the story allows them to go back to those places to find the details of the story.

There are other patterns—or mental pictures—that children will rely on too. For example, they will recall that each time Goldilocks tries things in the bears' house, it's in this order: Papa Bear, Mama Bear, Baby Bear.

The reason children like to hear the story again and again is to gain mastery over the story. They like and want to be able to anticipate and predict what will happen. This is why children don't like it when adults "mess" with the story by skipping a page or making up different events. Children need to hear a story multiple times to embed this neurological thinking pathway, this cognitive structure, in their brain. They can then use this pathway again and again.

Discussion

1. Notice the difference between the circular story pattern (described in Discourse Patterns earlier in this module) and the linear fairy tale structure. Might the circular story structure give children a less reliable or memorable thinking pathway than a linear story structure?

2. Imagine kids going to their first day of kindergarten, meeting their teacher, spending their day doing things with other kids, and learning the rules of school. How important is it for them to feel like they fit in, that they belong? What part does language play in their feeling of belonging?

3. What does all this have to do with poverty?

4. To what degree does the information about story structures apply in all regions and countries?

Language Experience

Betty Hart and Todd Risley researched how children learn to talk. They studied youngsters in professional, working-class, and welfare homes. Researchers went into the homes as a child was approaching his or her first birthday, then studied the language experience of the child for nearly three years. The families in the study were all considered healthy and loving; there were no obvious addiction issues or mental illness in any of the families, and all of the families had stable housing. Hart and Risley published their findings in Meaningful Differences in the Everyday Experience of Young American Children (1995).

In all the homes the children learned to talk, but there was a big difference in language experience and development by economic class. The following findings illustrate the principal differences.

Research About Language in Children, Ages 1 to 4, in Stable Households by Economic Group				
Economic Class	Number of Words Children Exposed To	Encouragements vs. *Prohibitions**		Working Vocabulary
Professional	45 million	6	1	1,200 words at 36 months
Working Class	26 million	2	1	No information
Welfare	13 million	1	2	900 words for adults

Definitions

Number of words that children are exposed to: As noted previously, the research tells us that the more words children hear from their parents and other significant adults, such as grandparents in the home (TV and radio don't count), in the early years of life, the more neural pathways are developed in the brain.

Encouragements (affirmations/'strokes') vs. prohibitions (criticisms/reprimands):* An encouragement is when an adult positively responds to a child's interest in something and encourages him/her to explore and talk about it. A prohibition is when an adult stops a child with "Be quiet," "Shut up," or "Don't do that." The more encouragement the child receives, the more words he/she has, the more learning structures are built.

Working vocabulary: The more words children learn, the easier and faster they can learn more words. For example, learning the word "bird" can lead to naming different birds, then learning the categories of birds, and perhaps even discovering the various life patterns of birds.

Discussion

1. Standardized tests typically place children from poverty two years behind their peers from middle class and wealth—and thus not ready for school. How does the information above explain part of the reason why?

2. Hart and Risley say it's impossible to suddenly make up 20 million words when a child is 4 or 5, but we also know that it isn't "over" for children who come to school with weak language background.

   a. What are some of the things found in the Mental Model of Poverty that make it difficult to provide children with a rich language experience?

   b. What are some of the barriers to providing children with a rich language experience as a result of child poverty rates and income segregation?

3. What are some things families can do right away to help their children? Make a list on the chart paper.

4. What are some things communities can do to support parents so that children can get a rich language experience?

Mediation: the *What*, the *Why*, the *How*

There are many things parents can do to help their children develop learning structures in the brain. One of the most effective strategies is called mediation. When parents do mediation with their children, they are helping build thinking structures in the brain. It's done by helping children see the reason why they need to do something (Sharron & Coulter, 2004).

When parents are encouraging their children, they need to give them three steps: the what, the why, and the how. The "what" is when you point out to children what they are doing, the content of their actions or words. The "why" is when you explain the mean-

> *We identify and address language issues that affect learning.*

ing of it. Before children are willing to learn, it helps to have the "why gate" open in their minds. Why should I do something differently? ("Because I said so" is a common response but not helpful to the child.) The "how" is when you suggest alternative strategies or behaviors for them.

Here's how it looks in a chart. In this example, a little boy is standing on the seat of a bus, looking out the window. It's late at night, and everyone on the bus is bleary-eyed and tired—except this 4-year-old boy. The dad says:

WHAT	WHY	HOW
"Hey, you're standing up in your seat."	"When the bus takes off, you might fall down."	"So ... why don't you kneel down or sit on my lap."

The boy, who obviously was used to his dad talking to him in this way, knelt down on the seat and happily counted the cars as the bus moved along.

In this mediation, the father offers the boy a choice between two strategies: to kneel down or sit on his lap. Given a choice, the little boy was less likely to feel forced to do something. At the same time, the young fellow could practice taking responsibility for his choice.

This is much different from another travel experience. In this case another father and 4-year-old boy were in an airplane traveling across the country—a very long flight. The boy was fidgeting, fussing, and asking a lot of questions. The dad says:

WHAT	WHY	HOW
		"Shut up. Be quiet. Settle down. Stop that" (repeated dozens of times over the next several hours).

In mediation, all three steps are necessary to build thinking structures. If this father had mediated the situation for his son, what might he have said?

In the space below write your mediation for the little boy on the airplane.

Mediation takes time, but when parents and kids get used to it, they get along better, and discipline is more about learning than punishment.

Discussion

1. How does this information relate to you?

2. Is mediation something you do with children already?

3. Do you think mediation can be used with adults?

4. As with other skills, it takes a while to use mediation easily. Do you think it has enough value to make it something you would like to use on a more regular basis?

Using Language to Resolve Differences

Discipline and Change

How we develop self-discipline and how we discipline our children is based in part on our hidden rules for destiny. In a stable environment where families have a lot of resources, children get to practice making choices. Children can choose what to eat, what to wear, which after-school activities they want to pursue, and how to behave. As they grow older and prove (by making good choices) that they're responsible, children can be given more freedom to try new things.

Mediation is a tool for developing the hidden rule that your choices make a difference. The man who used mediation with his son who was standing on the bus seat was disciplining his son—but in a way that subtly helped his son learn a life lesson about cause and effect. If parents do this form of mediation regularly, children will get a sense that their choices can change things. The understanding that our choices make a difference is empowering.

In an unstable world where resources are low, there are fewer choices to be made. There may be one only brand of cereal to eat and only one shirt to wear. When children don't practice making choices or when they do make choices but don't have the resources to turn a choice into a reality, they're more likely to feel fated. A common statement might be: "No matter what I do, things stay the same."

Parents who believe that choices matter tend to discipline their children using the choice-

> *"One of the priority resources that I am building is language. What is that for me? One of the sessions we learned that children from poor families often enter school with a serious language handicap. And they often times never catch up. This is because there isn't the interaction that engages the children to think. So, for me, the language resource means what I will do to help my children. I want my kids to grow into mature adults. So I decided to spend time reading with them. I learned mediation skills that help my children learn better ways to process thoughts. I had always thought that I was the one who needed help. Now I realize that to improve the quality of my own life, I will reach out to others."*
>
> –Bernard, Getting Ahead Graduate, Billings, MT

Penance/Forgiveness Cycle

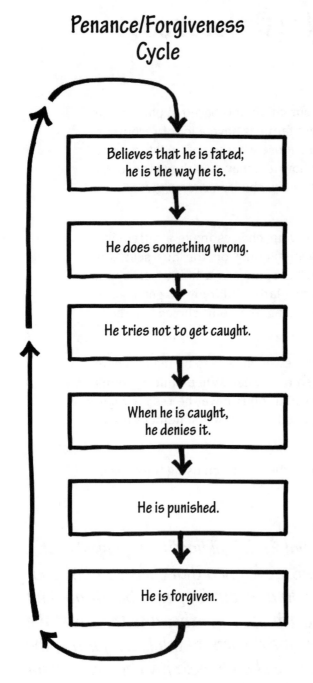

Believes that he is fated; he is the way he is.

He does something wrong.

He tries not to get caught.

When he is caught, he denies it.

He is punished.

He is forgiven.

and-consequence approach. This, coupled with a *future orientation**, allows a parent to base discipline on the choices a child makes. The parent expects that the child's behavior will change in the future. Parents, of course, must hold the child—even a teenager—accountable for his/her choices, for example: "You chose to drive too fast, so I'm taking your keys away for two weeks. I expect you to drive safely, and I expect you to change this behavior. If this happens again, you won't be allowed to drive for a month."

Parents (or grandparents) who feel controlled by fate, or fated, tend to engage in the *penance/forgiveness cycle** (Payne, 2012). Using the diagram, imagine a man in his early 30s who has had a series of service-sector jobs, none of which he has kept very long. He lives with his grandmother who cooks and cleans for him. When he decides he needs a truck for a job, he gets her to cosign on a loan for him. Before long she's making the truck payments. Later he decides he's going to get married and asks his grandmother for her credit card so he can get things he needs for the wedding and a new apartment. He maxes out her card at $10,000. His grandmother is pushed by other members of the family to kick him out and demand he repay the money. After he has been gone for a week, he calls and says he's living in his truck and has no place to stay or money to live on. He says he'll get a job and help pay the rent, so she takes him back.

The grandson felt there was nothing he could do differently from what he was already doing, so he took money from his grandmother. He didn't want other members of the family to catch him using her money and made excuses when they found out. When he was finally caught, and they pressured Grandma to kick him out, he took his punishment. For a week. And then Grandma forgave him. Soon the cycle repeated itself. Why? Because what is more important to the grandmother than the truck payments and the $10,000 is the relationship with her grandson.

In poverty the penance/forgiveness cycle is about maintaining relationships and seldom about long-term changes in behavior; it's about the relationship returning to the way it was.

In middle class, on the other hand, discipline is about consequences and change. If you don't change your behavior, you may lose the relationship. Middle-class people often do "tough love" better than people in poverty because there's more of a history in middle class of living with the consequences of decisions.

Getting Ahead in a Just-Gettin'-By World

Discussion

1. Someone once said, "No matter what economic class, we all strive to earn the respect of our peers." How might that attitude make it difficult for us to change the way we do things?

2. What is it about poverty and its impact on families that makes it difficult for people to change?

3. Have any of the aspects of language (discussed in this module) caused you problems? If so, what might you do to reduce the problem or improve the situation?

4. If you've seen examples of parents who use the choice/consequence approach and other parents who use the penance/forgiveness approach, describe the differences you observed in their children's behavior and in the parent's relationship with the child.

5. What might happen when someone who is part of the penance/forgiveness cycle gets into trouble with the law or with school officials?

The Basics of Negotiating

Economic class matters: GA graduates have said that one of the first things they could use from Getting Ahead was the information on language. While it may be hard to use formal register perfectly, it is possible to code switch on the choice of words and discourse patterns.

Even if vocabulary is somewhat limited, it's still possible to use language to negotiate. Using language to build relationships of mutual respect and to solve problems are the core skills of negotiation.

Information about economic class differences is information that most experts on negotiation do not cover. Understanding economic class issues may give you insights and skills that others don't have.

Discussion

How comfortable are you with the information about economic class—and using that information in your life? For example:

1. Language use can be different for people in poverty, middle class, and wealth. This applies to the five registers, discourse patterns, story structure, and vocabulary.

    a. Can you think of a time when casual register was used during a negotiation?

    b. How did that work for the people involved?

2. The environments we live in and the hidden rules we use to navigate are different and will affect the way we negotiate.

    a. How does the hidden rule on power influence negotiations?

    b. What happens when someone feels disrespected?

3. The resources we have or don't have will have an impact on negotiations too. The unstable environment of poverty that leads to the tyranny of the moment will affect negotiations.

    a. What does it do to someone's bargaining position if he/she is in the tyranny of the moment?

    b. How balanced is a negotiation going to be if one person has lots of resources (financial, emotional, social, physical, etc.) and the other person doesn't?

4. The fact that most institutions and businesses operate on middle-class rules and norms matters too.

    a. How do negotiations work when one of the two negotiators had normalized the middle-class mindset and didn't know that the other person had experienced life in significantly different ways?

Intentions matter: John Barkai, in his paper "The Savvy Samurai Meets the Devil" (1996, p. 706), says we must sometimes change our perspective when negotiating. Some people go into a negotiation thinking an angel, backed up by two more angels, is on one side of the table, while on the other side of the table is a devil backed up by two more devils: good against evil, right against wrong. To negotiate we must change our perspective to see that there is merit on both sides. Barkai is referring to more formal negotiations, such as those engaged in by attorneys and mediators, but many of these **principles*** apply to everyday situations as well.

Feelings matter: We all know we shouldn't drive under the influence of alcohol; we don't want a DUI. According to Barkai, negotiating under the influence (NUI) of strong feelings isn't a good idea either. When we're angry, hurt, or disgusted, we're much less likely to keep listening. We might go into the parent or the child voice. We're also less likely to ask questions to discover the other person's point of view and more likely to pound away on our own points. We'll want a win-lose solution. Here are some things to know about emotions when negotiating:

- There will be both positive and negative feelings during negotiations.

- Expect to hear things that you may not like; determine before entering into a negotiation that you won't take them personally.

- Negative feelings reduce our capacity to think, learn, and remember. We can't afford to get stuck in negative feelings.

- Don't allow your feelings to be hijacked. Sometimes all it takes is a word or phrase; sometimes it's the tone of voice or a gesture—and our feelings take over.

- Try to stay in the adult voice. Find the calm spot by detaching, by being objective: "How important is this issue to me?" Not every issue is a big one. Pick your battles.

- Recognize your feelings as you go into a negotiation and during the negotiation, then name them to yourself: I'm beginning to feel tense, annoyed, angry, etc.

- Naming your feelings means you are taking responsibility for them. Owning them means you can choose what to do with your feelings.

- Find a way to briefly express your feelings (usually not to the other party) if that will help you return to the **process*** of effective negotiation. Make a plan for dealing with strong emotions; ask for a break so you can walk or call someone.

- Look for the positive feelings; good things happen too, leading to good solutions.

- Appreciate the other side's point of view, finding value in those ideas as well.

- Remember, win-lose solutions, even the ones that go your way, can be expected to have an effect on your relationships into the future.

- Make personal connections with the other side; sometimes going through hard times, including conflicts, can lead to strong friendships.

Discussion

1. Whom do you find it hardest to negotiate with? Your ex-husband or ex-wife? Your children? Sister or brother? Boss? Probation officer? Associates at work? How do you account for the differences?

2. How good are you at handling your emotions? In the next module we'll look at 11 resources, including emotional resources, which are considered among the most important. Share with others what works for you.

Listening matters: Many experts in negotiation say that listening is the most important skill. If you aren't open to the merits or qualities of the other side's point of view, if you enter into negotiations with the intention of coming to a win-lose, and if you get emotionally hijacked, it isn't likely that you'll be able to reach a negotiated solution. Here are some things to know about listening:

- If you're primarily thinking about what you're going to say next, you're not listening.

- If you ask questions skillfully, you might find out very important information about the other side's point of view and **values.***

- Barkai, a lawyer who knows the reputation that lawyers have for talking, reminds us of the old saying, "You were born with two ears and one mouth, and that is the proportion in which you should use them" (1996, p. 721).

- Emotional blocks (see "Feelings matter" above) can keep us from listening.

- When we really listen, we can rephrase in our own words what the speaker just said—to his/her satisfaction.

- When we are actively listening we can encourage others to elaborate, explain, and clarify their points fully.

- Active listening means leaning forward, making eye contact, and having an open mind to learning. It doesn't mean frequently interrupting, though occasionally a question can be asked "midstream" for clarification.

- How to negotiate by asking questions:

    —Prepare some of your questions beforehand.

    —Can you tell me about that? (This is called an open-ended question. It encourages a person to expand on his/her thoughts. A closed question gets a one-word answer: yes or no.)

    —What do you mean by that? (This is a follow-up question; use it when you aren't sure you understand.)

    —Can you put that in other words? Could you state that another way? (These are clarifying questions. They can help you understand the answer more fully.)

    —How do you feel about that? (Questions about feelings are appropriate in some settings and not in others. Especially with family and friends, it's important to know how people feel.)

    —*What, where, when,* and *how* are usually good questions.

    —Asking *why* usually isn't a good question; it sounds like a challenge and tends to make people defensive.

Discussion

1. How comfortable are you with the idea of negotiating?

2. How hard was it to listen to the other person during a recent negotiation?

3. What listening skill is the most important one to you?

Information matters: Information is power. Think about the predatory businesses that we investigated earlier. Individuals selling mortgages have a lot more information about the products, processes, fees, and interest rates than a customer ever will. Selling mortgages is something they do every day, all day. They take classes to learn more about the business. They see hundreds of customers in a year and can categorize and name the "types" of homebuyers within minutes of seeing them coming through the door. They know which tricks to use on a customer to sweeten the deal for themselves. Most people buying a house go through the process only a few times in their lives. So who has the power in this situation?

- When negotiating, the person with the best information about the issue has most of the power.

- Do your homework, know the facts.

- Get help from experts.

- The information the other side has is important to you and can be discovered by asking questions.

Communicating (including body language) matters: Negotiating is all about communicating, but communicating is about more than just words. A study by Albert Mehrabian of UCLA on ways people communicate found that there's much more to sending and receiving information than just the words that are used, especially when emotional content is important. His findings show that when communicating, words count for 7%, the tone of voice 38%, and body language 55%. Style, expression, tone of voice, facial expression, and body language convey a great deal of the meaning (Mehrabian, 1981, pp. 43–44).

> *Getting Ahead can empower investigators to navigate the world effectively.*

How does this information fit with what we've covered in Getting Ahead? Consider these points:

- When using casual register we rely heavily on nonverbal (tone of voice and body language) communication. Casual register is a very powerful register for this reason.

- The "voices" we use can come from our internal parent, child, or adult. People will react to us differently, depending on the voice we use.

- Feelings are expressed through our choice of words, tone of voice, and body language. If we can't manage our feelings in a healthy or skillful way, we'll have trouble communicating and negotiating.

- Our mindsets or mental models about different topics change the way we communicate. If individuals think poverty is caused only by the choices of the poor, their mindsets will become apparent through their words, tone of voice, and body language.

- Knowing all of this can help us negotiate more skillfully—whether at home, in the neighborhood, at work, or at college ... in short, wherever we are.

Activity: Self-Assessment of Negotiating Skills

Time: 10 minutes
Materials: Self-assessment chart (next page), pen or pencil

Procedure: In the following chart, rank yourself by drawing a circle around the number (1–5) that applies to you.

1 = Don't understand the concept/don't have the skill

2 = Need a lot of work to understand it/to use it

3 = Getting the idea/starting to use the idea

4 = Understand the idea/can use it when I think about it

5 = Got it/can do it almost automatically with very little thought

Self-Assessment of Negotiating Skills		
Concept	**Understand Concepts**	**Ability to Use Concepts**
Hidden rules of economic class	1　2　3　4　5	1　2　3　4　5
Identifying intentions	1　2　3　4　5	1　2　3　4　5
Managing feelings/emotions	1　2　3　4　5	1　2　3　4　5
Skillful listening and questioning	1　2　3　4　5	1　2　3　4　5
Gathering important information	1　2　3　4　5	1　2　3　4　5
Verbal and nonverbal communication	1　2　3　4　5	1　2　3　4　5

Discussion

1. What negotiations are going on right now in your life?

2. What are your negotiating strengths?

3. What are your negotiating weaknesses?

4. Do you need to improve any skills? If so, which one(s)?

Exploring How to Plan

This module touched on many ideas and fields of study; think of it as a crash course in language and communication through the lens of economic class. Language is a resource that you can use to build other resources. All this is central, for example, to building relationships across class and race lines.

Reflecting on everything covered here, where are your strengths? Are you bilingual, meaning Are you able to use both casual register and formal register skillfully? Can you express yourself well both orally and in writing? Are you good at resolving conflicts and negotiating? Are there areas within this module that you want to strengthen? In the plans you make at the end of this Getting Ahead workshop, you may choose to pursue some of the ideas we talked about here.

Time Management and Planning—Setting a Goal and Working a Plan

Having investigated how you really spend your time and having thought about how you can be more effective, the next step is learning to make a plan to get things done.

Sometimes it's hard to know where to start. Or maybe you get started all right, but then you don't have time to put the finishing touches on the project before it's due. Whatever the case, you aren't alone. It takes time and practice before it feels natural to work a plan and manage a project.

Managing a project means knowing what the end result will look like (maybe a homework assignment, a research paper, or a personal goal) and knowing what needs to happen, in what order and by when, for the result to be achieved. It's having a vision, then working the plan.

In this activity, you'll practice the steps of *"planning backwards"** as they relate to a GA investigation. The example we will use comes from Module 8 where your group will be investigating community conditions. You and one other investigator have volunteered to investigate "Jobs, Wages, and Wealth-Creating Conditions" and to provide a report to the whole group.

Activity: Planning Backwards

Time: 1 hour, probably outside of group time
Materials: Paper, your workbook, a calendar, pen or pencil

Procedure:

1. *Set the goal:* In this example the goal is "Report to the GA group on 'Jobs, Wages, and Wealth-Creating Conditions' in Module 8, Table 4, on February 28."

2. *Determine the steps:*

   a. What are the major things that need to happen before you've completed the task?

   b. What information do you need to collect? (Hint: See Module 8, Table 4.)

   c. Where can you find the information?

   d. What should the written report look like?

   e. What materials do you need?

   f. How will you present the information to the group?

   g. How will this information help the GA group?

   h. What motivates you to achieve the goal?

   i. What actions will you need to take?

   j. What order should you do them in?

   k. Work through the list more than once to add new ideas and adjust the order.

3. *Place the steps on the timeline:* Work backwards from the date the project is due. In this case, that would be February 28.

Example of Planning Backwards Timeline						
Feb. 7	Feb. 8	Feb. 14	Feb. 17	Feb. 22	Feb. 24–25	Feb. 28
Brainstorm ideas with other GA investigators Do Steps 1 and 2 Prepare list of items to investigate Prepare list to show to reference librarian	Meet with reference librarian to get advice	Conduct online investigations	Meet with county officials for confirmation of local data	Conduct online investigations	Review with your partner and prepare written report	Share report with GA group

4. *Create a "To Do" list:* Each day prepare a "To Do" list with the important things for you to get done. Some of them will be in the "Steps" section of your plan, while some won't. Keeping a daily list of things that need to be done, then crossing them off as you go along, helps you keep track of what you have done and what you still need to do.

To Do on February 8:

1. Get library card (if necessary)

2. Pay fine for overdue books (if necessary)

3. Show Steps 1 and 2 to reference librarian

4. Make notes on how to use computer and other resources at library

5. Ask librarian about agencies or county offices that might have recent local data

---

*Vocabulary List for Module 5

Affirmations: positive responses or statements

Bilingual: able to code-switch and/or use both casual and formal register

Circular story pattern: a way of telling stories that doesn't present a linear sequence of events, but might emphasize characters or the importance of certain events; it's a more flexible, spontaneous, and interesting(!) form of storytelling

Code switching: the ability to use both Standard American English and community languages and, in bilingual fashion, move between/among them easily

Discourse patterns: the social boundaries for what groups can talk about, how they talk, and what their view is about different topics

Future orientation: focused on what is up ahead, makes plans and decisions based on what will happen later

Knowledge sector: a part of the job market where workers largely use their heads to produce and manage ideas, data, and information, as opposed to the manual worker who largely uses his/her hands and body; knowledge sector workers often are involved in information technology and education

Language experience: the exposure to words that a child gets in the first years of life; this includes vocabulary, discourse patterns, storytelling patterns, mediation, and exposure to books and reading

Mediation: the way parents help their children understand the meaning of the actions they need to take as they encounter new situations

Penance/forgiveness cycle: a pattern that deals with bad behavior by punishing the offender, expecting the offender to do penance (be in the doghouse for a while), then forgiving the offender; it doesn't usually require a change in behavior

Planning backwards: the steps to completing a task that begins with the end/date and overall goal in mind

Principles: the underlying laws or assumptions required in a system of thought

Process: a series of actions or steps directed toward a specific aim

Prohibitions: in this context, orders to stop a behavior—or to criticize

Service sector: a part of the job market that doesn't produce something you can hold in your hand; rather, it involves such services as housekeeping, tour guides, clerks, tax preparation, and truck driving

Values: what is of great importance, significance, or worth to you; the set of principles that guide your life and define what life means to you

Readings

Fisher, Roger, & Ury, William. (1983). Getting to yes: Negotiating agreement without giving in. New York, NY: Penguin Books.

Hart, Betty, & Risley, Todd R. (1995). Meaningful differences in the everyday experience of young American children. Baltimore, MD: Paul H. Brookes Publishing Co.

Levine, Mel. (2002). A mind at a time. New York, NY: Simon & Schuster.

Wheeler, Rebecca S., & Swords, Rachel. (2006). Code-switching: Teaching Standard English in urban classrooms. Urbana, IL: National Council of Teachers of English.

Eleven Resources

We can do something about poverty by building individual, institutional, and community resources.

WHAT'S COVERED

We will:

Define poverty

Define the resources

Create a "Mental Model of Social Capital"

Use case studies to practice doing assessment of resources

Explore ways to use this information

WHY IT'S IMPORTANT

We can stabilize our lives and get out of poverty by building resources. Money is only one of them.

If we want a high quality of life, we need to build all resources.

Investigating resources leads naturally to ideas for improving our lives.

HOW IT'S CONNECTED TO YOU

Defining poverty as "the extent to which an individual does without resources" gives individuals, institutions, and communities something to do about poverty—build resources.

One way to build resources faster is to develop bridging social capital and relationships of mutual respect with diverse groups of people.

The resources cover all areas of life. When we're good at analyzing resources, we'll be ready to do a self-assessment of our own resources. We can then begin making our plans.

Defining Poverty

In Module 1 we investigated the Federal Poverty Guidelines that define poverty by income.

As noted above, Ruby K. Payne (1996) **defines poverty*** as "the extent to which an individual does without resources"—the 11 resources we'll be exploring in this module. This is helpful because it widens our thinking about instability and poverty beyond just money, income, and wealth. While money is important to stabilizing lives, Payne's definition takes in the quality of life in all its aspects. Also as mentioned above, this definition gives GA investigators and their communities something they can do about poverty—build resources.

Considering our investigations into the environments of class and the importance of stability in family life, we could describe the three economic classes this way (all in terms of the "stability factor," or we might even say the "fear factor"):

- *We are in poverty when we're afraid for today.* Our homes, neighborhoods, and community are so unstable that we can't see much past today.

- *We are in middle class when we have today covered, but we're afraid for the future.* Savings accounts and insurance can stabilize today, but pensions and retirement funds aren't as secure as they once were and unforeseen crises (like medical problems or layoffs) can blow up our tomorrow.

- *We are in wealth when we have both today and tomorrow covered, but we fear instability itself.* We fear instability in the financial, social, and political world. We fear the loss of our assets and perhaps even the connections that have come along with our lifestyle.

Our experiences, of course, don't fall into three perfect mental models of class. They stretch across the continuum (from instability to stability) that we used in Module 2. The goal of Getting Ahead is to help us become economically stable by improving all areas of our lives. Building a solid balance of resources will free us from the tyranny of the moment.

Defining Resources

The more resources a person has in all areas, the easier it is to make changes and live well. Resources are interconnected, so having high levels of some (or many) resources makes it easier to build the rest.

Eleven Resources	
Financial	Having enough income to purchase goods and services and to save or invest money. Having an educated understanding of how money works—being financially literate.
Emotional	Being able to choose and control emotional responses, particularly to negative situations without engaging in self-destructive behavior. This is the "state of mind" that determines the way we think, feel, and behave at any given moment. This is a resource that shows itself through stamina and choice. This is about interpersonal skills like teamwork, teaching others, leadership, negotiation, and working with people from many backgrounds.
Mental/Cognitive	Having the mental ability and acquired skills (reading, writing, computing) to deal with daily life. This includes how much education and training individuals have in order to compete in the workplace for well-paying jobs or run their own business.
Language	Having the vocabulary, language ability, and negotiation skills to succeed in the work and/or school environments.
Social Capital	Having friends, family, and backup resources available to access in times of need. Sometimes this resource is called "Support Systems."
Physical	Having physical health and mobility.
Spiritual	Believing in divine purpose and guidance and/or having a rich cultural connection that offers support and guidance.

Eleven Resources	
Integrity and Trust	Trust is linked to two issues: *predictability** and safety. Can I know with some certainty that this person will do what he/she says? Can I predict with some accuracy that it will occur nearly every time? The second part of the question is safety: Will I be safe with this person?
Motivation and Persistence*	Having the energy and drive to prepare for, plan, and complete projects, jobs, and personal changes.
Relationships/Role Models	Having frequent access to adults who are appropriate, who are nurturing, and who don't engage in self-destructive behavior.
Knowledge of Hidden Rules	Knowing the unspoken cues and habits of poverty, middle class, and wealth.

Additional Information on Four Key Resources

In Modules 4 and 5 we investigated knowledge of hidden rules and language, both of which are resources. Now we're going to investigate four others. While we're doing this, you might start thinking about which resources to work on and where you would go to find help.

Financial Resources

Money, income, and wealth are the first things people think of when talking about instability, near poverty, and poverty. To build this resource, you need to be able to play the money game. You need to be financially literate—know the rules of money. In the money game there are no fans in the bleachers and no cheerleaders; everyone is a player. The only question is: How well can you play? And can you play it well at every stage of your life?

Most high schools don't teach this important information. Yet it's crucial to the economic security of each of us. That means either our parents or guardians taught us about money (and they may not be very good at the game themselves), or we learned it on our own.

Further, what we needed to know coming out of high school was different from what we need to know when starting college, buying a house, planning to have children, or preparing for retirement.

The good news is that there are a number of workbooks and books about financial literacy available in the library and at the bookstore.

In Module 1 we did the calculations for three important measures of our financial resources (percentage of income that goes to housing, savings cushion, and debt-to-income ratio). These calculations are a great first step on the road to financial literacy.

Emotional Resources

Emotional resources are very important, among the most important resources. Sometimes intelligent, healthy people with great job skills lose their job because they had low emotional resources. In other words, they couldn't handle their feelings well. Low emotional resources also damage family relationships.

In addition, abuse, addiction, and other dangerous situations can create in us reactions and patterns of behavior that work against us. They can create thoughts, feelings, and behaviors that have negative consequences.

Learned helplessness is a behavior noticed among people who feel that their problems are permanent, pervasive, and personal (Seligman, 2002). Someone feeling that way might say (or think), *I'll never make it; I mess up everything, and I'm so stupid.* Such individuals might feel sorry for themselves or blame themselves. Or they might blame others or manipulate them.

> *"How can resources help you move forward, not stand still?"*
>
> –GA Graduate

In "Empowerment: A Course in Personal Empowerment" the writers say:

> The single most important skill of the Empowerment Skills Training is the ability to regulate what you think and feel inside yourself—meaning that you decide the content, nature, and intensity of what you think, feel, and do.
>
> Regulating what you think and feel inside yourself does not mean "suppressing," "keeping the lid on," "putting up with it," "ignoring it," or "holding it in."
>
> To regulate feelings means to adjust the degree, intensity, and meaning of internal experiences. It works like an internal thermostat that keeps the temperature inside where you want it, regardless of the temperature outside.
>
> *Note.* From *Empowerment: A Course in Personal Empowerment* (p. 25), by Twin Cities RISE!, 2009, Minneapolis, MN: Twin Cities RISE! Copyright 2009 by Twin Cities RISE!

For one GA investigator, his older brother taught him how to regulate his own emotions. The following story illustrates that it's not so much what happens to us in life, it's how we respond to it that matters most, starting with our thoughts and attitudes. The investigator said:

> For some reason, my older brother loved to beat me up. To get me mad, he would push my buttons. And believe me, he knew all my buttons! I would explode and start swinging; then he could "defend" himself and happily twist me into knots. One day, in a rare moment of kindness, he said, "Why do you let me do that to you? You know I love to piss you off so I can beat you up. Why do you fall for it every time?" At that moment I realized that the control for what happened was in me, not in him. I had always said, "He makes me lose my temper. He made me do it." From that day forward my thinking changed. I never gave that power to someone else again, including my brother. The power over my thinking and feeling is in me.

Another way to look at emotional resources is to assess *"emotional intelligence."** Daniel Goleman (1995) describes emotionally intelligent people as being very aware of their own feelings. Because they can identify and manage their feelings, they also can check their impulses and control their actions.

Emotionally intelligent people can relate to other people's emotions. They can help manage the difficult emotions that come up in relationships so that those relationships stay healthy.

It's interesting that you don't have to be educated academically to have high emotional intelligence.

Social Capital

In *Bowling Alone* (2000) Robert Putnam describes social capital (or support systems) as something that is just as important as financial capital. He is talking about our connections with others, our networks, the things we do for each other with the trust and knowledge that they would do the same for us. Well-connected people feel a mutual obligation to help others; they have "favor banks." One man said, "It's like the golden rule. I'll do this for you now knowing that, down the road, you will return the favor."

Individuals have social capital, and so do communities. While individuals have many connections with other individuals, communities have a number of clubs and organizations like bowling leagues, service clubs, unions, religious organizations, and so forth.

Bridging social capital, developed during GA, is often the first and strongest support for change.

There are two types of social capital: bonding and bridging. *Bonding social capital** is what we have with our tightest friends. It's *exclusive,* usually keeping others out. It is about belonging and identity. Others in our bonded group have many of the same resources and connections we do. Some examples of bonding capital are ethnic fraternal organizations, church-based reading groups, and country clubs. Some bonding groups are harmful, such as gangs, the Ku Klux Klan, or certain neighborhood groups that form to exclude others. These individuals and groups tend to have the NIMBY (not in my back yard) attitude.

Bridging social capital, on the other hand, is what we have with people outside our usual circle. It's *inclusive* of people from different backgrounds. Examples of bridging capital are civil rights movements, youth service clubs, organizations that promote the arts, United Way, block parties (if you live in a neighborhood where there are people from different classes), etc. When you have bridging capital, you have relationships of mutual respect, many acquaintances, and lots of connections—along with your numerous bonding connections.

Putnam cites Xavier de Souza Briggs who says bonding capital is good for getting by, while bridging capital is good for getting ahead. By this he means that our bonding-capital friends will have the same contacts and knowledge of job opportunities as we have. But someone outside our normal circle will have a number of contacts that we don't have and might be able to give us good leads for jobs and access to other resources.

Activity: 'Mental Model of Personal Social Capital'

Time: 10 minutes
Materials: Paper and pencil

Procedure: Use a full sheet of paper to create a mental model. Draw a small circle inside a larger circle. The center of the circles represents you.

1. Thinking of the circles as a pie, draw eight pieces of pie and write the following labels around the outside of the larger circle: Household, Other family, Friends, Work, Religious/spiritual, Schools, Clubs, and Agencies.

2. In each section of the pie, put the initials of the people who are in your life. Those with bonding relationships will be in the inner circle, while those with bridging social capital will go in the outside circle.

3. After group discussion, place this mental model and your notes and reflections inside your Future Story Portfolio.

Mental Model of Personal Social Capital

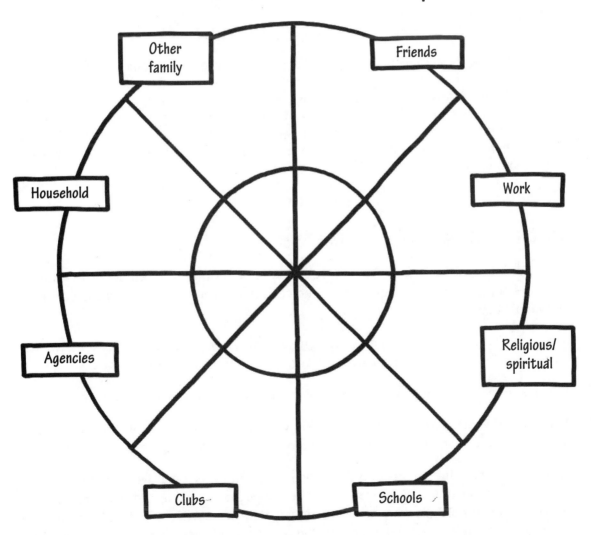

Discussion

1. How many people did you name as bonding capital? Why did you name them? How many people did you name as bridging capital? Why did you name them?

2. What are the positive things you see in your relationships when you look at this mental model?

3. What are the negative things you see in your relationships?

4. If you decided to make a change in the future, how might this information help you?

5. How does this pattern today impact what you see in your future?

6. How might you strengthen your social capital?

7. Bonding social capital may be important to people who are struggling financially. If you don't have money to solve problems, you'd better have lots of bonding capital; your people will make it possible to survive. Bridging social capital may be more valuable to people in wealth because of the value placed on connections. How do the social realities of different groups support or maintain their economic status?

Investigate This!

Bridging social capital is a resource that can be utilized to build other resources. To build social capital we need to know how to network. Some networking skills you've already learned—things like knowledge of the hidden rules of class, an understanding of different economic environments, and language skills. Yet there's much more to learn about networking. Investigate networking skills by finding no fewer than three approaches to networking, compare and contrast them, and report back to the group on your findings.

Motivation and Persistence

Motivation and persistence—the ability to keep pursuing something—are internal resources that an individual can make choices about. They are resources over which individuals have control.

Change is always going to happen. Some changes we have no control over; some we do. Change is seldom easy. It takes wisdom, courage, and motivation to change.

Here are some other things we know about motivation, persistence, and change.

Wisdom and values: We need wisdom to know what we should and can change. And to figure out what we should change, we need to understand our values.

Values define what life means to us, what is important to us, what we hold dear. Values influence our motivation. We move toward the things that we value and away from things we don't. For example, if a woman values money highly, she will make decisions and take action toward things that make money. She will be motivated to make money or find ways to have money. If a woman dreams of and values a certain house in a certain neighborhood, she will make choices and take steps to get that house. She is motivated to get that particular house. If a woman values relationships highly, she will make choices and do things that maintain and enhance those relationships. She will be motivated by the importance to her of those relationships.

When we become disconnected from our values, it's as if we've lost our purpose for living. When that happens we spend lots of time doing things that don't really make us happy. The things we do may just be distractions from our unhappiness with the ways things are. We may do too much of things that aren't very good for us (drinking, drugs, sex, watching TV, playing endless video and computer games).

Willing: When we first think about changing something, we tend to put the idea on a scale, whether we actually realize it or not. On one side of the scale is what we have now, and on the other is what we could have—or what we want, what we value.

Miller and Rollnick (2002) describe motivation as being "willing, able, and ready." For us to be willing to change, the scale has to be tipped toward the "what we want" side, toward the future. The scale tips back and forth while we figure out if the change is going to be worth all the effort it will take. Sometimes the change we want might be in conflict with other things we value. For example, we've already learned that to *achieve* we might have to give up some relationships, at least for a time. So ... if we want to go back to school (because we value education and because it will mean a better job and provide more security for ourselves and our family), the scale may rock back and forth between going to school and our desire to be with our old friends.

> *"You'll know you're motivated when it's your voice making the argument for change and not someone else's."*
>
> –Phil DeVol

The key to being willing is the size of the gap between what we have now and what we might have—the difference between what is and what could be. The bigger the difference, the more willing we tend to be to change.

Able: To be *able* to change, we must know the steps—and have the strength, skill, and the resources to take action. We must imagine ourselves moving ahead and feel confident enough that we can do what it takes. We have to think positively and be persistent. When we are willing to change but then aren't able to because of personal barriers or barriers in the community, we often shift back into thinking that we're fated. It's easy to lose motivation and slip again into living for the moment.

Ready: To be *ready*, we have to move beyond the "I'll do it tomorrow" and the "Yes, but" phase. This requires that we overcome our fear of failure and our fear of success and push through toward what we want.

Andreas and Faulkner (1994) say that motivation is a relatively simple mental strategy that we can learn to use ourselves. They point out that we are always motivated for something. In fact, sometimes we are too motivated. Some of us are too motivated for chocolate, sex, cigarettes, and so on. In that case, we have to learn some anti-motivation strategies, which includes self-control and impulse control.

But what happens when we see that big gap between what we have now and what we could have? What happens when the things we value seem out of reach? What do we need to do to get motivated?

Andreas and Faulkner also say there are two basic thinking strategies about motivation. Those who "move toward" what they want and those who "move away from" what they don't want.

Characteristics of 'moving toward' thinkers

- Jump out of bed in the morning, ready to go!
- Plan ahead for things they want to do, such as meet friends, go fishing, etc.
- Pick friends who keep them going, who interest them
- Take advantage of opportunities when they arise

Pros of being 'moving toward' thinkers

- Goal-oriented
- Get things done
- Get the jobs because they match what most employers are looking for

Cons of being 'moving toward' thinkers

- Don't think through the problems carefully enough
- Rush into things, putting the "pedal to the metal"
- Have to learn things the hard way

Characteristics of 'moving away from' thinkers

- Lie in bed until the threats of what will happen become too great
- Wait to change things until it gets really uncomfortable
- Pick friends who don't bother them
- Wait to change jobs until they just can't stand their job another minute

Pros of being 'away from' thinkers

- Careful about getting into things
- Remember the bad times to stay motivated
- Good at identifying and fixing problems

Cons of being 'away from' thinkers

- Afraid to try things
- Get fixated on problems
- When the pain and pressure to change are lessened, so is the motivation
- Motivation comes and goes with the threats
- Less attention is given to where they'll end up when they're looking back at the problem instead of looking ahead
- Much higher stress levels and risk of health problems

It's best if you learn to use both motivational strategies, with an emphasis on the "moving toward" strategy. You can do this by monitoring your motivational strategies and practicing new ways of thinking and acting.

Focus and persistence: Staying focused means you control your thinking while being persistent means you control what you do. Let's say you decided to go back to school but found yourself thinking your books or teachers were boring or stupid, that you could be doing something more fun than being in school. You've lost focus. If you combine that with negative feelings of fear, doubt, and impatience, you are likely to drop out. But if you persist in your actions, if you keep going to class and reading and turning in assignments, you still have a chance. Someone once said 90% of success is simply showing up.

Courage: The Serenity Prayer, attributed to Reinhold Niebuhr, has something to say about motivation:

> *"God, grant me the serenity to accept the things I cannot change, the courage to change the things I can, and the wisdom to know the difference."*

When we think about change and motivation, we have to consider what we'll do with our own life, as well as what we'll do about poverty in our community. What can we change about ourselves? What can we change about our community? When we've answered these questions, we'll know what it will take in the way of courage to move toward prosperity. By the way, the prosperity we're talking about here isn't just financial; it's an overall sense of well-being, success, contentment, and (yes) happiness.

Discussion

1. How does poverty impact what a person values?

2. What are some things that cause people to lose their motivation?

3. How will you know when you are willing to change?

4. What might help you feel confident about moving toward economic stability?

5. Which motivational strategy do you tend to use the most?

6. What would it be like for you if you used the "moving toward" strategy more often?

Activity: Case Studies

Time: 30–90 minutes
Materials: Case studies below and perhaps additional case studies
provided by the facilitator, pen or pencil

Case studies give you a chance to practice analyzing a person's resources. Soon you'll do a self-assessment of your own resources.

Procedure:

1. Do one case study at a time.

2. Read and score each case study using the upcoming three-page chart. You will notice that for each resource there are five levels: (1) Urgent/Crisis, (2) Vulnerable/High-Risk, (3) Stable, (4) Safe/Secure, (5) Thriving/Giving Back. Read the five descriptions of each resource and decide which description best matches the information in the two case studies.

3. Share your scores with others and discuss how you came to your decision. It's important that each person gets good at "tight thinking." One of the best ways is to hear what others think, so you can sort out and explain your own ideas. It's OK to build on the ideas of others. Try to be specific.

Case Study—Carl

Carl's memories of his early family life are of an abusive and disturbed father who heard voices and had mental health problems that became progressively worse over time. His father taught his three sons to steal from malls. He also beat his wife and sons. Carl's mother couldn't handle the beatings anymore and, taking her three boys, left his father.

Carl's family moved frequently and went from having lots of toys and material things to being hungry and not having enough clothes. Every time they settled into a new place to live, his father would find them, and they would have to move again. They lived in dumpy apartments, shelters, and with family members and strangers. During this time Carl learned to protect himself from being hurt by building walls and isolating himself from others.

Carl has a vivid memory of his mother standing in front of a gas station looking at the boys, trying to smile, but with tears rolling down her face as she told them they were going to live with a different family.

Carl and his brothers were taken from his mother and put into a foster home. The first foster placement was for three years, but then the children were split up. The second foster parents were Christians who went to church every Sunday and Wednesday and enrolled Carl in a Christian school. That was a good experience for him—both for the religious foundation and academically. He was a good student and made good grades. The family lived on a farm where he was given chores.

His mother brought the family together again only to continue the life of moving from neighborhood to neighborhood with a series of men. She was heavily involved in drug use. As the oldest child, he protected his brothers as best he could.

When Carl was in high school he skipped school frequently and began experimenting with alcohol, drugs, and sex. He went to parties and was in lots of fights. He dropped out of school his senior year.

He moved from place to place, job to job, and girlfriend to girlfriend. Carl found it easy to find work and always learned the work quickly. If he had stayed at any of the jobs, he could have worked his way up quickly. But he was heavily into drugs, which took a toll financially and physically.

Toward the end of his drug use Carl was homeless and described himself as spiritually bankrupt. He had developed a terrible reputation and all kinds of enemies. At the time he went into treatment for drug addiction, his nose, cheekbone, eye socket, and hand were all broken. Carl said he had hit bottom. His recovery began with a renewal of his spiritual life.

He now has two part-time, low-wage jobs. His money goes to paying child support and rent, leaving very little for keeping his car running and food. He is basically healthy but doesn't have health insurance. His social life is centered around 12-step meetings and reconnecting with his family. He enjoys helping people with fix-it projects, moving, and giving them rides. He wants to get a GED but is busy with his two jobs, along with helping family and friends. His mother is very ill and still using drugs; his brothers always need money. They aren't supportive of his efforts to stay clean and sober.

Despite his conflicting feelings about his mother and the hard times they have lived through, Carl remembers some good times too. They would go for walks and to the park. He finds himself laughing over the silliest things they did. Carl has deep bonds with his brothers and maintains a relationship with them. He has learned to turn hard experiences into strengths; he has the ability to survive and find the humor in things. He is generally self-assured and able to make friends easily.

Case Study—Sandy

Sandy is the product of a one-night stand. Her father was Vietnam veteran and, for a short time, a member of the Black Panthers. Her mother was a white girl from Tennessee. He was married at the time of their encounter and went on to marry two other women. She was married twice; they both had several children from each of their marriages.

They were living in a small town in Indiana when, at the age of 8, Sandy's father took her to California, telling her that her mother was in jail for welfare fraud. Her father spent most of his time living with girlfriends and using drugs. He became addicted to cocaine and would leave her alone in motel rooms or with strangers for long periods of time. Before her mother was able to find her, Sandy experienced homelessness, spent her ninth Christmas living in a car, learned how to fend for herself, and got herself to school using the bus and rail system in San Francisco.

Sandy's mother also had a hard childhood. When she was 12 she was raising her 6-year-old sister and 14-year-old brother who had mental health problems. She didn't get along with Sandy's father or his family and had to fight to keep Sandy. After she got Sandy back from California, they lived in Chicago where she worked long hours and left Sandy to her own devices. Sandy joined a gang where she found love, support, and acceptance. But gang life was a struggle, with frequent fights with members of other gangs; Sandy was hungry most nights and in almost constant pain from fighting. Soon she became pregnant.

Six months into her pregnancy Sandy was jumped by another gang and was spared from being killed by a girl who told the would-be shooter that the baby didn't deserve to die. That crisis led to them returning to Indiana. Sandy promised to go back to school and stay out of trouble. However, she dropped out of school and got involved in abusive relationships. When she was 17, she had an apartment and was the target of every hustler and drug dealer around. She was abused physically, sexually, and mentally on a daily basis. She had five children who were forced on her by men who wanted to keep her in a relationship. She survived by doing what others did to her: exploiting and terrorizing others.

> "Getting Ahead is like stopping and looking at luggage; unpack it and look at it—or don't look at it. Your choice."
>
> —GA Investigator, Syracuse, NY

Eventually Sandy realized that she was starting to do to her children what had been done to her. She worked a series of low-wage jobs and went to school at the same time. She did well in school, getting a GED and going on to a community college. Her children have excelled at school; all five are on the honor roll. She figured that she had role models of "what not to do" and determined that it was more important to be a role model than to have one. It was having children that made her realize that she had to manage her emotions in a less destructive way.

Sandy's relationships with men have settled down considerably. There is no violence, but her life is complicated by relationships that have led to lost jobs, indebtedness, and moves to new apartments. She has borrowed money from payday lenders four times and now must pay them first on payday, leaving little money for necessities.

Sandy is now working 30 hours a week at a "big box" store; there are relatively few companies that pay good wages in her community, and she feels fortunate to have the job she does. At work she has always caught the eye of supervisors and has moved up quickly. Sandy thinks that being biracial has helped her learn to manage herself in different settings—both the 'hood and the workplace. She is quite verbal.

She uses food stamps and Medicaid. She has been diagnosed with diabetes and is trying to manage it with diet and exercise, but she is finding it difficult because of the crises that often interrupt her days and all the demands on her to manage her children, three of whom are now in high school. Her relationships with workers at local agencies generally aren't good because she confronts those who don't treat her with respect as she is trying to improve her life.

Resources Scoring Chart

	(1) Urgent/Crisis	(2) Vulnerable/High-Risk	(3) Stable	(4) Safe/Secure	(5) Thriving/Giving Back
Financial	Doesn't have enough income to purchase needed goods and services	Has some, but not enough, income to purchase needed goods and services—and to save money	Has enough income to purchase needed goods and services—and to have money saved for crisis	Has enough income to purchase needed goods and services, to save for emergencies, and to invest for future	Actively seeks to increase personal financial assets over time and help build community assets
Emotional	Can't choose and control emotional responses; often behaves in ways that are harmful to others or self	Can sometimes choose and control emotional responses; sometimes behaves in ways that are harmful to others or self	Can almost always choose and control emotional responses; almost never behaves in ways that are harmful to others or self	Is good at choosing and controlling emotional responses; engages in positive behaviors toward others	Actively seeks to improve emotional health in self and others
Mental	Lacks ability, education, or skills to compete for well-paying jobs	Has some ability, education, or skills to compete for well-paying jobs	Has enough ability, education, or skills to compete for well-paying jobs	Has plenty of ability, education, or skills to compete for well-paying jobs	Actively seeks to improve on existing ability, education, or skills—and build mental resources in community
Language	Lacks vocabulary, language ability, and negotiation skills needed for workplace settings	Has some of vocabulary, language ability, and negotiation skills needed for workplace settings	Has enough of vocabulary, language ability, and negotiation skills needed for workplace settings	Has plenty of vocabulary, language ability, and negotiation skills needed for workplace settings	Actively seeks to improve upon already strong vocabulary and language ability foundation—and works to develop language resources in community
Social Capital	Lacks positive friends, family, and connections that can be accessed to improve resources	Has some positive friends, family, and connections that can be accessed to improve resources	Has enough positive friends, family, and connections that can be accessed to improve resources	Has plenty of positive friends, family, and connections that can be accessed to improve resources	Actively develops networks and social resources that can be accessed to improve personal and community resources
Physical	Lacks physical health and mobility for workplace settings	Has some physical health and mobility problems that could limit effectiveness in workplace	Has physical health and mobility needed for workplace settings	Consistently maintains physical health and mobility needed for self and others in workplace	Actively develops physical resources for self, workplace, and community

Resources Scoring Chart

	(1) Urgent/ Crisis	(2) Vulnerable/ High-Risk	(3) Stable	(4) Safe/Secure	(5) Thriving/ Giving Back
Spiritual	Lacks cultural connections or sense of spiritual purpose that offers support and guidance	Has some cultural connections or sense of spiritual purpose that offers support and guidance	Has sufficient cultural connections or sense of spiritual purpose that offers support and guidance	Has plenty of cultural connections or sense of spiritual purpose that offers support and guidance	Actively seeks cultural connections and/or spiritual growth
Integrity and Trust	Cannot be trusted to keep one's word, to accomplish tasks, and to obey laws even when under supervision	Can sometimes be trusted to keep one's word, to accomplish tasks, and to obey laws when under supervision	Can be trusted to keep one's word, to accomplish tasks, and to obey laws, without supervision	Can invariably be trusted to keep one's word, to accomplish tasks, to obey laws, and to inspire others to do same	Actively seeks to build integrity and trust—and sets high ethical standards at work and in community
Motivation and Persistence	Lacks energy or drive to prepare for, plan, and complete projects, jobs, and personal change	Has some energy or drive to prepare for, plan, and complete projects, jobs, and personal change	Has enough energy or drive to prepare for, plan, and complete projects, jobs, and personal change	Has plenty of energy or drive to prepare for, plan, and complete projects, jobs, and personal change	Actively seeks to maintain motivation and persistence—and to assist others in finding theirs
Relationships/ Role Models	Lacks access to others who are safe, supportive, and nurturing	Has limited access to others who are safe, supportive, and nurturing	Has enough access to others who are safe, supportive, and nurturing	Has plenty of access to others who are safe, supportive, and nurturing	Actively seeks out others who are safe, supportive, and nurturing—and is safe, supportive, and nurturing of others
Knowledge of Hidden Rules	Lacks knowledge of hidden rules of other economic classes	Has some awareness of hidden rules of other economic classes but can't use them	Knows rules of other economic classes and can use some of them in personal ways	Knows rules of all three economic classes and can use most of them effectively in limited settings	Actively seeks to understand rules of all three economic classes—and to use them effectively in variety of settings

Note. Adapted from work of Jennifer Clay, Opportunities Industrialization Center of Clark County, Springfield, OH.

Discussion

1. In the cases of Carl and Sandy, which resources did you learn the most about? Which the least?

2. What were the strongest or highest resources for Carl and Sandy?

3. What were the weakest or lowest resources?

4. If Sandy and Carl were each to pick one resource to build up, which do you think it would be?

5. Which of their strongest resources could they use to build the others? How would they build resources? How long do you think it would take?

• • •

When the group has analyzed the case studies—enough to be able to do tight thinking about the resources—discuss these questions.

1. Would it be possible for someone to have high financial resources but to have other resources that are very low? If so, how would that look? How might that occur?

2. Would it be possible to have very low financial resources but have other resources that are very high? How would that look?

3. How are an individual's resources interconnected? What happens to other resources when someone has a sudden decline in health or loses a job?

4. Which resources does poverty impact the most severely?

5. Which resources are the hardest to assess?

6. Does it matter what community, state, or nation you live in? Do some states or nations provide easier access to resources?

7. Which resources do you think are the most important in order to have a well-balanced life?

8. As the group has worked through the case studies, in what ways did the thinking about the resources get tighter?

9. How well does this definition of well-being and poverty include or account for the many variables that people experience? How does it work for men and women, for the young and old, for people from different races and cultures, for the disabled, for those who are GLBT (gay, lesbian, bisexual, transgender), and for immigrants?

Explore Ways to Use This Information: Case Study—Dale

Dale is a 34-year-old man who was raised in poverty. He's still in poverty, but this story is about the beginning of his transition out. He's a high school dropout who has worked a series of jobs, the best one a manufacturing job in a mid-size city in Ohio. He has moved frequently, living in a number of states with a number of different women. After a recent divorce, he returned to Ohio looking for work and is living with some friends. Dale wants custody of his daughter because his ex-wife has a serious mental health problem. The only way to get custody, though, is to establish a home. Dale's strongest resources are emotional, physical, and motivational. His weakest resources are financial, social capital, and knowledge of the hidden rules of middle class.

Dale applied at the manufacturing plant several times with no results before beginning Getting Ahead. He decided to try again, using what he had learned in the workshop about economic class.

He went to the plant to apply, this time not just dropping off the application and walking away, but staying to talk to the secretary taking the forms. He explained why he wanted the job (establish economic security, get custody of his daughter) and told the office worker that he had worked there before and knew how to do the work. He then asked about a man who had worked at the plant when he first worked there years earlier. It turned out that the man was now in management. The secretary made a call and arranged for Dale to see the manager right then.

When Dale first went into the manager's office, he was fidgeting and stumbling over his language. He then thought, I've got to just go for it. Again he explained himself, how he wanted to provide for his daughter, get and keep a good job, establish a home, and how he was at the point in his life where he knew he had to make a major change. The manager was impressed and told Dale he could have the job, but there was one thing he would have to do first. He would have to cut off his ponytail. The plant was under new management, and one of the rules that had changed was the one about ponytails. One man who had worked there for years quit his job rather than cut his hair. Dale recognized this as a conflict in hidden rules and chose to give up his ponytail for the job. The job pays a living wage and provides benefits. Dale moved to a small apartment near the plant so he could save money.

Discussion

1. What resources was Dale trying to build?

2. What resources did he use? How did he use them?

3. What hidden rules did he use? How did he use them?

4. How did Dale use mediation when talking with the manager?

5. How much did it matter that the manager had no idea about the hidden rules as they're taught here?

6. Which motivational strategy did Dale use?

7. What will Dale need to do to maintain his changes?

8. How does this information apply to you?

> *"Bonding social capital is good for 'getting by,' but bridging social capital is good for 'getting ahead.'"*
>
> —Xavier de Souza Briggs

*Vocabulary List for Module 6

Bonding social capital: the people in our closest circle, the ones most like us

Definition of poverty: the extent to which an individual, family, institution, or community does without resources

Emotional intelligence: those who can identify feelings and manage them well

Persistence: when you don't give up even when faced with opposition and difficulty—having the energy or drive to prepare for, plan, and complete projects, jobs, and personal change

Predictability: when something turns out the way you expected it to

Readings

Davidson, Richard J., & Begley, Sharon. (2012). *The emotional life of your brain: How its unique patterns affect the way you think, feel, and live—and how you can change them.* New York, NY: Hudson Street Press.

Coontz, Stephanie. (2000). *The way we never were: American families and the nostalgia trap.* New York, NY: Basic Books.

Covey, Stephen R. (1989). *The 7 habits of highly effective people: Powerful lessons in personal change.* New York, NY: Fireside Books, Simon & Schuster.

Goleman, Daniel. (2006). *Social intelligence: The new science of human relationships.* New York. NY: Bantam Dell.

Sapolsky, Robert M. (1998). *Why zebras don't get ulcers: An updated guide to stress, stress-related diseases, and coping.* New York, NY: W. H. Freeman and Company.

Self-Assessment of Resources

In Getting Ahead, we do a self-assessment of our resources instead of having people in the helping agencies do the assessment.

LEARNING OBJECTIVES

WHAT'S COVERED

We will:

Do a self-assessment of your resources

Create a "Mental Model of Resources"—a summary of your resource levels

WHY IT'S IMPORTANT

The 11 resources cover all aspects of life. It's important to do your own assessment instead of having others assess your situation.

HOW IT'S CONNECTED TO YOU

We have covered the information we need in order to have an accurate picture of our economic situations.

We've investigated political/economic structures and learned about hidden rules, language issues, and resources.

Now it's time to summarize the results of our investigations.

The first step is to do this assessment. When we're done, we'll do an assessment of the community, then start making our personal and community plans.

Activity: Self-Assessment of Resources

Time: 45–60 minutes
Materials: Worksheets, pen or pencil

Procedure:

1. Review all the activities we did in Getting Ahead and the mental models in your Future Story Portfolio. Make any necessary revisions in order to keep them accurate and up to date.

2. Following are 11 charts. Each chart contains one of the 11 resources. Each resource is broken down into the five levels that we used in Module 6.

   (1) Urgent/Crisis

   (2) Vulnerable/High-Risk

   (3) Stable

   (4) Safe/Secure

   (5) Thriving/Giving Back

   For each level, there's a description. For each description, there are a number of illustrations of the description.

3. Complete the Self-Assessment of Resources. Work on your own, not as a group. If a question needs to be clarified, ask the facilitator.

4. Put an "X" mark by every illustration that is true for you. You might end up having several check marks in each level.

5. After you've completed the self-assessment for the resource, look back over your answers and decide which of the five levels most closely represents your situation. For example, if you have three "X's" in Level 1 and four in Level 2, decide that, on the whole, you are in Level 2. Circle your level number in the resource-level chart that is below the Self-Assessment of Resources.

6. Take the level number in the resource-level chart and transfer it to the Mental Model of Resources bar chart that follows the Self-Assessment.

NOTE: Do these worksheets as if your situation were just another case study, as if you were objectively looking from the outside at your life. "Detaching" yourself from any problem will help you see it more clearly. Sometimes doing this kind of self-assessment can be painful, especially if a number of your resources are in the crisis/vulnerable level. It would be natural to want to reduce the pain by scoring your resources higher than they really are, but this is the time to do tough and tight thinking.

This is also the time to identify your strongest resources because it is those resources that will help you build the bridge out of the urgent and vulnerable ones.

After you're finished, you can share your thinking and scores with others, but only if you want to. Sometimes listening to others can help clarify one's thinking. Remember too that this assessment is yours, not what someone else is saying about you. Best wishes as you do this important exercise.

---

1. Self-Assessment of Financial Resources			
Level	Description	Statements	X
(1) Urgent/Crisis	Doesn't have enough income to purchase needed goods and services.	When an adult in my household works, the job usually pays less than $8 an hour.	
		Members of our household have been homeless or have doubled up with others who are not related to us in the past 12 months.	
		My family uses one or more government subsidies, such as cash assistance, food stamps, medical card, and/or HEAP (Home Energy Assistance Program).	
		Someone in my household goes to payday lenders, check-cashing places, and/or lease-purchase services.	
		The transportation that my household uses isn't reliable.	
		Our family's income is at or below the Federal Poverty Guidelines;(*) see Module 1.	
(2) Vulnerable/High-Risk	Has some, but not enough, income to purchase needed goods and services—and to save money.	When an adult in my household works, the job usually pays less than $10 an hour.	
		Half (50%) of my household income comes from earnings and/or child support.	
		More than a third (33%) of my household income goes toward housing.	
		I live in subsidized housing.	
		We don't have insurance for the family car(s).	
		Our household's income is 200% of the Federal Poverty Guidelines.(*)	
(3) Stable	Has enough income to purchase needed goods and services—and to have money saved for a crisis.	At least one adult in my household has a job that pays a living wage or a self-sufficient wage.	
		All of my household income (100%) is from earnings and/or child support.	
		My household's housing costs are 30% of the household income.	
		Our household is reducing our debt and works from a budget.	
		Our household has liability insurance for our car(s) and renters insurance.	
		Our family's annual income is 300% of the Federal Poverty Guidelines.	

(4) Safe/Secure	Has enough income to purchase needed goods and services, to save for emergencies, and to invest in the future.	My household's employer(s) contribute to the pension/retirement investments.	
		My household has affordable health insurance.	
		My household has a savings account for emergencies.	
		Our household has insurance for our home and businesses.	
		Working adults in my household are making investments to support retirement.	
		Our family's annual income is 400% of the Federal Poverty Guidelines.(*)	
(5) Thriving/Giving Back	Actively seeks to increase personal financial assets over time—and to help build community assets.	The provider(s) in the household build(s) assets: housing, business, investments.	
		Our household can access all the healthcare services we need.	
		Our household uses financial services to assist in building assets.	
		Our household has no debt that isn't part of a financial plan.	
		Our household helps other community members build their financial assets.	
		Our family's annual income is well above 500% of the Federal Poverty Guidelines.(*)	

(*) Calculate the percentage of income using the Federal Poverty Guidelines chart in Module 1.

Financial Resource Level				
Urgent/Crisis	Vulnerable/ High-Risk	Stable	Safe/Secure	Thriving/ Giving Back
1	2	3	4	5

Instructions:

1. Put an "X" mark by every statement that is true for you.

2. Circle your level number in the resource-level chart that is below the Self-Assessment of Resources.

3. Write the level number in the Mental Model of Resources bar chart that follows the Self-Assessment.

		2. Self-Assessment of Emotional Resources	
Level	Description	Statements	X
(1) Urgent/Crisis	Can't choose and control emotional responses; often behaves in ways that are harmful to others or self.	I have trouble naming the feelings I'm having.	
		I often lose my temper.	
		I regularly try to control the thoughts, feelings, and actions of others.	
		I often feel anxious or depressed.	
		I have trouble getting along with others at work/school.	
		I have been in legal trouble because of my anger.	
(2) Vulnerable/High-Risk	Can sometimes choose and control emotional responses; sometimes behaves in ways that are harmful to others or self.	I sometimes use positive self-talk to help me deal with problems.	
		I seldom get into fights or threaten others.	
		I usually control my temper.	
		I sometimes feel anxious or depressed.	
		For the most part, I accept responsibility for my actions.	
		I get along with others at work/school more often than not.	
(3) Stable	Can almost always choose and control emotional responses; almost never behaves in ways that are harmful to others or self.	I identify my feelings quickly.	
		I use my thoughts to control my feelings.	
		I usually choose positive behaviors, even in stressful situations.	
		I rarely feel anxious or depressed.	
		I can solve problems with others by talking things through.	
		I get along well with people at work/school most of the time.	

(4) Safe/Secure	Is good at choosing and controlling emotional responses; engages in positive behaviors toward others.	I almost always manage my thoughts and feelings in positive ways.	
		I can almost always set aside emotional issues so that I can focus on immediate issues.	
		I make most of my choices based on future results rather than on the feelings of the moment.	
		I almost always get along well at work/school.	
		I can help others when they are distressed or emotional.	
		I almost always get along with people with whom I disagree about issues that are important to me.	
(5) Thriving/Giving Back	Actively seeks to improve emotional health of self and others.	I have worked through difficult emotional events in my life.	
		I can identify, own, and take responsibility for my feelings.	
		I have healthy ways of dealing with stressful emotions.	
		I help others to grow emotionally, to empower them.	
		I get along well with people who come from different backgrounds, classes, races, and political points of view.	
		I am able to work through major differences and emotional issues with others.	

Emotional Resource Level				
Urgent/Crisis	Vulnerable/High-Risk	Stable	Safe/Secure	Thriving/Giving Back
1	2	3	4	5

Instructions:

1. Put an "X" mark by every statement that is true for you.

2. Circle your level number in the resource-level chart that is below the Self-Assessment of Resources.

3. Write the level number in the Mental Model of Resources bar chart that follows the Self-Assessment.

3. Self-Assessment of Mental Resources

Level	Description	Statements	X
(1) Urgent/Crisis	Lacks ability, education, or skills to compete for well-paying jobs.	I have trouble learning new things.	
		I have a learning disability that I haven't had help for yet.	
		I don't see the point of learning math.	
		I have a hard time organizing information and deciding what's important.	
		I like to be able to see, feel, or touch what it is I'm trying to learn.	
		I don't usually have a plan for things I have to do.	
(2) Vulnerable/High-Risk	Has some ability, education, or skills to compete for entry-level jobs.	I can learn some new things, but there are many subjects I'd rather not have to learn about.	
		I have a learning disability and know how and where to get help.	
		I know enough math to be able to do things like measure, weigh, add up expenses, and make change.	
		I can see connections between different stories, and I have strategies for how to get my (school) work done.	
		I like to be able to talk about how I feel about learning and compare it to other things.	
		I make and carry out plans for solving daily problems.	
(3) Stable	Has enough ability, education, or skills to compete for well-paying jobs.	I can learn new things and am willing to study subjects that aren't very interesting to me personally.	
		I have a learning disability that I can manage, and it no longer interferes with my ability to learn.	
		I know enough math to be able to do abstract calculations and understand statistics.	
		I can easily understand what information is important and what will work to solve a problem using proven rules.	
		I like to think about how I think and make models to describe how parts work together to make a whole.	
		I make detailed plans for work and/or school and home, then carry them out.	

(4) Safe/Secure	Has plenty of ability, education, or skills to compete for well-paying jobs.	I love learning new things and can usually find a way to make any subject interesting to me personally.	
		I don't have a learning disability.	
		I did well in math through high school and am able to learn new math concepts quickly.	
		I see patterns among all sorts of problems and stories that make it easy for me to make judgments and generalizations.	
		I think about systems and how new information fits into the systems knowledge I have.	
		I have detailed plans to achieve my future story, as well as plans to prevent bad things from happening.	
(5) Thriving/Giving Back	Actively seeks to improve existing ability, education, or skills—and builds mental resources in the community.	I help others learn.	
		I know strategies to help people with learning disabilities master new information.	
		I'm good at math and able to teach others how to do math.	
		I can do complex problem solving without even thinking about it; solutions come easily.	
		I use my understanding of systems and how to build knowledge to help individuals and community groups do their work.	
		My personnel plans are solid and work well, and I help the community make plans to solve problems.	

Mental Resource Level				
Urgent/Crisis	Vulnerable/ High-Risk	Stable	Safe/Secure	Thriving/ Giving Back
1	2	3	4	5

Instructions:

1. Put an "X" mark by every statement that is true for you.

2. Circle your level number in the resource-level chart that is below the Self-Assessment of Resources.

3. Write the level number in the Mental Model of Resources bar chart that follows the Self-Assessment.

4. Self-Assessment of Language Resources

Level	Description	Statements	X
(1) Urgent/Crisis	Lacks vocabulary, language ability, and negotiation skills needed for workplace and school settings.	I don't speak English well.	
		I cannot read.	
		My vocabulary is mostly made up of concrete, specific terms.	
		I use only the casual register in my native language.	
		I use only the casual register in English.	
		I have trouble using language to negotiate with people at work or school.	
(2) Vulnerable/High-Risk	Has some vocabulary, language ability, and negotiation skills needed for workplace and school settings.	I use the casual register in English.	
		I can use the formal register in my native language.	
		I can read notices and directions at school or work.	
		I understand most of the instructions I get from teachers and supervisors.	
		I can explain myself well enough to solve most problems at school and work.	
		I can hold a job that doesn't require much language knowledge.	
(3) Stable	Has enough vocabulary, language ability, and negotiation skills needed for workplace and school settings.	My vocabulary includes some abstract terms, particularly those needed in school or the workplace.	
		I can write in the formal register.	
		I can sometimes translate from the formal to the casual register and vice versa.	
		I'm able to use language to explore the point of view of others and to negotiate solutions.	
		I can present ideas in a linear, sequential manner.	
		I can use the "voices" (child, parent, adult) appropriately.	

(4) Safe/Secure	Has plenty of vocabulary, language ability, and negotiation skills needed for workplace and school settings.	I have the vocabulary to be comfortable in a variety of work and school settings.	
		I use language to express complex ideas.	
		I use language to develop and maintain a career.	
		I can function easily in both casual and formal registers.	
		I provide children with a varied and rich language experience.	
		I use language to negotiate at work and school, as well as in personal settings.	
(5) Thriving/Giving Back	Actively seeks to improve upon already strong vocabulary and language ability foundation—and works to develop language resources in the community.	I'm reasonably fluent in at least one language besides my native language.	
		I use language to debate and persuade.	
		I use language to resolve conflicts.	
		I can use both the casual and formal registers appropriately.	
		I use language to develop relationships of mutual respect.	
		I work in the community to develop language resources for everyone.	

Language Resource Level				
Urgent/Crisis	Vulnerable/High-Risk	Stable	Safe/Secure	Thriving/Giving Back
1	2	3	4	5

Instructions:

1. Put an "X" mark by every statement that is true for you.

2. Circle your level number in the resource-level chart that is below the Self-Assessment of Resources.

3. Write the level number in the Mental Model of Resources bar chart that follows the Self-Assessment.

5. Self-Assessment of Social Capital Resources

Level	Description	Statements	X
(1) Urgent/Crisis	Lacks positive friends, family, and connections that can be accessed to improve resources.	Some people in my home are dangerous to me and others; I have been a victim of others.	
		Most of my family members and friends don't support my efforts to make positive changes in my life.	
		Situations with my family often interfere with work and/or my education—such as truancy, drug use, or violence.	
		My neighborhood is unsafe.	
		I have very little positive contact with people from the community: social services, police, healthcare, etc.	
		I have no influence or voice on important community issues.	
(2) Vulnerable/High-Risk	Has some positive friends, family, and connections that can be accessed to improve resources.	People in my home are sometimes, but not often, dangerous to me and others; I am a survivor.	
		Many, but not all, of my family members and friends support my efforts to make positive changes.	
		Situations with my family—such as truancy, drug use, or violence—rarely interfere with my work and/or my education.	
		I have some positive contact with people from the community: social services, police, healthcare, etc.	
		Sometimes my neighborhood is unsafe.	
		I have very little influence or voice on important community issues.	
(3) Stable	Has enough positive friends, family, and connections that can be accessed to improve resources.	Nearly all of my family members and friends support my efforts to make positive changes.	
		Serious problematic behaviors by my family members are not completely under control.	
		I have positive relationships with some people in community organizations and agencies.	
		My neighborhood is safe.	
		I have relationships of mutual respect with several people outside of my usual circle of family and friends.	
		I have influence or a voice in important community issues that matter to me.	

(4) Safe/Secure	Has plenty of positive friends, family, and connections that can be accessed to improve resources.	I live in a neighborhood that is safe—in part because of the close relationships I have with my neighbors.	
		My family and friends encourage and support my efforts to make positive changes.	
		My siblings and I are usually engaged in positive social activities with peers and adults.	
		I belong to groups or organizations that improve community life.	
		I help people at work or school gain influence and voice on important work and community activities.	
		I build bridging social capital intentionally.	
(5) Thriving/Giving Back	Actively develops networks and social resources that can be accessed to improve personal and community resources.	I have a large circle of friends and family who support me and help me raise my family.	
		I have a strong network of positive, professional co-workers.	
		I have many social and financial connections.	
		I help people from other backgrounds and economic classes gain influence and power on important community issues.	
		I live in a mixed community with people from various backgrounds and economic classes.	
		I support and advocate for policies that build communities where everyone can live well.	

Social Capital Resource Level				
Urgent/Crisis	Vulnerable/ High-Risk	Stable	Safe/Secure	Thriving/ Giving Back
1	2	3	4	5

Instructions:

1. Put an "X" mark by every statement that is true for you.

2. Circle your level number in the resource-level chart that is below the Self-Assessment of Resources.

3. Write the level number in the Mental Model of Resources bar chart that follows the Self-Assessment.

6. Self-Assessment of Physical Resources

Level	Description	Statements	X
(1) Urgent/Crisis	Lacks physical health and mobility for workplace and school settings.	I regularly do things that are bad for my health.	
		I have a drinking/drug problem and/or mental health illness.	
		I have a disease that is stress-related or chronic and/or a disability.	
		I have problems with my teeth that aren't being addressed.	
		I am not always sure that I'll have enough to eat.	
		I spend a great deal of time on health issues and getting healthcare, which often affects my ability to work or attend school.	
(2) Vulnerable/High-Risk	Has some physical health and mobility problems that could limit effectiveness in the workplace or school.	I'm getting treatment for an addiction and/or a mental illness.	
		I'm receiving medical care for a disease that is stress-related or chronic and/or a disability.	
		I'm receiving dental care.	
		I rarely exercise, but I can do light physical work.	
		More often than not I eat highly processed foods and unbalanced meals.	
		Health problems sometimes interfere with my work or school schedule.	
(3) Stable	Has the physical and health mobility needed for workplace and school settings.	I do preventive healthcare and dental care.	
		I am maintaining my recovery program for addiction and/or mental health issues and/or follow medical advice to manage my chronic illness.	
		More often than not I eat healthy foods and balanced meals.	
		I exercise or play sports fairly often.	
		I can do hard physical work.	
		Health problems seldom interfere with work or school.	

(4) Safe/Secure	Consistently maintains physical health and mobility needed for self and others in the workplace and/or school.	I have no ongoing physical health concerns; except for the occasional cold, I'm in excellent health.	
		I have no addiction issues or mental health issues.	
		I use preventive and early-detection strategies.	
		I exercise at least three times a week.	
		I am an above-average athlete.	
		Health concerns almost never interfere with work or school.	
(5) Thriving/Giving Back	Actively develops physical resources for self, workplace, school, and community.	I am in the peak of health.	
		I have outstanding athletic ability.	
		I eat healthy and well-balanced meals.	
		I exercise daily.	
		I support healthy lifestyle programs in the workplace and school.	
		I have worked toward the development of high-quality and affordable community facilities and healthcare systems for all members of the community.	

Physical Resource Level				
Urgent/Crisis	Vulnerable/ High-Risk	Stable	Safe/Secure	Thriving/ Giving Back
1	2	3	4	5

Instructions:

1. Put an "X" mark by every statement that is true for you.

2. Circle your level number in the resource-level chart that is below the Self-Assessment of Resources.

3. Write the level number in the Mental Model of Resources bar chart that follows the Self-Assessment.

7. Self-Assessment of Spiritual Resources

Level	Description	Statements	X
(1) Urgent/Crisis	Lacks cultural connections or a sense of spiritual purpose that offers support and guidance.	I believe in fate—that my choices really don't make any difference.	
		My actions are guided by my immediate needs.	
		I go to religious institutions when I need clothes, food, housing, or other emergency assistance.	
		I don't feel a sense of belonging to any particular group or culture.	
		I often feel hopeless.	
		I often feel that I don't have a purpose in my life.	
(2) Vulnerable/High-Risk	Has some cultural connections or a sense of spiritual purpose that offers support and guidance.	I think choices can sometimes make a difference but that there's little point in trying to make changes.	
		I go to church or other religious institutions for help with emergency needs and support during hard times.	
		I identify with a cultural or ethnic group, but I don't participate in its activities.	
		I sometimes feel hopeless.	
		I don't have a strong sense of belonging with other people.	
		I sometimes feel that I have a purpose in my life.	
(3) Stable	Has sufficient cultural connections or a sense of spiritual purpose that offers support and guidance.	I believe in a higher power that is larger than I.	
		I read spiritual texts for guidance.	
		I attend services at a church, temple, synagogue, or mosque.	
		I have some social relationships with people from my religious group.	
		I have some relationships with people from my cultural or ethnic group.	
		My spiritual beliefs guide my actions and my choices.	

(4) Safe/Secure	Has plenty of cultural connections or a sense of spiritual purpose that offers support and guidance.	I engage in a daily spiritual practice based on a particular religious faith.	
		I regularly participate in services at a church, temple, synagogue, or mosque.	
		I have many social relationships with people from my religious group.	
		I regularly participate in the cultural or ethnic events of my group.	
		I feel hopeful most of the time.	
		I engage in regular spiritual activities outside of organized religion.	
(5) Thriving/Giving Back	Actively seeks cultural connections and encourages spiritual growth in self and others.	My spiritual practice is a very important part of my life.	
		My spiritual life motivates me to devote time and money to helping others.	
		I am accepting of people from other beliefs and faiths.	
		I actively work to develop understanding and compassion among groups in the community.	
		I feel optimistic nearly all of the time.	
		I have strong connections with a religious, cultural, or ethnic group and participate fully in its activities.	

Spiritual Resource Level				
Urgent/Crisis	Vulnerable/ High-Risk	Stable	Safe/Secure	Thriving/ Giving Back
1	2	3	4	5

Instructions:

1. Put an "X" mark by every statement that is true for you.

2. Circle your level number in the resource-level chart that is below the Self-Assessment of Resources.

3. Write the level number in the Mental Model of Resources bar chart that follows the Self-Assessment.

8. Self-Assessment of Integrity and Trust Resources

Level	Description	Statements	X
(1) Urgent/Crisis	Cannot be trusted to keep one's word, to accomplish tasks, and to obey laws, even when under supervision.	I often lie and deceive others.	
		I find ways to get around the law that aren't exactly legal.	
		I don't give my employer my full effort.	
		I obey the laws but only when they're being enforced.	
		I often don't do what I say I'll do.	
		I don't want to be accountable to anyone.	
(2) Vulnerable/High-Risk	Can sometimes be trusted to keep one's word, to accomplish tasks, and to obey laws when under supervision.	I sometimes lie and deceive others.	
		I rarely steal from others or from work or school.	
		I obey laws most of the time.	
		Few people trust me.	
		I give my employer a full day's effort most of the time.	
		I'm accountable to those who have power.	
(3) Stable	Can usually be trusted to keep one's word, to accomplish tasks, and to obey laws without supervision.	I'm truthful.	
		I try to do what is fair and right for all concerned.	
		I obey laws, unless it's a law with which I have a philosophical or moral disagreement.	
		Many people trust me.	
		I almost always give my employer a full day's work.	
		I generally accept responsibility for myself and don't blame others.	

(4) Safe/Secure	Can invariably be trusted to keep one's word, to accomplish tasks, to obey laws, and inspire others to do the same.	I have earned the trust of others at work or school.	
		I take on difficult problems and accept responsibility for myself.	
		I live by high ethical standards.	
		Most people trust me.	
		I don't cheat on taxes or try to circumvent the law.	
		I do what I say I'll do.	
(5) Thriving/Giving Back	Actively seeks to build integrity and trust—and sets high ethical standards at work, school, and in the community.	I'm accountable to myself.	
		I make myself accountable to others.	
		I work with others to set high ethical standards at work or school and in community life.	
		I lead by example.	
		I actively work with others to change laws and policies that I consider immoral or unjust.	
		I don't misuse my power or position.	

Integrity and Trust Resource Level				
Urgent/Crisis	Vulnerable/ High-Risk	Stable	Safe/Secure	Thriving/ Giving Back
1	2	3	4	5

Instructions:

1. Put an "X" mark by every statement that is true for you.

2. Circle your level number in the resource-level chart that is below the Self-Assessment of Resources.

3. Write the level number in the Mental Model of Resources bar chart that follows the Self-Assessment.

9. Self-Assessment of Motivation and Persistence Resources

Level	Description	Statements	X
(1) Urgent/Crisis	Lacks energy or drive to prepare for, plan, and complete projects, jobs, and personal change.	I avoid work or school when possible.	
		I have low energy most of the time.	
		I would rather not be promoted at work, and I hate training events.	
		I don't like the hassle of learning new things.	
		I work hard sometimes but often goof off while at work or school.	
		I usually wait until things get really bad before I make changes.	
(2) Vulnerable/High-Risk	Has some energy or drive to prepare for, plan, and complete projects, jobs, and personal change.	I have low energy some of the time.	
		I'm cautious about taking on new duties at work or school.	
		I don't enjoy training events, but I usually attend because it's expected.	
		I work just hard enough to keep supervisors and instructors off my back.	
		I work hard if I like the people I'm working for.	
		I'll work at making changes in my life if things will get better right away.	
(3) Stable	Has enough energy or drive to prepare for, plan, and complete projects, jobs, and personal change.	I work hard most of the time.	
		I set short-term goals.	
		I usually stick with the goals I set until I finish them.	
		I have fairly steady energy.	
		I seek promotion for the power or recognition.	
		I attend and value most training opportunities.	

(4) Safe/Secure	Has plenty of energy or drive to prepare for, plan, and complete projects, jobs, and personal change.	I have high energy almost all of the time.	
		I try to do the right thing for the business or school or organization.	
		I sometimes seek out training on my own.	
		I seek promotions because they reflect excellence.	
		I have planning strategies that usually work very well for me.	
		I'm self-motivated.	
(5) Thriving/Giving Back	Actively seeks to maintain motivation and persistence— and to assist others in finding theirs.	I see the big picture and can make plans for the organization or school.	
		I see opportunities for the organization and other individuals and prepare the organization and others for such opportunities.	
		I work with others to set goals, and I enjoy achieving positive results in an atmosphere that emphasizes teamwork.	
		I promote motivation and persistence by creating quality improvement structures at the organizational and community level.	
		I'm self-motivated and persistent in my personal life.	
		I walk the talk.	

Motivation and Persistence Resource Level				
Urgent/Crisis	Vulnerable/ High-Risk	Stable	Safe/Secure	Thriving/ Giving Back
1	2	3	4	5

Instructions:

1. Put an "X" mark by every statement that is true for you.

2. Circle your level number in the resource-level chart that is below the Self-Assessment of Resources.

3. Write the level number in the Mental Model of Resources bar chart that follows the Self-Assessment.

10. Self-Assessment of Relationship/Role Models Resources

Level	Description	Statements	X
(1) Urgent/Crisis	Lacks access to others who are safe, supportive, and nurturing.	Many people I know personally are negative and unsuccessful people.	
		Many people I know say negative things about themselves and others.	
		Many people I know think life happens to them—that they really don't have much control over things.	
		Many people I know let fear and obstacles stop them from trying to pursue their dreams.	
		Many people I know don't like to learn new things.	
		Many people close to me will undercut just about any efforts I make to improve my life.	
(2) Vulnerable/High-Risk	Has limited access to others who are safe, supportive, and nurturing.	Some people I know personally are negative and unsuccessful people.	
		Some people I know say negative things about themselves and others.	
		Some people I know think life happens to them—that they really don't have much control over things.	
		Some people I know let fear and obstacles stop them from trying to pursue their dreams.	
		Some people I know don't like to learn new things.	
		Some people close to me will undercut just about any efforts I make to improve my life.	
(3) Stable	Has enough access to others who are safe, supportive, and nurturing.	Some people I know often think, "By my choices I can create my life."	
		Some people I know are eager to change and to succeed.	
		Some people I know like to learn.	
		Some people in my life will support the changes I want to make to improve my life.	
		I have several relationships of mutual respect with people at work and school.	
		I have someone I can model myself after in one or more areas of life.	

(4) Safe/Secure	Has plenty of access to others who are safe, supportive, and nurturing.	Most people I know usually think, "By my choices I can create my life."	
		Most people I know are eager to change and succeed.	
		Most people I know like to learn.	
		Most of the people in my life support the changes I want to make to improve my life.	
		I have many relationships of mutual respect with people at work and school.	
		I have someone who is a strong role model, mentor, ally, or sponsor to me.	
(5) Thriving/Giving Back	Actively seeks out others who are safe, supportive, and nurturing—and is safe, supportive, and nurturing to others.	Most people I know focus on opportunities.	
		Most people I know are positive, successful people.	
		Most people I know are continually learning and growing.	
		I have mentors, allies, or sponsors with whom I meet regularly.	
		I'm a mentor, ally, or sponsor to others in the community.	
		I assist the community in building relationships that are supportive of people from all economic classes and backgrounds.	

Relationship/Role Models Resource Level				
Urgent/Crisis	Vulnerable/ High-Risk	Stable	Safe/Secure	Thriving/ Giving Back
1	2	3	4	5

Instructions:

1. Put an "X" mark by every statement that is true for you.

2. Circle your level number in the resource-level chart that is below the Self-Assessment of Resources.

3. Write the level number in the Mental Model of Resources bar chart that follows the Self-Assessment.

11. Self-Assessment of Knowledge of Hidden Rules Resources

Level	Description	Statements	X
(1) Urgent/Crisis	Lacks awareness of economic class issues; lives an unexamined life.	I get along with others in my own environment.	
		I know how to survive in my environment.	
		I know how to get my needs met in my environment	
		I haven't given much thought to the economic class in which I live.	
		I've lived in the same economic class my whole life.	
		I haven't learned about economic class issues.	
(2) Vulnerable/High-Risk	Has some awareness of economic class issues in term of the environment and hidden rules.	I have experienced some new environments and realize that I am more comfortable in some places than in others.	
		I've noticed that I don't know how to handle new environments as well as those who "belong" there.	
		I try to fit in by observing others or by asking for help.	
		I tend to judge and dislike people from other classes.	
		I have given some thought to economic class issues.	
		I am beginning to learn about people in other economic classes.	
(3) Stable	Has examined people from other economic classes to better understand their behavior and hidden rules; seeks to apply that understanding at institutional and community levels.	I realize that there are different living environments based on economic class.	
		I've learned about the hidden rules of class.	
		I seek to understand how others think and behave.	
		Sometimes I use my knowledge to have relationships of mutual respect across economic class lines.	
		I'm getting better at navigating new environments.	
		Sometimes I use my knowledge of people in other economic classes to influence how programs are designed and run.	

Getting Ahead in a Just-Gettin'-By World

(4) Safe/Secure	Has begun to examine one's own life in terms of privilege, power, and opportunity through the lens of economic class; seeks to make changes in one's own thinking and behavior.	I've read books and/or attended classes on economic issues.	
		I've examined my family history in terms of resource and asset development and stability of the environment.	
		I've examined my life in terms of privilege, power, and opportunity.	
		I'm aware of how I fit in the class structure.	
		I'm learning how to help create an environment where people from all classes can work together effectively.	
		I have a number of relationships of mutual respect across class lines.	
(5) Thriving/Giving Back	Continues to examine one's own life in terms of privilege, power, and opportunity through the lens of economic class; seeks to make changes at institutional and community levels.	I'm increasingly comfortable being at the planning and decision-making table with people from all classes.	
		I participate in making changes at the institutional level that will help create an environment where everyone can do well.	
		I participate in making changes at the community level that will help create a community where everyone can live well.	
		I utilize the hidden rules of class to resolve conflicts and to build relationships of mutual respect across economic class lines.	
		I'm changing my lifestyle to be more consistent with my growing understanding of economic class issues.	
		I participate in making policy changes at the highest level possible so everyone can live well.	

Knowledge of Hidden Rules Resource Level				
Urgent/Crisis	Vulnerable/High-Risk	Stable	Safe/Secure	Thriving/Giving Back
1	2	3	4	5

Instructions:

1. Put an "X" mark by every statement that is true for you.

2. Circle your level number in the resource-level chart that is below the Self-Assessment of Resources.

3. Write the level number in the Mental Model of Resources bar chart that follows the Self-Assessment.

Activity: Mental Model of Resources

Time: 10 minutes
Materials: Colored markers

Procedure: Using a colored marker, fill in the spaces. For example, if your financial resources are Vulnerable/High-Risk (2), color in rows 1 and 2 in the "Financial" column so that you create a bar. When you have done all 11 resources, you will have completed the Mental Model of Resources.

	Financial	Emotional	Mental	Language	Social Capital	Physical	Spiritual	Integrity and Trust	Motivation and Persistence	Relationship/Role Models	Knowledge of Hidden Rules
Mental Model of Resources											
5											
4											
3											
2											
1											

Discussion

1. Looking at the mental model, which are your strongest resources?

2. Where did each of your resources come from? To what extent were they from family, organizations (schools, clubs, associations), and cultural or ethnic groups?

3. How did your community help your family build resources?

4. To what extent does your community provide fair opportunities for good jobs, good healthcare, a good education, and fair credit?

5. Did you build your resources yourself? Was it something inside you, a decision you made, a way of thinking, a talent, a gift?

6. What did you learn about your situation and your life by doing this exercise?

7. How are certain resources linked to each other in relation to your situation?

8. Which resources are your lowest?

9. How might you use your higher resources to build your lower resources?

10. Thinking back over everything that we have investigated so far, how does the Mental Model of Resources fit into it?

11. Where are you with regard to the Stages of Change?

GA investigators deal critically and creatively with reality—and participate in the transformation of their world.

Community Assessment

In Getting Ahead, there are two main story lines: the individual and the community. We assessed our own resources; now it's time to assess the strengths and weaknesses of our community.

WHAT'S COVERED

We will:

Investigate the community's ability to provide a high-quality life for everyone, including people in poverty and near poverty

Complete a "Community Assessment Mental Model"

Identify community assets (individuals, associations, and institutions) that can help Getting Ahead investigators build resources.

Create the "Group One-on-One Relationships Mental Model"

Create the "Personal One-to-One Relationships Mental Model"

WHY IT'S IMPORTANT

When it comes to building resources, the community you live in matters. Resource development is done locally.

The community contributes to the quality of life by helping people build resources. An accurate assessment is needed that includes information from people in poverty and those who are experiencing instability.

It's important to identify people and organizations that can help build resources.

It's important to hold the community accountable for its quality of life.

It's important that members of the GA group participate in solving community problems, not just their own.

It's important that GA investigators also focus on systemic issues involving poverty beyond the local community.

HOW IT'S CONNECTED TO YOU

There are two themes in Getting Ahead: the individual and the community. We've done a self-assessment; now let's do a community assessment.

When studying the Research Continuum in Module 3, we found that we must develop strategies not only for ourselves but also for the community.

In the next module we're going to focus on how to build resources: who can help us and where to go. This module is the beginning of that investigation.

When we make our final plans, we'll need to include what needs to be done in the community—alongside what needs to be done in our personal lives and what needs to be done at the systemic level.

Assessing the Community

One of the unique features of Getting Ahead is the two story lines: the personal and the community. Now we shift from looking at our own resources and examine the community. To do an accurate assessment of the community, keep these points in mind:

1. The facilitator may have suggested that you start these investigations earlier. If so, you had a head start. If not, you will need to do much of this investigation between GA workshop settings.

2. We define the community as your county, not just your city or town. This means you are assessing the opportunities for everyone in the county, not just those living in an upscale suburb or subsidized housing.

3. Not very many counties or states provide reports on the social and economic health of the communities that combines all the information in one place. Such reports go by different names, but in general they are called *Social Health Index.**

Find out if there is a single report that covers wages, unemployment, poverty, health and safety information, housing availability, educational opportunities, recreation and civic opportunities, and environment conditions in your community. Some small towns may not have this information readily available. Sometimes these facts and figures are available from state level departments and databases. If they aren't, you'll need to dig deeper using the strategies below.

4. This is an opportunity for GA investigators to meet local leaders and get to know them, building bridging social capital in the process. The fact that solutions usually must be found at the local level is a good thing because it's at the local level that GA investigators can make connections and have influence.

> *"If you have come to help me, you can go home. But if you see my struggles as a part of your own survival, then perhaps we can work together."*
>
> –Lila Watson, an Aboriginal Woman from Australia

Activity: Community Assessment

Time: 3 hours (2 hours collecting data for each investigator and 1 hour compiling the data into a single bar chart/mental model)
Materials: Assessment forms (following pages), pen or pencil

Procedure:

1. Read and discuss the following charts that make up the survey of community assets.

2. Divide up the investigations so that everyone shares in the work. As much as possible pick indicators that interest you.

3. Conduct the investigations outside of group time and write a brief summary of the evidence you found for each indicator.

4. Report your findings to the whole group.

5. The entire group should decide on the answer (True? or False?) for each indicator.

6. Use chart paper to create the Community Assessment Mental Model (bar chart at end of this exercise).

7. Scoring: All "T" (True) answers are positive and all "F" (False) answers are negative. Add up the "T" answers and divide by 2 to get the score. For example, if under Economic Conditions there were 8 "T" answers, divide 8 by 2 to get a score of 4. Circle the "4" in the bar below this assessment. Then turn to the page with the bar chart titled "Community Assessment Mental Model." Use a colored marker to fill in spaces 1 through 4 of the bar for Economic Conditions. When you have done the nine sets of questions you will have completed the Community Assessment Mental Model.

1. Community Assessment of Economic Conditions

Indicators	T	F	?
1. The percentage of people in poverty is going down.			
2. The percentage of people in or near poverty (200% of the Federal Poverty Guidelines) is going down.			
3. The free and reduced lunch rate in all schools is going down.			
4. Income disparity is decreasing.			
5. The number and value of business loans in low-income areas is growing.			
6. There's growing diversity in employment sectors, such as manufacturing, service, technology, knowledge, health, construction, tourism, etc.			
7. The number of people employed by locally owned businesses is growing.			
8. There's a mix of employment opportunities so more people can move up economically.			
9. The annual investment in the community's infrastructure is rising.			
10. The downtown vacancy rate is declining.			

Scoring: All "T" (True) answers are positive, and all "F" (False) answers are negative. Add up the "T" answers and divide by 2 to get the score. For example, if there were 8 "T" answers, divide 8 by 2 to get a score of 4. Circle the "4" in the bar below. Then turn to the page with the bar chart titled "Community Assessment Mental Model." Use a colored marker to fill in spaces 1 through 4 on the bar for this assessment.

1	2	3	4	5

2. Community Assessment of Housing Conditions

Indicators	T	F	?
1. Rental units for low-income renters that are 30% of income is more available than in previous years.			
2. Percentage of households able to afford a median single-family house is rising.			
3. Utilization of homeless shelters is going down.			
4. Doubling up (people living together) is going down.			
5. The number of vacant and abandoned houses and other structures is going down.			
6. Segregated housing by economic class is going down.			
7. Housing cooperatives and mutual rental or home ownership (people not related to each other) are going up.			
8. Housing that is inadequate, overcrowded, or costs more than 30% of income is going down.			
9. Waiting time for subsidized housing is getting shorter.			
10. The number of homeless people is going down.			

Scoring: All "T" (True) answers are positive, and all "F" (False) answers are negative. Add up the "T" answers and divide by 2 to get the score. For example, if there were 8 "T" answers, divide 8 by 2 to get a score of 4. Circle the "4" in the bar below. Then turn to the page with the bar chart titled "Community Assessment Mental Model." Use a colored marker to fill in spaces 1 through 4 on the bar for this assessment.

1	2	3	4	5

3. Community Assessment of Financial/Banking Conditions

Indicators	T	F	?
1. Bank loans for small-business start-ups is going up.			
2. *Community Reinvestment Act** (CRA) scores for local banks are improving.			
3. Participation in the CRA plans of banks by people in poverty and near poverty is going up.			
4. More banks are providing typical and fair financial services to low-wage workers.			
5. More credit unions and banks are offering fair loans to low-wage workers.			
6. More financial literacy classes are available to people in poverty and near poverty.			
7. Micro loans are more available to low-income people.			
8. Percentage of disposable personal income that is being saved is rising.			
9. The dollars spent in the local economy (local businesses, local labor, and local resources) is growing.			
10. Per-capita debt is going down.			

Scoring: All "T" (True) answers are positive, and all "F" (False) answers are negative. Add up the "T" answers and divide by 2 to get the score. For example, if there were 8 "T" answers, divide 8 by 2 to get a score of 4. Circle the "4" in the bar below. Then turn to the page with the bar chart titled "Community Assessment Mental Model." Use a colored marker to fill in spaces 1 through 4 on the bar for this assessment.

1	2	3	4	5

4. Community Assessment of Jobs, Wages, and Wealth-Creating Conditions

Indicators	T	F	?
1. Median household income is going up.			
2. Weekly average earnings are going up.			
3. Hours of labor required to meet basic needs is going down.			
4. The number of employee-owned businesses is on the rise.			
5. The ratio of CEO salary to front-line staff employee wages is going down.			
6. Employers are using fewer temporary and part-time employees.			
7. The availability of affordable, high-quality childcare is on the rise.			
8. Transportation to work and agencies is becoming more reliable and affordable.			
9. The community has a living-wage ordinance.			
10. The number of businesses using Bridges concepts is on the rise.			

Scoring: All "T" (True) answers are positive, and all "F" (False) answers are negative. Add up the "T" answers and divide by 2 to get the score. For example, if there were 8 "T" answers, divide 8 by 2 to get a score of 4. Circle the "4" in the bar below. Then turn to the page with the bar chart titled "Community Assessment Mental Model." Use a colored marker to fill in spaces 1 through 4 on the bar for this assessment.

1	2	3	4	5

5. Community Assessment of Protection from Predators Conditions

Indicators	T	F	?
1. The number of payday lenders, cash-advance shops, and check-cashing outlets is going down.			
2. Alternatives to payday lenders, cash-advance shops, and check-cashing outlets are going up.			
3. Employers are developing low-interest loans and savings strategies for low-wage workers.			
4. Alternatives are being developed for buy-here/pay-here car dealers.			
5. The *Better Business Bureau**, Chamber of Commerce, and other business leaders are taking a stand against predatory businesses.			
6. The number of employers who "ask" employees to work "off the clock" without pay is declining.			
7. *Minimum-wage violations** are going down.			
8. *Workers'-compensation violations** are going down.			
9. Human trafficking is going down.			
10. Drug trafficking is going down.			

Scoring: All "T" (True) answers are positive, and all "F" (False) answers are negative. Add up the "T" answers and divide by 2 to get the score. For example, if there were 8 "T" answers, divide 8 by 2 to get a score of 4. Circle the "4" in the bar below. Then turn to the page with the bar chart titled "Community Assessment Mental Model." Use a colored marker to fill in spaces 1 through 4 on the bar for this assessment.

1	2	3	4	5

6. Community Assessment of Education Conditions

Indicators	T	F	?
1. High-quality, affordable preschool opportunities are on the rise.			
2. The percentage of children enrolled in Early Head Start is going up.			
3. The graduation rate of high school students is on the rise.			
4. School *"report cards"** on standardized test scores is rising.			
5. The graduation rate of first-generation, low-income college students is going up.			
6. Apprenticeship and certificate programs that lead to well-paying jobs are on the rise.			
7. Worker skills are increasingly meeting the needs of the employers.			
8. The cost of a college education is declining.			
9. The *digital divide** (the gap between those with access to computers and the Internet and those without access) is narrowing.			
10. The number of community colleges, colleges, and universities using Bridges concepts is on the rise.			

Scoring: All "T" (True) answers are positive, and all "F" (False) answers are negative. Add up the "T" answers and divide by 2 to get the score. For example, if there were 8 "T" answers, divide 8 by 2 to get a score of 4. Circle the "4" in the bar below. Then turn to the page with the bar chart titled "Community Assessment Mental Model." Use a colored marker to fill in spaces 1 through 4 on the bar for this assessment.

1	2	3	4	5

7. Community Assessment of Public Sector Conditions

Indicators	T	F	?
1. The tax base for maintaining high-quality police and fire services is secure.			
2. The tax base for maintaining high-quality schools and recreational facilities is secure.			
3. The tax base for public transportation, water, sewer, garbage collection, and street cleaning is secure.			
4. Public transportation is adequate to move people to and from the workplace, school, healthcare facilities, and grocery stores.			
5. Governmental services usually treat everyone in a respectful and timely manner.			
6. Agencies collaborate to serve clients more effectively and efficiently.			
7. Governmental and non-profit organizations are providing a safety net (financial support for the aged, disabled, young, unemployed, et al.) and increasingly providing support for those who are making the transition out of poverty.			
8. The percentage of taxpayer satisfaction with services is going up.			
9. The percentage of people who trust local government is going up.			
10. The public sector is increasingly using Bridges concepts in programming and service delivery.			

Scoring: All "T" (True) answers are positive, and all "F" (False) answers are negative. Add up the "T" answers and divide by 2 to get the score. For example, if there were 8 "T" answers, divide 8 by 2 to get a score of 4. Circle the "4" in the bar below. Then turn to the page with the bar chart titled "Community Assessment Mental Model." Use a colored marker to fill in spaces 1 through 4 on the bar for this assessment.

1	2	3	4	5

8. Community Assessment of Health Conditions

Indicators	T	F	?
1. The number of uninsured community members is declining.			
2. The cost of healthcare is declining.			
3. High-quality food is accessible and affordable to all.			
4. Environmental safety is improving for everyone.			
5. Transportation and easy access to healthcare is improving.			
6. Neighborhood crime is going down.			
7. Mental health and addiction treatment is affordable and accessible.			
8. Preventive healthcare is on the rise for all.			
9. The overall fitness of community members is rising.			
10. Health disparities are on the decline.			

Scoring: All "T" (True) answers are positive, and all "F" (False) answers are negative. Add up the "T" answers and divide by 2 to get the score. For example, if there were 8 "T" answers, divide 8 by 2 to get a score of 4. Circle the "4" in the bar below. Then turn to the page with the bar chart titled "Community Assessment Mental Model." Use a colored marker to fill in spaces 1 through 4 on the bar for this assessment.

1	2	3	4	5

9. Community Assessment of Leadership Conditions

Indicators	T	F	?
1. The leadership in each sector increasingly ensures that people from all classes and races are engaged in planning, program design, implementation, and evaluation of major initiatives.			
2. The leadership in each sector is increasingly intentional about helping people in poverty make the transition to a stable economic situation.			
3. The leadership increasingly creates a culture of mutual respect for people of all classes and races.			
4. The leadership is increasingly collaborative and less prone to operating in "silos."			
5. The leadership is increasingly able to work across political lines to serve the whole community.			
6. The leadership increasingly supports locally owned and small businesses with incentives and tax breaks.			
7. The leadership is increasingly representative of the population in terms of race, ethnicity, and class.			
8. Citizen participation in community projects is increasing.			
9. The community has a Bridges Steering Committee or a similar group by another name that coordinates the work on poverty based on the Ten Core Bridges Constructs (see Appendix I).			
10. The leadership is increasing the application of Bridges concepts in its area of influence.			

Scoring: All "T" (True) answers are positive, and all "F" (False) answers are negative. Add up the "T" answers and divide by 2 to get the score. For example, if there were 8 "T" answers, divide 8 by 2 to get a score of 4. Circle the "4" in the bar below. Then turn to the page with the bar chart titled "Community Assessment Mental Model." Use a colored marker to fill in spaces 1 through 4 on the bar for this assessment.

1	2	3	4	5

Community Assessment Mental Model

	Economic	Housing	Financial	Jobs, Wages	Predators	Education	Public Services	Health	Leadership
5									
4									
3									
2									
1									

Discussion

1. What are the strengths and weaknesses of your community?

2. What does this investigation suggest about the quality of life (Social Health Index) in the community? What about the nation?

3. What opportunities might your community have in the near future?

4. List individuals, associations, and organizations that stand out as potential partners for building resources.

5. List local leaders who are committed to a wide range of strategies to eliminate poverty.

6. How does this information relate to you?

Additional discussion questions: In your community how easy will it be to build resources? Are there opportunities for each resource? Is there access in terms of cost, availability, and transportation? Is there support in terms of relationships, childcare, and follow-up?

Asset-Based Community Development

In Module 7 you completed a self-assessment of resources that named the current realities of your life. You can use that assessment to hold yourself accountable for your resources and for what happens next in your life. If you hold yourself accountable, it's only reasonable that your community should be held accountable too. The Community Assessment that we just completed was in part about holding the community accountable.

The next investigation is to find the individuals, associations, and institutions that have the vision, knowledge, and connections to help solve community problems in new, exciting ways.

Getting Ahead is based on the idea that people who live in poverty are problem solvers who have unique skills, talents, and knowledge that can help them in any setting. John Kretzmann and John McKnight, authors of *Building Communities from the Inside Out: A Path Toward Finding and Mobilizing a Community's Assets*, share that philosophy. They take a "capacity" approach that "… leads toward the development of policies and activities based on the capacities, skills and assets of lower income people and their neighborhoods" (Kretzmann & McKnight, 1993, p. 5).

They have shown that poverty neighborhoods are full of unrecognized assets. They say,

> The key to neighborhood regeneration, then, is to locate all the available local assets, *to begin connecting them with one another in ways that multiply their power and effectiveness*, and to begin harnessing those of local institutions that are not yet available for local development purposes [emphasis added]. (Kretzmann & McKnight, 1993, p. 5)

The Community Assets Map is a way to organize an inventory that unlocks the gifts and talents available from individuals, associations, and institutions.

Community Assets Map

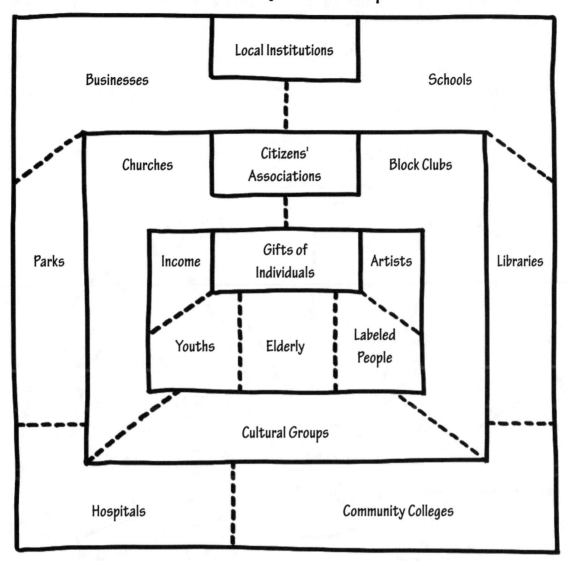

Local Institutions

Businesses

Schools

Churches

Citizens' Associations

Block Clubs

Parks

Income

Gifts of Individuals

Artists

Libraries

Youths

Elderly

Labeled People

Cultural Groups

Hospitals

Community Colleges

Note. Adapted from *Building Communities from the Inside Out: A Path Toward Finding and Mobilizing a Community's Assets* (p. 7), by J. P. Kretzmann and J. L. McKnight, 1993, Chicago, IL: ACTA. Copyright 1993 by ACTA.

The information in Getting Ahead helps GA investigators make connections. Having already identified our strongest resources, investigated our social capital, and named the hidden rules that have helped us navigate our world, we know the value of one-on-one relationships. Combining the relationships-based approach of poverty with the achievement-based approach of the middle class allows us to form and build new relationships of mutual respect and expanded opportunities for everyone.

In the next chart, Kretzmann and McKnight represent how to develop one-on-one relationships. This example is for "local youths." In their book there are similar charts for senior citizens, disabled individuals, welfare recipients, and artists. The point is that each "group" interacts with a variety of community associations and institutions. And within each of those groups are people who might share a concern or interest with the associations and institutions. Each of the interactions, represented by the arrows going in two directions, illustrates a matching of the gifts and capabilities of "local youths" with those in various organizations and institutions.

The purpose of this activity is to develop one-on-one relationships that have the potential to turn into partnerships that will help you (1) complete the plan you'll make in Module 10, (2) stabilize your environment, (3) build personal resources, (4) benefit people in poverty, and (5) benefit your community.

One-on-One Relationships

Note. Adapted from *Building Communities from the Inside Out: A Path Toward Finding and Mobilizing a Community's Assets* (p. 44), by J. P. Kretzmann and J. L. McKnight, 1993, Chicago, IL: ACTA. Copyright 1993 by ACTA.

Getting Ahead in a Just-Gettin'-By World

Analyze the chart in order to expand your thinking of how you can build relationships with associations and institutions in your community. It is in those relationships where you might find the key to new solutions.

Activity: Creating a Group One-on-One Relationships Mental Model

Time: 45 minutes
Materials: Paper, pencils, community directories, campus directories

Procedure:

1. Working as a group, use flipchart paper and draw a circle in the center of the paper, labeling the circle GETTING AHEAD INVESTIGATORS.

2. Brainstorm the local associations, institutions, and organizations with which investigators might partner.

3. Review the following Sample Community Map for additional ideas regarding the associations, institutions, individuals, physical spaces, and activities in the local economy that might be considered.

4. List the local individuals and organizations that came up in Steps 1–3. If possible, find and document the contact information for each.

5. Create a Group One-on-One Relationships Mental Model by drawing lines between a center circle (GETTING AHEAD INVESTIGATORS) and the various community assets. Write brief descriptions of the possible connections. Where might there be matches of gifts, resources, and capabilities?

6. Develop a Personal One-on-One Relationships Mental Model for your individual use—one that is specific to your interests, gifts, capabilities, and connections.

7. This is a time to identify people who can be bridging social capital for you. Create a list of those people, including their contact information. Review what you learned about networking skills and prepare to contact them.

8. Place your Personal One-on-One Relationships Mental Model and your bridging social capital list in the Future Story Portfolio.

Getting Ahead investigators do a self-assessment of their resources and an assessment of the community before building plans for both themselves and their communities.

Sample Community Map

Physical Spaces

Gardens
Parks
Playgrounds
Parking Lots
Bike Paths
Walking Paths
Forests/Forest Preserves
Picnic Areas
Campsites
Fishing Spots
Duck Ponds
Zoos
Wildlife Centers
Natural Habitats—coastal, marine,
amphibious
Bird Watching Sites
Housing
Vacant Land and Buildings
Transit Stops and Facilities
Streets

Associations

Animal Care Groups
Anti-Crime Groups
Business Organizations
Charitable Groups
Civic Events Groups
Cultural Groups
Disabilities/Special Needs Groups Education
Groups
Elderly Groups
Environmental Groups
Family Support Groups
Health Advocacy/Fitness
Heritage Groups
Hobby and Collectors Groups
Men's Groups
Mutual Support Groups
Neighborhood Groups
Political Organizations
Recreation Groups
Religious Groups
Service Clubs
Social Groups
Union Groups
Veterans' Groups
Women's Groups
Youth Groups

Physical
Associations
My Community
Individuals
Institutions
Local Economy

Individuals

Gifts, Skills, Capacities, Knowledge, and
Traits of:

Youths
Older Adults
Artists
Welfare Recipients
People with Disabilities
Students
Parents
Entrepreneurs
Activists
Veterans
Ex-Offenders

Local Economy

For-Profit Businesses
Consumer Expenditures
Merchants
Chamber of Commerce
Business Associations
Banks
Credit Unions
Institutional—purchasing power
and personnel
Barter and Exchange
Community Development
Corporations (CDCs)
Corporations and Branches

Institutions

Schools
Universities
Community Colleges
Police Departments
Hospitals
Libraries
Social Service Agencies
Non-Profits
Museums
Fire Departments
Media
Foundations

Note. Adapted from "Discovering Community Power: A Guide to Mobilizing Local Assets and Your Organization's Capacity" (p. 15), by J. P. Kretzmann and J. L. McKnight, with S. Dobrowolski and D. Puntenney, 2005, Evanston, IL: Asset-Based Community Development Institute. Copyright 2005 by Asset-Based Community Development Institute.

Discussion

1. This is information that can be used by the entire group. How might it be used by other groups in the community?

2. What community assets did this investigation uncover that surprised you?

3. Who are some of the individuals identified by the group who can address policy issues in the institution or community?

4. Which individuals are in a position to help GA investigators build resources?

5. What associations and institutions can help GA investigators build resources?

6. Are there state or national programs that have local offices or initiatives?

7. Are there foundations that could be a resource?

REFLECTIONS

*Vocabulary List for Module 8

Better Business Bureau: a national organization with local chapters that is a go-between for consumers and businesses to resolve disputes; it provides alerts about possible fraudulent activity against consumers and businesses

Community Reinvestment Act: the U.S. Congress passed the CRA in 1977 to encourage commercial banks and savings associations to help meet the needs of borrowers in all segments of the community, including low-income and moderate-income neighborhoods

Digital divide: the gap between groups in access, use, and knowledge of information and communication technology

Minimum-wage violations: the U.S. Department of Labor takes complaints about employers who break the minimum-wage laws—infractions like being asked to work off the clock but not getting paid for it, having to pay for a uniform, and being expected to work during lunch periods

School "report cards": most schools have report cards too! Typically they report on attendance, graduation rates, and academic performance of the students on key subjects—math, science, reading, social studies, and writing

Social Health Index: some (very few) counties and states have a Social Health Index that measures quality of life; these indexes use data to assess quality of life and cover such indicators as health, education, safety, poverty, and the environment

Workers'-compensation violations: when someone is injured on the job but doesn't get any financial compensation for the medical expenses and work time lost

Readings

Burd-Sharps, Sarah, Lewis, Kristen, & Martins, Eduardo Borges. (2008). *The measure of America: American human development report 2008–2009.* New York, NY: Columbia University Press.

Kretzmann, John, & McKnight, John. (1993). *Building communities from the inside out: A path toward finding and mobilizing a community's assets.* Chicago, IL: ACTA Publications.

McKnight, John. (1995). *The careless society: Community and its counterfeits.* New York, NY: Basic Books.

Miringoff, Marc, & Miringoff, Marque-Luisa. (1999). *The social health of the nation: How America is really doing.* New York, NY: Oxford University Press.

Building Resources

*The next step in making plans for our future story is
to investigate how to build our resources.*

WHAT'S COVERED

We will:

Analyze the difference between resources that are for "getting by" and resources that are for "getting ahead"

Develop ways to build each resource

WHY IT'S IMPORTANT

Building resources is a way to build a better life.

Brainstorming with the whole group will help individuals think of various ways of building resources for themselves.

HOW IT'S CONNECTED TO YOU

We will use this information when creating our future stories and making our plans for economic stability and resource development.

Key Points About Building Resources

We have defined poverty as the extent to which individuals and communities do without resources. So the solution to poverty is to build resources. But building resources is easier said than done. We know that building resources and getting out of poverty are harder to do and take longer in the U.S. than in most European countries, for example. We know there are barriers we have to overcome and that they are different, based on where we live.

The investigations we're going to do in this module aren't as easy as finding a few books on how to build financial, emotional, mental, physical, and all the other resources. There are literally thousands of books on these topics. And while reading some of those books may be a necessary step in our investigations, we have to develop strategies that will work in our communities. We have to dig deeper.

Here are some points to keep in mind when doing our investigations.

1. Building resources can lead to a more balanced life. Have you ever known someone who was very intelligent but couldn't get along well with others? That person might have high mental resources and low emotional resources. Raising emotional resources would improve that person's quality of life.

2. It's natural to focus on building resources that are already high. For example, a woman who is already physically fit doesn't really need to build that resource any more. But it wouldn't be surprising if that's what she wanted to do—because she's familiar with going to the gym and feels comfortable there. When building resources we'll need to build primarily those that are low, and that means doing some new things that might be uncomfortable for us, at least at first.

3. *Resources* are connected or *interlocking**. The loss of one resource can lead to the loss of another. For example, a man who suffered brain and pelvic damage in a car accident lost his job and his ability to hike and climb. This eventually led to the loss

of his hiking friends. Resources are interlocking when we build them too. Building mental resources by learning a trade can lead to higher financial resources and more social capital.

4. Building resources begins when we form the intention to build them, when we decide to take action. Researchers are learning more about the ***"mere-measurement effect."*** This means that, by forming (and measuring) an intention, we're more likely to take action. So, if you're motivated to build resources—and you monitor your progress—you'll be more likely to be successful. It's interesting that many Getting Ahead graduates report that they redo the self-assessment of their resources once or twice a year to see how they're doing.

5. Before we begin the investigation into building resources, we should take a moment to examine the different resources that we use for "getting by" and those we use for "getting ahead."

Telling the Difference Between Resources That Help Us Get By and Those That Help Us Get Ahead

Getting-by resources are necessary for survival, but they don't necessarily help us get ahead. An example would be food stamps, cash assistance, or an unemployment check. These may help with day-to-day needs, but they aren't necessarily going to help us build resources. It could be that getting-by resources do little more than maintain us while we live in poverty. Or they may be a factor in keeping us in poverty.

There are organizations in the community that provide getting-by resources, such as food, clothing, cash, and lodging but don't provide long-term support for transition out of poverty. Another term for this is "needs based" services. The thinking behind this seems to be that if people are provided with a safety net, they'll be able to step on a ladder that will get them out of poverty. The problem is that stepping from a net to a ladder looks so risky it might feel safer to just stay on the net!

Getting-ahead resources are those that can take us to a whole new future as we build those resources. There are organizations in the community that offer "power based" resources. Getting Ahead is an example of this. When GA investigators make their own argument for change—and create a future story and a plan to build resources—they're taking charge of their own lives. GA investigators also will need to build social capital and teams of support for the risky step from the safety net to the ladder.

The following chart can be used to sort out the difference between getting-by and getting-ahead resources. For example, a one-time loan or gift of money is likely to be a getting-by resource while a class on financial literacy would be a getting-ahead resource.

Analyzing the Difference Between Getting-By and Getting-Ahead Resources		
	Getting-By Resources: 'Needs Based'	Getting-Ahead Resources: 'Power Based'
Financial		
Emotional		
Mental/Cognitive		
Language		
Social Capital		
Physical		
Spiritual		
Integrity and Trust		
Motivation and Persistence		
Relationships/Role Models		
Knowledge of Hidden Rules		

Activity: Analyzing the Difference Between Getting-By and Getting-Ahead Resources

Time: 20 minutes

Materials: Pen or pencil

Procedure:

1. As a group, give examples of getting-by and getting-ahead resources that are available in the community. Name the organizations that provide them.

2. In the two columns of the chart above, identify the organizations and resources that you personally use.

3. How many resources are in each column?

4. Are all of the 11 resources covered?

Discussion

1. What stands out in your mind about the difference between getting-by and getting-ahead resources?

2. To what extent are the differences between the two clear-cut?

3. Can some getting-by resources be turned into getting-ahead resources? If so, how?

4. What does this tell you about the resources that are available in your community?

5. How does this apply to you?

Now that we've done a self-assessment of our resources, as well as an assessment of community resources, it follows naturally to ask the question, "How do I build these resources?" Or as a GA investigator put it, "How can resources help you move forward and not stand still?"

> *"This class helped me with every single thing I needed for college. Everybody needs to learn what's in this book. It helped me focus on the key points of the situation and how to apply my lifestyle to my income. I am now more open-minded and more relaxed with people who aren't just like me."*
>
> —Remona Gordon, College Student

Strategies for Building Resources

A woman whose Mental Model of Social Capital revealed that she only had one person in her life she could trust, turned to the others and asked, "How do you build bridging capital?" The group immediately began brainstorming ideas. First they wanted to know what her interests were (she loved history and crafts). The group then began naming people and organizations that shared those interests. Next they talked about how she could fit in (the hidden rules of those people and organizations) and how she could get involved if there were costs to participate.

The following activities do the same thing but in more detail. They provide ideas on how to build each resource so that you can jump-start your thinking about building them. Each GA investigator will benefit from the work and wisdom of the group.

Activity: Building Resources

Time: 30–45 minutes
Materials: Chart paper, markers

Procedure:

1. As a group, choose one of the two following strategies to brainstorm ideas for resource development.

2. Break into small groups.

3. Assign as many resources to each group as necessary so that all 11 resources are covered.

4. As a group, brainstorm the resources assigned to you.

Option 1: Tic-Tac-Toe Technique

1. On chart paper re-create the following Tic-Tac-Toe diagram (without the examples) for each resource assigned to your small group. In the center circle of the center square, name the resource that the group will be working on. When naming each resource, add a more specific goal to help focus thinking. For instance, if your group is working on physical resources, the specific goal may be to "lose weight and exercise." In the following example, group members are working on mental resources, and their specific goal is earning a college degree.

2. Then brainstorm eight issues that will have to be addressed when building that resource. In one or two words, label the eight circles surrounding the resource named in the center. In the example, three of the eight issues are identified: (managing) time, (making good) grades, and (managing) relationships.

3. Now take the first issue (in the circle marked A in the center square) and rewrite it in the center circle marked A of the upper-left square. Do the same with each issue from the center square.

4. Continue brainstorming to identify strategies for each issue in circles A through H. In the example below for A (Time) members of the small group decided they would need to spend less (<) time at parties and more (>) time studying.

5. When the small groups are done brainstorming each resource assigned to them, they will share their results with the whole group.

6. The group will add more ideas to the charts developed by the small groups, which will result in capturing everyone's best thinking.

7. Individuals will be able to access these charts when they develop their own plans in Module 10.

8. Add this mental model to your Future Story Portfolio.

Example: Tic-Tac-Toe Diagram

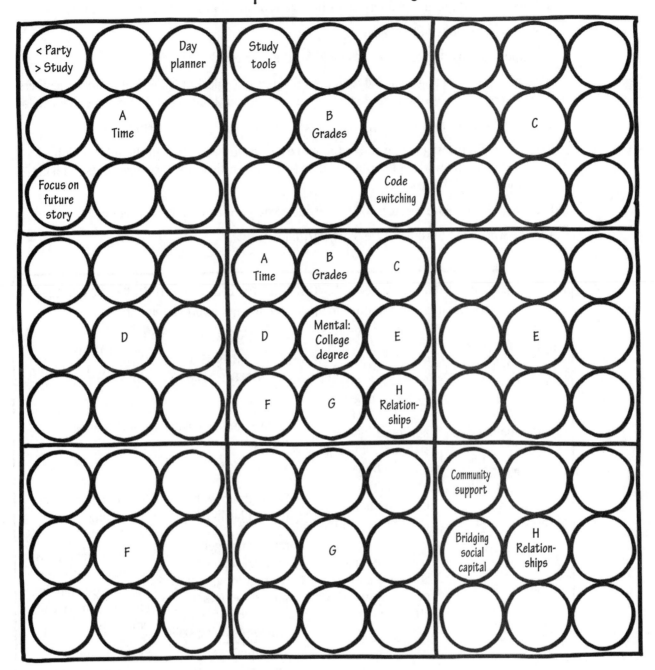

Option 2: Resource Development Worksheet

1. Working as individuals or in teams, use the following worksheet to identify where and how resources can be built.

2. Review the example below for "Building Emotional Resources" before starting. The names of the organizations and some of the details of their offerings have been changed. This investigation was done on the web, by phone, and through general knowledge of the local community.

3. The key elements of the worksheet are in bold print:

    a. Providers of Opportunity (individuals or organizations that help to build resources)

    b. Access (availability of the resource)

    c. Support (during the learning phase and for the long term)

    d. Steps to be taken to get started with the Providers of Opportunity and with family members and people who will be part of your support team, your bonding and bridging social capital

    e. Summary (determine if it's a getting-by resource or a getting-ahead resource)

    f. Selection (GA investigators will need to make a selection according to the information provided on the worksheet or by doing their own investigation). Visualize yourself taking action to build the resource.

4. The idea is to find local sources for the resource you have chosen to investigate.

5. Add the worksheet to your Future Story Portfolio.

Example: Resource Development Worksheet for Building Emotional Resources
Description: How to better manage feelings and improve relationships

Providers of Opportunity	Option #1: Online	Option #2: Therapists Partnership	Option #3: Private Counselor
Program names	Anger Management Class DotCom, approved by many state and national organizations	Change Your Thinking Program	Anger-management classes
Program description, key words, short phrases	20 online lessons, based on book that must be purchased	Small group with trained facilitator	Individual or group counseling
Mission or goal	Overcome anger issues, usually for people required to attend by a court	Anger management through cognitive restructuring, social-skills development, and development of problem-solving skills	Perceiving emotions, reasoning with emotions, understanding emotions, managing emotions
When offered	Anytime; it's online	Individual sessions can start anytime, groups offered three times a year	Evenings and Saturdays, 5 weeks individual, 5 weeks group
Number of sessions	20 lessons, work at your own pace	10–50 weeks, 1-hour individual or group sessions	5-week session, 2 hours each session

Access			
Target population	Adults	Adults, families, teens	General public
Eligibility	Willingness to pay and to complete test	Willingness to attend all sessions	Voluntary
Costs	$695	$50 per hour	Individual sessions: $200 total Group sessions: $175 total
Transportation	None required	30-minute drive	30-minute drive
Other			
Support			
Childcare	None required	None provided	None provided
Relationships	None	Individual counselor or group counselor	Individual counselor or group counselor
Follow-up	None	None	Individual sessions
Other			
Steps			
Enrolling	Online	Phone call, office visit	Phone call, office visit
Materials	Provided online	Provided in cost	Provided in cost
Schedule	At own pace		
Manage relationships			
Other			
Summary			
Getting-by resource			
Getting-ahead resource	X	X	X
Selection			
Visualize yourself taking action			
Planning (to be done in next module)			

Additional worksheet available in Appendix F.

Resource Development Worksheet for _____ Resource			
Providers of Opportunity	**Option #1**	**Option #2**	**Option #3**
Program names			
Program description, key words, short phrases			
Mission or goal			
Duration			
Number of sessions			
Access			
Target population			
Eligibility			
Costs			
Transportation			
Other			
Support			
Childcare			
Relationships			
Follow-up			
Other			

Steps			
Enrolling			
Materials			
Schedule			
Manage relationships			
Other			

Summary			
Getting-by resource			
Getting-ahead resource			

Selection			
Visualize yourself taking action			

Planning (to be done in next module)

Discussion

1. What ideas did you get from these exercises?

2. How might someone still be able to build resources even when his/her environment is very unstable?

3. How might someone build resources when community assets are low?

4. Which resources were the most difficult to build? Why?

5. Which resources were the easiest to build? Why?

6. Where are you now with regard to the Stages of Change?

7. What is the most important thing you've learned that will help you build the resources you are thinking of building?

*Vocabulary List for Module 9

Interlocking resources: connected parts in such a way that everything is impacted when one thing is

Mere-measurement effect: this happens when the act of responding to a question about intent will change behaviors and bring about the change; similar to bringing about a self-prophecy

Readings

Leondar-Wright, Betsy. (2005). *Class matters: Cross-class alliance building for middle-class activists.* Gabriola Island, BC: New Society Publishers.

Shuman, Michael H. (2007). *The small-mart revolution: How local businesses are beating the global competition.* San Francisco, CA: Berrett-Koehler Publishers.

Taylor-Ide, Daniel, & Taylor Carl, E. (2002). *Just and lasting change: When communities own their futures.* Baltimore, MD: Johns Hopkins University Press.

Personal and Community Plans

Investigators create a future story for themselves and a mental model for community prosperity.

WHAT'S COVERED

We will:

Review the mental models and investigations that we've done so far; list your highest and lowest resources; rank the resources you need to work on

Create SMART (Specific, Measurable, Attainable, Realistic, and Time-specific) goals

Develop plans for building the resource(s) you select; create immediate action steps and close the back doors

Complete a "Support for Change Mental Model"

Create a "Mental Model of My Future Story"

As a group, create a "Mental Model of Community Prosperity"

Complete the Future Story Portfolio

WHY IT'S IMPORTANT

It's important that you make your own plans—plans that fit your overall situation and that will help you achieve your future story.

HOW IT'S CONNECTED TO YOU

The investigations are done, and it's now time to move to the action phase.

Everything you've done in Getting Ahead up to this point is part of the foundation for this module. Now you can create a plan that works for you.

You and your co-investigators have what it takes to be at the planning and decision-making tables, to contribute to community solutions.

Taking Charge of Our Lives

Your plans will focus on building your personal resources—and also considering your role in the community. Consider this quote from Carl Upchurch:

> In reality, no single group has created the conditions of our inner cities. No single race can be charged with committing the whole array of economic, political and social crimes perpetrated against the poor and their children. We are all at fault, we who preach peace and justice yet enjoy the bounty of exploitation and oppression; we who don't give our national crises the same priority we give international ones; we who barter away human rights for a slice of the power pie; and we, the poor, who intentionally or not, help perpetuate our own condition by refusing to hold society accountable for what it does to us—and for refusing to hold ourselves accountable for what we allow it to do. (Upchurch, 1996, p. 198)

Activity: Personal Plan for Building Resources

Time: 15 minutes
Materials: Worksheets, mental models from your
Future Story Portfolio, pen or pencil

Procedure:

1. Review all the work you've done in Getting Ahead, including the mental models,
activities, and reflections. You will find these in your Future Story Portfolio.

The mental models and activities include:

- Mental Model of Floor Plan of My Apartment/House

- Affordable Housing Payment Threshold

- Debt-to-Income DTI Ratio

- My Life Now

- Theory of Change

- Predator worksheet

- My Economic Class Story

- Family Structure

- Self-Assessment of Negotiating Skills

- Social Capital Mental Model

- Resources Self-Assessment (bar chart)

- Community Assessment (bar chart)

- Getting-Ahead vs. Getting-By Resources

- One-on-One Relationships

- Tic-Tac-Toe and/or brainstorming worksheet

The time-management and planning activities include:

- Estimated Time vs. Actual Time

- Time Monitor sheets

- Time-Management Matrix

- Planning Backwards

Work through the following steps thoroughly, using the blank worksheets in Appendix
G. Talk things over with other group members and the facilitator as you see fit.

If you're comfortable disclosing your work, share it with other GA investigators so they
can use your ideas to help build their own plans.

2. Decide *What* to Work On

Consider what resource you want to work on and why it's important to you. Reviewing the Self-Assessment of Resources Mental Model (Module 7), identify and list your three highest and lowest resources.

Three Highest Resources	Three Lowest Resources

3. Define *Why* You Want to Work on These Resources

Choose the three lowest resources you want to work on and rank them with the most important one first. For example, if your financial resource is one of the lowest, you may choose to work on it. But should you work on it *first*? Imagine that you have just been offered a job. However, if the job is for minimal pay or has few hours, you might decide that it's more important to pursue your degree (building your mental resources) than to work another low-wage job right now. This step might take considerable thought because sometimes what seems obvious at first is not in your best interest in the longer term.

Rank your three most important resources to work on	How important is it to you that you change? 1–10 scale 1 = not important at all, 10 = extremely important	Explain in your own words why this change is important to you
1.	*circle your score:* 1 2 3 4 5 6 7 8 9 10	
2.	*circle your score:* 1 2 3 4 5 6 7 8 9 10	
3.	*circle your score:* 1 2 3 4 5 6 7 8 9 10	

Activity: Establish a SMART Goal

Time: 1 hour
Materials: Worksheets (found in Appendix G), pen or pencil

Step 1: SMART Goal

Here's how you can start building your lowest resources.

Establish a SMART goal for one of the resources on your list (you can do more later). Before listing your goals, refer back to the work the group did in Module 9, about how to build your particular three resources. It is very important that you set goals well. SMART goals are *Specific**, Measurable, *Attainable**, *Realistic**, and Time-specific. Use a worksheet to work on these goals first. When you have the first one exactly the way you want it, write it on the worksheet found in Appendix G. What follows is an example.

Example: Setting a SMART Goal

Resource: Social Capital

Goal: Three months from now I will have more bridging social capital. I'll join two groups or organizations where I will have regular (at least monthly) contact with a diverse group of positive people.

Monitor for SMART standards: Check each box that meets the standards of a SMART goal. Get feedback from at least one other person that it is in fact a SMART goal.

❑ Specific   ❑ Measurable   ❑ Attainable   ❑ Realistic   ❑ Time-specific

---

Analysis: Let's check to see if this example meets the SMART standard: Is it *specific?* Yes, it's about building bridging capital. Is it *measurable?* Yes, this person will join two groups and will have *monthly* contact. Is it *attainable* or *doable?* The answer to this is not so obvious. We would have to know more about the person setting the goal, but let's say that most people could find the time to join two groups if it was important to them. Is it *realistic?* The answer to this is similar to the "attainable" question. Is it *time-specific?* Yes, it must be done within three months.

Step 2: Procedural Steps

Create procedural steps for each goal. Write the goal in the appropriate space, then put the procedural steps in a logical order, first things first. What do you need to do to accomplish your goal? Identify the hidden rules that you may use. Finally, think through how long it will take to do each step, then pick the starting date for each.

Example: Procedural Steps

Goal: Three months from now I will have more bridging social capital. I'll join two groups or organizations where I will have regular (at least monthly) contact with a diverse group of positive people.

Steps	Starting Date	Hidden rules that can help build this resource:
1. Make a list of things that interest you personally and/or a list of community issues that you want to do something about.	Today	*Driving force: middle class = work and achievement*
2. Find organizations that deal with those issues and interests. Choose five organizations that interest you the most.	Today	*Language: casual and formal registers, language to negotiate*
3. Make contact (face to face or by phone, mail, or e-mail) with the organizations. Ask for information about when and where the next meeting is and if it's OK for you to attend.	Tomorrow	*Time: middle class = keep the future in mind; be on time, reliable* *Personality: poverty = entertainment and humor; middle class = stability and achievement*
4. Attend meetings and meet people from the organizations.	Two weeks from today	
5. Sign up with or join two of them.	Eight weeks from today	
6. Attend meetings and get involved in a regular way. Keep a journal to record your thoughts and feelings—and how you use information from Getting Ahead within these organizations.	Ten weeks from today	

Step 3: Where to Go to Get Help

Make a list of where you will get help. When we begin to make changes, we almost always need the help of other individuals, groups, organizations, and agencies. Review the ideas this group created on how to build resources. Make a list for each goal.

	Example: Where to Go to Get Help
Goal 1:	Three months from now I will have more bridging social capital. I'll join two groups or organizations where I will have regular (at least monthly) contact with a diverse group of positive people.
Resource: 1. Social Capital	1. For ideas on interests: I'll check with GA investigators, friends, family, people who are well-connected, newspapers, library, Internet. 2. For ideas on organizations and groups: I'll review the investigations done on the community and on building resources (Modules 8 and 9) to find organizations and people who interest me. Investigate community newspapers, library, Internet, agency lists, Chamber of Commerce lists, phone book. Also talk to people outside of my bonding circle. 3. For first meeting: I'll find someone who is already connected or a member of the group and go with him/her. Invite one of the people from the GA group to go along as well. 4. If I don't know anyone in the organization, I can ask a contact person to meet ahead of time in order to find out what to expect.

Step 4: Weekly and Monthly Plan

Develop a monthly and weekly plan. Put the action steps you need to take into a monthly and weekly plan. The first week of the month is laid out in an example below.

Example: Plan for First Week

Goal 1: Three months from now I will have more bridging social capital. I'll join two groups or organizations where I will have regular (at least monthly) contact with a diverse group of positive people.

Sun	Mon	Tue	Wed	Thu	Fri	Sat
Read newspaper; review investigations done in Modules 8 and 9; talk to family and friends; check phone book	Chamber of Commerce; agency lists; library; make lists of interests and organizations	Contact two of five organizations	Contact other three organizations	Research interests and organizations to find out what's expected	Talk with positive friends and/or family—people who support my changes	Talk with positive friends and/or family—people who support my changes; prepare plans for next week

Step 5: Daily 'To Do' List

Keep a daily plan or "To Do" list. On a 3x5 card, write down everything you're going to do today. Carry it with you and cross off the items as you get them done. You could have one card for each goal—or keep all your to do's on the same card. See the example on p. 114.

Step 6: Back-Up Plans for Closing Back Doors

Create backup plans for when things go wrong. It's very easy to slip back into old ways of functioning. Sometimes we make wonderful plans for change but keep a "back door" open to escape if the going gets tough. The following strategy comes from the American Lung Association, and it's used to help people stop smoking. There are hundreds of reasons to stop smoking, but people often relapse by leaving the back door open, using a phrase like, "If I start gaining weight … then I'll smoke again." The last half of that sentence often isn't spoken, but it's there. Well, many people who stop smoking gain some weight, at least at first, so there's the back door. You have to close the back doors so that you can stick with your plans.

Example: Closing 'Back Doors'	
Back Doors	How to Close Them
1. "If things don't go well, I'll throw in the towel." (It's always easier to give up than keep trying.)	1. Recognize that you are about to fly out the back door. 2. Tell yourself that you can do this. Wait a few minutes, and the negative feeling will pass. 3. Talk to someone who supports what you're doing. Have his/her phone number handy and tell this person ahead of time that it's his/her "job" to encourage you when things get rough. Have a sense of humor about this "job description," but still be firm in your expectations of your friend.
2. "I'll do it tomorrow. Too much is going on today. Gotta let it slide for now."	1. Recognize the negative thinking you're engaging in. 2. Make the phone call to your friend. 3. Tell yourself that nothing short of death or the house burning down is going to keep you from doing the things on your daily list.
3. "If the people around me don't support me, I won't be able to do it."	1. Recognize the inclination to do back-door thinking. 2. Make a list of people who do support your changes—and stay in touch with them. 3. Have more than one plan for getting things done. If Person A won't help, have Person B ready to go. If Plan A falls apart, be ready with Plan B.

Step 7: Establish Support Team

It's time to put together the team that will support you for as long as it takes to build your resources. The following Support for Change Mental Model will help you pick your team. Building different resources may require different people, so you'll want to make a model for each resource.

1. At the top of the paper, fill in the name of the resource that you're planning to build.

2. Put your name in the center circle.

3. Think of the people who will be affected by the changes you make: children, family, friends, employers, and so on. These are people who have influence on your life and people you influence. To refresh your thinking, go back to the earlier mental models you made: Floor Plan of My Apartment/House, My Life Now, My Family Structure, and Social Capital. Draw a circle for all persons and put their names in those circles.

4. Using a pen or pencil, draw a line between each person and yourself—the more support they are likely to give you the thicker the line. For example, if the person will give you total support and actively help you make the change, draw a thick line. If his or her support is halfhearted or weak, use a thin or dotted line. If the person will oppose the idea of your change and will work against you, leave it blank or draw an arrow going away from you.

5. Now begin to select the members of your support team.

   a. Look at the mental model and select people who are already supporting your efforts to change. List them as "current team members."

   b. Then think of fellow co-investigators from this class whom you want on your team. List them as "current team members" also.

   c. Think back to the Social Capital Mental Model created in Module 6 and the people you listed in the section on bridging social capital. Select and list the people from that mental model whom you need to "recruit."

   d. Review the investigation into community assets and the Personal One-on-One Relationships Mental Model you created in Module 8. Add the people and organizations whom you believe will support you as you build your resources; write down their names on your "recruit" list.

6. Share your plan with the people and organizations you have selected and ask for their commitment to be part of your support team.

Example: Support for Change Mental Model

"I'm going to build my ___SOCIAL CAPITAL___ resource."

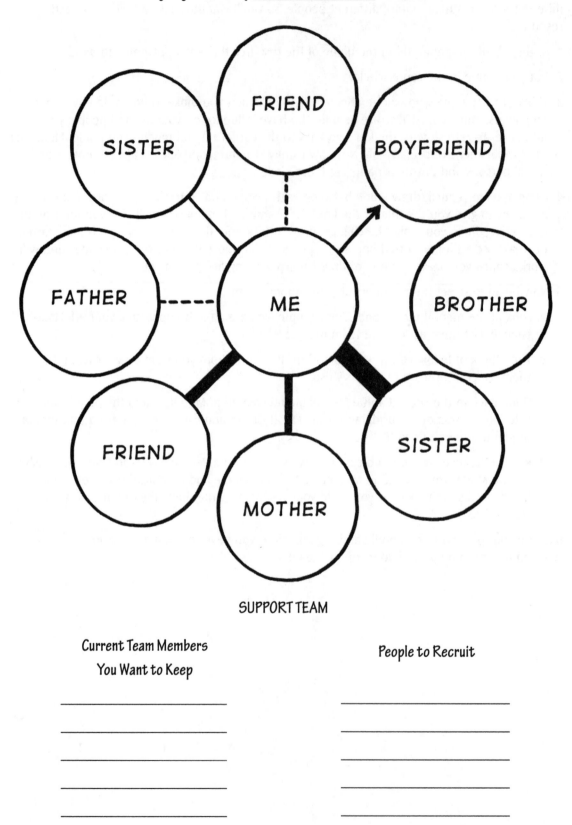

SUPPORT TEAM

Current Team Members
You Want to Keep

_____

_____

_____

_____

_____

People to Recruit

_____

_____

_____

_____

_____

Activity: Mental Model of My Future Story

Time: 1 hour

Materials: Worksheets, mental models, pen or pencil

Procedure:

1. Look back over the mental models that you've created and think about how far you've come. Also reflect on the story you were living when you started and the future story you are now making. This is the story of your life.

2. Look at the plans you just made—the goals and action steps, the people you are contacting to support you, and the work that lies ahead.

3. Using these thoughts, think of a way to draw a mental model or write a brief story of the changes you are already making and are going to keep making. This is a picture or vision of your coming journey and your goals. You can hold this mental model in your mind more easily than all the words that went into the SMART plan. This mental model will help you remember your plan. The vision will help you persist and avoid back-door escapes.

   Some GA investigators have drawn a mental model that includes both My Life Now and My Future Story. In this way they illustrated on one piece of paper what life is like now (on the left side) and what the future will be like (on the right side).

4. If you wish, share your mental model with others. How many times have we found that building on each other's ideas helps to improve our thinking? Consider their ideas, and perhaps use them in your mental model.

5. Your latest vision might help you see missing pieces in your plan—people who could support you, things to do, organizations to work with, or even specifics about your goals. Revise anything that needs to be revised.

Discussion

1. When you think back over the investigations, what things stand out as the most important for you?

2. When you think about what it took for you to create your own path, what did you learn about yourself?

3. Where are you now in relation to the Stages of Change?

4. When was it that you became most motivated to change?

5. What changes have you already made in the way you think and act?

6. Who is going on the journey with you?

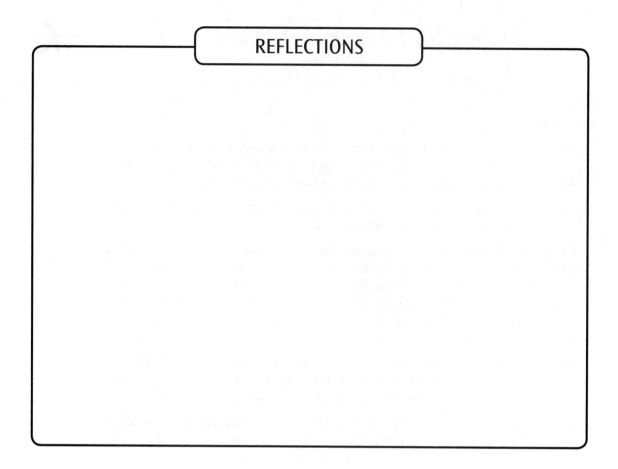

Activity: Mental Model for Community Prosperity

Time: 45 minutes

Materials: Chart paper, markers

Procedure:

1. Have a group discussion about the difference between taking responsibility for solving personal problems (such as taking action to build your own resources) and taking responsibility for community solutions (like fighting poverty or discriminatory housing practices). We've often said that poverty is about more than the choices of the individual. If we hold the community responsible for creating a wide range of strategies to fight poverty, then we can help the community create those strategies. Now that we're taking responsibility for our own choices, it's time to consider how we also can be problem solvers in the community.

2. Discuss what it means to have prosperity and economic security for all people. What would it take for that to happen? Think back over the information on the wealth gap, the research on poverty, and the Community Sustainability Grid. What strategies are needed? How can we get the community to work on those strategies?

3. Make a list of the ideas generated by the group.

4. Work on a mental model together.

5. Decide how to share this mental model and your ideas with the community.

Discussion

1. Did the Mental Model for Community Prosperity include strategies from all four areas of research on the causes of poverty?

2. Has your attitude toward the community changed since beginning this workbook? If so, in what ways?

3. Has your perspective about the middle class changed? Toward the wealthy? If so, how?

4. How might you build more and stronger partnerships with people from other economic classes?

5. In what ways do you think of yourself differently now that you have contributed ideas for the betterment of yourself and the community?

Getting Ahead initiatives promote sustainable communities where everyone can live well.

*Vocabulary List for Module 10

Attainable: something that can be reached, done

Realistic: is it truly possible; can it be done?

Specific: exact, detailed

A closing word from Phil DeVol:

The next time you get together will probably be at the graduation ceremony. It will give you a final opportunity to show your appreciation to all members of the group for their participation and for the special qualities they shared with you.

I thank you for doing Getting Ahead, being an investigator, taking charge of your own learning, and being part of the entire learning experience. The information you created as a group will be of help to your community, and what you do in the future will no doubt help you and your families.

I hope you'll consider joining the growing number of GA investigators who are sharing their ideas, gifts, talents, and stories on the Getting Ahead website.

Congratulations on completing Getting Ahead; I know it was hard work. My hope is that it has been worthwhile for you.

Phil DeVol

APPENDIX: TABLE OF CONTENTS

APPENDIX A: Getting Started (on Your Future Story)

THIS IS THE BEGINNING, NOT THE END ...

It may seem a little odd to come to the end of Getting Ahead only to see something titled, "Getting Started." But if you remember the Triangle at the beginning of every module, you'll realize that the action phase of Getting Ahead doesn't begin until we've finished the workbook.

PLAN A GRADUATION PARTY

The best way to get started is to throw a party. Getting Ahead groups have celebrated in parks, prisons, restaurants, meeting halls, courtrooms, churches, community centers, and at worksites.

They have invited families, children, friends, sponsors, and funders of Getting Ahead. They've also included elected officials, community leaders, employers, media representatives (see below), and people from the Bridges initiative in the community who will be providing support for transitions.

Some common themes are to have GA graduates and facilitators speak, share the mental models created by the group, award certificates of completion, and share a meal. Sometimes a community leader will be asked to speak a few words. But the real focus is on the GA investigators and what they have to say.

Often a media release is sent (to newspapers, TV stations, radio stations) that might cover the event (all GA investigators must agree to media attention).

Planners usually record the celebration with photos and video clips. These are often posted on the Getting Ahead website, as well as websites of the sponsoring organization(s). Many Bridges communities have their own websites and so also can post these pictures and clips.

SHARE THE RESULTS OF YOUR WORK

Investigators have two reasons to share the results of their investigations with planners and decision makers in local institutions and the community:

1. Planners and decision makers may not have an accurate mental model of what poverty is like in their community.

   Like everyone else, local leaders form their understanding of poverty and near poverty through their individual experience, the data they look at, and the people they listen to and learn from. Their understanding of poverty is likely to be filtered by what drives them in their work and by their political lens.

2. GA graduates can't afford not to be at the planning and decision-making tables.

> GA graduates understand this statement attributed to N. Smith (as noted earlier): "When you live in reaction, you give your power away. Then you get to experience what you gave your power to." Another way of putting this is: "Nothing about us, without us, is for us."

Investigators now have a common language, relationship skills, partners, and information that are needed to address poverty in a comprehensive way.

1. A common language: GA graduates and people trained in Bridges concepts know the mental models of class, the causes of poverty, the definition of poverty, the hidden rules of class, language registers, and the importance of resources.

2. Relationship skills: having a common language gives communities a way to bring people together across class lines to solve problems. We can have relationships of mutual respect.

3. Partnerships: the GA facilitators, sponsors, funders, and others who are attracted to and use Bridges are potentially powerful partners.

4. The tools:

   a. Mental Model of Poverty

   b. Community Assessment

   c. Mental Model of Community Sustainability

OBTAINING SUPPORT FOR TRANSITION AND FOR BUILDING RESOURCES

Let's look at the issue of support from three vantage points: individual, institutional, and community.

1. Individual Initiatives

   Some GA groups have organized on their own, meeting monthly or quarterly to:

   - Share meals and continue the kitchen-table learning experience. One group met at each other's homes for potluck dinners.

   - Provide resources for one another, such as childcare, transportation, help with educational coursework, and connections to other resources.

   - Review and update their plans and mental models.

   - Do (redo) the Self-Assessment of Resources to see what changes they have made.

   - Solve community problems.

   Some GA grads have:

   - Shared their future stories with agencies they go to.

   - Spoken at conferences, workshops, training events, and other meetings.

   - Become GA facilitators.

2. Institutional Initiatives

Organizations that sponsor Getting Ahead have often trained their staff in Bridges concepts. This provides a common language for poverty and class issues in the organization. To support GA grads, sponsoring organizations have:

- Offered space and time for in-house meetings of GA graduates where they can connect and make plans.

- Built bridging social capital, such as coaches, mentors, and partners from various backgrounds.

- Provided raises of 50 cents an hour upon completion of Getting Ahead.

- Encouraged GA grads to move up to better jobs within the organization.

- Included GA grads on planning and decision-making teams.

- Offered classes in financial literacy, emotional resources (such as anger management), and parenting classes.

Some organizations, such as Habitat for Humanity, offer GA graduates an opportunity to buy a home. Other organizations offer Getting Ahead as part of training course that will result in a job, such as STNA (state tested nursing assistant).

3. Community Initiatives

Almost all communities that offer Getting Ahead begin the initiative by conducting Bridges workshops at agencies and in the community. In this way hundreds of people learn the same type of information that GA investigators learn from Getting Ahead. This gives people from all classes a common language. These communities have developed a number of strategies and programs to support GA grads.

To learn about them, go to:

a. The Getting Ahead Network website, www.gettingaheadnetwork.com

b. Bridges Out of Poverty website, www.bridgesoutofpoverty.com

c. Monthly networking meetings of South Bend, IN, www.sjcbridges.org

d. Schenectady Bridges: schenectadybridges.com

e. Stillwater CARES: stillwatercares.org

f. Columbiana County, OH, www.gettingaheadcolumbiana.com/Home.aspx

How employers, courts, colleges, and healthcare providers are applying Bridges concepts and how that helps Getting Ahead graduates:

- Imagine that in your community there were employers who were using Bridges concepts to help stabilize the world of low-wage employees so they could stay on the job and advance within the company.

- Imagine that the courts in your community were using Bridges concepts to redesign procedures and programs so that low-income offenders were supported in their efforts to comply with sentencing.

- Imagine that technical schools, community colleges, and universities were using Bridges concepts to support low-income, first-generation students by reducing the barriers that keep students from attending classes semester by semester until they graduate (if they do).

- Imagine that healthcare providers in your community were using Bridges concepts to help low-income patients navigate the healthcare system and to support recovery and disease management that took into account the instability and stress caused by poverty.

Think of the preceding four sectors—and the ones that will follow—as widening and strengthening the bridge out of poverty. People in unstable environments and poverty benefit when they go to and work for organizations that use Bridges and Getting Ahead concepts.

As more people from all sectors embrace Bridges and Getting Ahead concepts, relationships are changed for the better. This fact can lead to a change in the environment and culture of an organization and a community.

The organizations within these sectors exchange ideas—using the Bridges and Getting Ahead websites, phone conferences, and the annual conference. Learn more about this movement by going to the websites and joining the phone calls.

THANK YOU

Thank you for the work you have done and the information you have developed for yourself, your co-investigators, and for the community. You will be part of a movement that can put people in charge of their lives and transform our communities.

APPENDIX B: Tips for Getting Ahead Investigators

Module 1

Definition: An investigator is someone who seeks facts. An investigator digs into details to form a complete and logical picture of a particular situation.

1. As an investigator you examine your own life. This can be painful and challenging; it takes courage and honesty. It also can empower and challenge you.

2. You have contacts in the community that are a source for information. Journalists and researchers would love to have the connections you have.

   a. Talk with friends, neighbors, and others in the community about their experiences.

   b. Take notes.

3. Libraries can be an investigator's best friend.

   a. They have access to many sources of information.

   b. They have computers you can use.

   c. Librarians can teach you how to find the information you need.

   d. Librarians are master investigators and it's their job to help you.

   e. Most librarians love their work.

4. How to work with libraries and librarians:

   a. If you don't have a library card, get one at your first visit.

   b. Libraries have reference librarians (super investigators), but other librarians can help you too.

   c. Don't be afraid to ask for help (that's what they are there for). Don't be afraid to ask for help with computers either.

   d. When you go to the library:

      i. Tell them what you are going to do with the information, for example:

         a) You will report to the Getting Ahead group.

         b) Write a summary paragraph.

         c) Copy a few pages to take with you.

ii. Be ready to answer these questions about your search (for example, let's say you are investigating the poverty rates in the United States over the last 40 years):

    a) *Who?* U.S. citizens

    b) *What?* Poverty rates

    c) *When?* 1972–2012

    d) *Where?* United States

    e) *Why?* To see the trend lines, when poverty rates were high and low

iii. Show up with something to write with and write on.

5. Using a computer on your own:

a. Use many of the same strategies you learned from the librarian.

b. Find websites and sources that provide information that comes from reliable sources, such as government reports.

c. To find out about the source, do a search on the institute or think tank by its name, then read several descriptions of the organization. That way you can understand how it may slant the information it presents—liberal, conservative, libertarian, or neutral/objective.

APPENDIX C: Who Pays the Most Taxes? What Does It Mean to the Community?

Module 3

Most people feel that taxes are pretty complicated and are happy if they can just get their own income taxes filed correctly each year. But there is key information about taxes that applies to our investigation into the causes of poverty and the development of sustainable communities.

Corporations vs. individuals: The share of federal revenue being paid by corporate income tax has been declining since the 1950s. In 1962 it was 21% of the federal revenue; in 2007 it was 14%. This is the result of lower rates and loopholes. The share of federal revenue paid by individuals (including income tax, Social Security, and Medicare taxes) rose from 72% to 83%. (The percentages do not add up to 100% because excise taxes aren't included.) This means that much of the tax burden is being shifted to the middle class.

> *Note.* Adapted from *The Growing Divide: Inequality and the Roots of Economic Insecurity,* 2009, Boston, MA: United for a Fair Economy. Copyright 2009 by United for a Fair Economy.

Estate and capital gains tax on individuals: Estate taxes, sometimes called the inheritance tax or death tax, are paid on assets that pass on to the next generation upon a person's death. The laws are changing: In 2009 the federal rate was 45%; the amount exempted was $3.5 million. In 2010 there was no estate tax, but in 2011 the rate was 55%, and the exempted amount could be anywhere between $1 million and $7 million.

> *Note.* Adapted from "Taxes Are More Certain Than Death?" by E. Istook, 2009. Copyright 2009 by E. Istook.

Capital gains taxes are paid on profit realized from the sale of stocks, bonds, precious metals, and property. In the U.S. the wealthiest 10% own 75% of stocks and mutual funds. Since 1980 estate taxes decreased by 46%, capital gains taxes by 31%. Meanwhile, payroll tax on workers has increased 25%. Again, the tax burden is being shifted to the middle-class individual.

> *Note.* Adapted from *The Growing Divide: Inequality and the Roots of Economic Insecurity,* 2009, Boston, MA: United for a Fair Economy. Copyright 2009 by United for a Fair Economy.

Individual income tax on adjusted gross income: The U.S. Internal Revenue Service figures show that the top 10% of individuals paid 71.22% of all federal income taxes in 2007. The bottom 50% paid 2.89% of taxes.

> *Note.* Adapted from "Summary of Latest Federal Individual Income Tax Data," by G. Prante, 2009. Copyright 2009 by Tax Foundation.

This information on taxes, as another indication of how great income disparity is in the U.S., is important to the long-term stability of communities. When a community loses high-paying jobs because of business closings or relocations, or the people with those jobs move to better school districts and safer communities, their contributions to the community are lost.

Upper- and middle-class flight to the suburbs continues to strip the budgets of cities that are losing population. Without a sustainable tax base, cities cannot remain viable. Services are cut, infrastructure isn't maintained, people are laid off, and wages are reduced. These factors contribute to the downward trend experienced by many U.S. cities today.

The inability of a community or school system to raise taxes is a sign of a weakening community. Schools that give up extracurricular activities (such as band, art classes, and sports) or turn to the "pay to play" strategy are depriving children of resources that build their bodies and minds—and create social connections that can last a lifetime. The community itself suffers when families leave in order to put their children in schools that can offer extracurricular activities. Those who are least able to move are people in poverty and low-wage workers.

Discussion

1. What has happened to the tax base in your community?

2. How much difference is there in extracurricular activities and educational achievement among the school districts within an hour's drive of your home?

3. Which businesses employ the most workers in your community? Where do the workers in those businesses live?

4. Discuss local current events in terms of taxes collected in the community. Are school levies being passed? How are city/county governments doing with respect to service provision? What's being cut and what's being saved?

APPENDIX D: The Community Sustainability Grid: A Planning Tool for Addressing All Causes of Poverty

Module 3

The idea for the Community Sustainability Grid came from Getting Ahead (GA) investigators and other community members in Burlington, VT. The Community Sustainability Grid is a mental model that presents three themes:

1. Address all the causes of poverty. In the U.S. we're confused about the causes of poverty, so we're confused about what to do. It's not enough to blame individuals or the whole system. That is either/or thinking. We need to use both/and thinking. Poverty is caused by the choices of people in poverty and it's caused by political/ economic structures—and everything in between.

2. Create a sustainable community where everyone can live well. The Community Sustainability Grid is a tool that can be used to engage people from all classes, organizations (agencies, schools, healthcare providers, courts, etc.), and sectors (elected leaders, businesses, faith-based entities, and cultural groups).

3. Getting Ahead graduates play an important part when using this tool. They should be at the table with other community leaders.

Beginning on the next page is an example of how the Community Sustainability Grid can be used. In this case the topic is predatory lending and what can be done about it. The notes below the table explain how each level (individuals, organizations, and community groups) can take action.

Community Sustainability Grid				
	Individual Choices, Behaviors, and Circumstances	Community Conditions	Exploitation	Political/ Economic Structures
Individual Action	Attend fiscal literacy class	Participate in discussions, educate	Stop going to predators, find alternatives	Lobby, vote
Organizational Action	Support fiscal literacy classes	Get active on Bridges Steering Committee	Offer alternative loans and typical banking services	Influence legislators
Community Action	Offer fiscal literacy class	Develop media campaign, engage banking industry to develop solutions, support GA graduates	Prosecute predators, offer alternatives (like credit unions)	Influence legislators
Policy Changes	Make personal commitments to confront predatory practices	Implement policy changes at institutional and community levels where possible	Make commitment that members of community won't be exploited	Pass legislation

We can take action in three areas:

1. Individual action

a. *Individual choices, behaviors, and circumstances:* Individuals can attend to their own learning. Any individual, but most importantly people who are targeted by the predators, will need to learn the rules of the game, the rules of money. They can attend financial literacy classes that are available in almost every community. These are sometimes offered by credit unions, consumer groups, banks, and Bridges Steering Committees. Don't be embarrassed to go to these classes. Very few people are taught much about money in high school or college, even though the U.S. has a capitalist economy.

b. *Community conditions:* GA graduates can share their experiences with people who have never had to use the services of the predators. Those who have enough financial resources don't go to payday lenders or check-cashing outlets. They need to be educated by people who do. In fact, this is an educational topic for the whole community.

c. *Exploitation:* Stop going to the predators. Even though they're offering a concrete solution to your concrete need, you're only worsening your situation in the long run by going to them. One GA graduate said, "My furniture may not be pretty, but it's mine. I don't go to the lease/purchase story anymore."

d. *Political/economic structures:* GA graduates can have a voice on policy matters by joining with others who want to see legislative changes. This is a democracy; be part of it.

2. Organizational action

a. *Individual choices, behaviors, and circumstances:* Organizations can support individuals by offering financial literacy classes and making it easier for them to get fair loans. "Working Bridges," a group of employers in Vermont, works with credit unions and banks that provide the employers' workers with fair loans. Payments toward those loans are deducted automatically from the employees' paychecks. Employees have used this program to purchase cars, appliances, and trailers. They have opened checking and savings accounts and repaired their credit ratings.

b. *Community conditions:* Organizations can form or join Bridges Steering Committees in their city or county. These are designed to address poverty using concepts from the books Bridges Out of Poverty and Getting Ahead in a Just-Gettin'-By World. They can act as a group to educate the community and reduce the barriers that people encounter when they're trying to build resources.

c. *Exploitation:* Organizations can help create alternatives to the "services" provided by predators and take a stand against predatory practices.

d. *Political/economic structures:* Through their associations and connections, organizations can influence people in positions of power.

3. Community action

a. *Individual choices, behaviors, and circumstances:* Bridges Steering Committees can ensure that financial literacy classes are affordable and easy to attend.

b. *Community conditions:* The local Bridges Steering Committee can work with bankers and credit unions to offer alternative products. The bigger the Bridges initiative in the community and the more sectors (such as business, health, government, colleges, and schools) that are involved, the more momentum there will be for fighting poverty.

c. *Exploitation:* The Bridges Steering Committee can sometimes act more easily than individual organizations by speaking "with one voice" as a group about the need to stop exploitation. Sometimes, however, exploitation must be addressed in a concrete way; in one community an attorney did pro bono work, taking on predators and their practices.

d. *Political/economic structures:* GA graduates who are part of the Bridges Steering Committee can help make changes by providing information that people in other economic situations may not have.

Activity: Practice Using the Community Sustainability Grid to Address the Causes of Poverty

Time: 30 minutes
Materials: Chart paper

Procedure:

1. Go back to the first activity in Module 3 and review the list of the causes of poverty that you made. Answer these questions:

   a. To what extent might your list have favored a particular area of research?

   b. Has your thinking changed? If so, how?

   c. Do you think the information in this module could help you change another person's mindset or way of thinking? If so, in what way or ways?

2. Imagine that you're on a Bridges Steering Committee in your community. Sitting around the table with you are people from all economic classes and from many sectors of the community. Everyone knows and buys into the Bridges/Getting Ahead concepts. You have relationships of mutual respect with those at the table with you.

3. Pick a cause of poverty or a barrier to making the transition out of poverty. For example, the lack of public transportation to and from work—or the lack of affordable childcare while at school or work. Another possibility would be the difficulty that convicted (and now released) felons have finding employment.

4. Draw a copy of the following grid on chart paper.

5. Have a volunteer fill in the grid as you brainstorm how individuals (GA graduates and other members of the community) can take action. Do the same for organizational and community action. Be sure to include a role at those levels for GA graduates. You might use ideas and programs from your community, the nation, or from other countries. You also are invited to develop new ideas.

Community Sustainability Grid				
	Individual Choices, Behaviors, and Circumstances	Community Conditions	Exploitation	Political/ Economic Structures
Individual Action				
Organizational Action				
Community Action				
Policy Changes				

Discussion

1. How can investigators use the information in this module to help build their future stories?

2. How can they use the information about the causes of poverty and mental models of economic class to build relationships of mutual respect with people from diverse backgrounds?

3. How might the Community Sustainability Grid help you solve community problems?

APPENDIX E: What Does It Mean to Be a Getting Ahead Graduate?

Getting Ahead is meant to be agenda-free. That means that no one—not the facilitator, not the organization that provides Getting Ahead—is going to tell you what to do. That also means investigators who "opt in" define their future story and come up with their own plans to make that story come true.

Having said that, some organizations that provide Getting Ahead do have an agenda; they do have a goal or outcome in mind for the investigator. For example, Circle programs want you to become a Circle Leader, an employer may want you to become a long-term employee, a drug court may want you to establish a strong recovery program, and so on. If you know their purpose going into Getting Ahead and you agree to it, you'll still find that there's space for you to personalize your future story and plan.

Since 2004, thousands of people have been through Getting Ahead, and we've made some observations about what it means to be a Getting Ahead (GA) grad. Most people coming out of Getting Ahead seem to be energized about their lives. Rather than becoming compliant members of society who mainly strive to fit into the system, GA grads are coming out empowered. They want to help transform their communities. It's as if many of them are living every day as if their hair was on fire!

They understand this statement (used earlier) by N. Smith: "When you live in reaction, you give your power away. Then you get to experience what you gave your power to." Most GA grads know about living in reaction or being stuck in the tyranny of the moment and the consequences of that.

Also as used earlier, another phrase that fits is: "Nothing about us, without us, is for us." Most GA grads want to be involved in things that are about them. Graduates of the workshop have ways of seeing the world and analyzing situations that make it possible for them to form relationships of mutual respect with all sorts of people. Understanding environments, hidden rules, causes of poverty, language issues, and the importance of resources gives people from unstable environments and poverty a powerful voice. With those skills and insights, GA grads can help transform discussions and participate in high-level decision making.

This doesn't mean that transition to stability and higher resources is easy. The move from the safety net to the bridge is almost always hard. It's hard in many ways:

- Giving up benefits like housing assistance, health insurance, and childcare

- Learning new information

- Scheduling your days differently

- Changing some relationships

- In many ways reshaping your identity

Support for yourself and others is crucial during this difficult period.

Many Getting Ahead graduates seem to find ways to work at both ends of the poverty problem at the same time—at the individual level and at the community level.

APPENDIX F: Resource Development Worksheet (Blank)

Resource Development Worksheet for _____ Resource

Providers of Opportunity	Option #1	Option #2	Option #3
Program names			
Program description, key words, short phrases			
Mission or goal			
Duration			
Number of sessions			
Access			
Target population			
Eligibility			
Costs			
Transportation			
Other			

Support			
Childcare			
Relationships			
Follow-up			
Other			
Steps			
Enrolling			
Materials			
Schedule			
Manage relationships			
Other			
Summary			
Getting-by resource			
Getting-ahead resource			
Selection			
Visualize yourself taking action			
Planning (to be done in next module)			

APPENDIX G: Personal Plan for Building Resources (Blank)

Step 1: SMART Goals

<table>
<tr><td colspan="5" align="center">Setting a SMART Goal</td></tr>
<tr><td colspan="5">Resource:</td></tr>
<tr><td colspan="5">Goal:</td></tr>
<tr><td colspan="5">Monitor for SMART standards: Check each box that meets the standards of a SMART goal. Get feedback from at least one other person that it is in fact a SMART goal.</td></tr>
<tr><td>❑ Specific</td><td>❑ Measurable</td><td>❑ Attainable</td><td>❑ Realistic</td><td>❑ Time-specific</td></tr>
</table>

Step 2: Procedural Steps

Procedural Steps

Goal:

Steps	Starting Date	Hidden Rules

Step 3: Where to Go to Get Help

Where to Go to Get Help	
Goal:	
Resource:	

Step 4: Weekly and Monthly Plan

Plan for First Week						
Goal:						
Sun	*Mon*	*Tue*	*Wed*	*Thu*	*Fri*	*Sat*

Plan for First Month

Sun	Mon	Tue	Wed	Thu	Fri	Sat

Sun	Mon	Tue	Wed	Thu	Fri	Sat

Sun	Mon	Tue	Wed	Thu	Fri	Sat

Sun	Mon	Tue	Wed	Thu	Fri	Sat

Step 5: Daily 'To Do' List

Keep a daily plan or "To Do" list on a 3x5 card.

Step 6: Back-Up Plans for Closing Back Doors

Closing 'Back Doors'	
Back Doors	How to Close Them
1.	
2.	
3.	

Support for Change Mental Model

"I'm going to build my _____ resource."

SUPPORT TEAM

Current Team Members
You Want to Keep

People to Recruit

_____

_____

_____

_____

_____

_____

_____

_____

_____

_____

APPENDIX H: Films, Literature, and Poetry on Economic Class

Films

Allen, W. (Director). (1969). *Take the money and run* [Motion picture]. USA: American Broadcasting Company. Cast: Woody Allen, Janet Margolin, Marcel Hillaire. Uses documentary style to tell the story of a compulsive thief.

Apted, M. (Director). (1980). *Coal miner's daughter* [Motion picture]. USA: Universal Pictures. Cast: Sissy Spacek, Tommy Lee Jones, Beverly D'Angelo, Levon Helm. Life story of country singer Loretta Lynn, chronicling her rise from poverty to fame and her struggles with identity.

Avildsen, J. G. (Director). (1976). *Rocky* [Motion picture]. USA: Chartoff-Winkler Productions. Cast: Sylvester Stallone, Burgess Meredith, Talia Shire, Burt Young. Story of a prizefighter who makes it back to the top through spirit and hard work. Won an Academy Award for best picture, director, and editing. Followed by four sequels.

Bauman, S., & Heller, R. (Directors). (1986). *The women of summer* [Motion picture]. USA: The National Endowment for the Humanities. Documentary of 1920s Bryn Mawr Summer School for Women Workers in Industry. Present-day interviews are used to reflect back on this period of labor schools in America.

Benedek, L. (Director). (1951). *Death of a salesman* [Motion picture]. USA: Stanley Kramer Productions. Cast: Fredric March, Cameron Mitchell, Mildred Dunnock. Arthur Miller's Pulitzer Prize-winning drama of a middle-aged salesman facing age and business decline.

Biberman, H. (Director). (1954). *The salt of the earth* [Motion picture]. USA: Independent Production Company. Cast: Will Geer, David Wolfe, Rosaura Revueltas. New Mexico mineworkers are abused for going on strike. Strong women characters help them survive. Docudrama tone. Film resulted in blacklisting of Geer, Biberman, producer Paul Jarrico, and screenwriter Michael Wilson.

Bird, S., & Shaffer, D. (Directors). (1979). *The Wobblies* [Motion picture]. USA: Joint Federation for Support. Documentary of Industrial Workers of the World. History intermixing archival footage and present-day interviews with old Wobblies.

Borden, L. (Director). (1986). *Working girls* [Motion picture]. USA: Alternate Current. Cast: Louise Smith, Ellen McElduff, Amanda Goodwin. Depicts a New York City brothel in docudrama style.

Brown, P., & Jason, W. (Directors). (1951). *The Harlem Globetrotters* [Motion picture]. USA: Columbia Pictures Corporation. Cast: Thomas Gomez, Dorothy Dandridge, Bill Walker, Angela Clarke. Documentary-style tale of exhibition black basketball team as it struggles for recognition in racist 1950s America.

Burnett, C. (Director). (1990). *To sleep with anger* [Motion picture]. USA: SVS Films. Cast: Paul Butler, Danny Glover, Carl Lumbly, Mary Alice. African American working-class family struggles with a wicked visitor in their Los Angeles home.

Cassavetes, N. (Director). (2002). *John Q* [Motion picture]. USA: New Line Cinema. Parents are financially ruined by their child's illness.

Cattaneo, P. (Director). (1997). *The full monty* [Motion picture]. United Kingdom: Redwave Films. Cast: Robert Carlyle, Tom Wilkinson, Mark Addy, Paul Barber, Steve Huison. An unlikely bunch of out-of-work steel laborers decide to reverse their fortunes by performing as male strippers in a local club.

Chapman, M. (Director). (1983). *All the right moves* [Motion picture]. USA: Lucille Ball Productions. Cast: Tom Cruise, Craig T. Nelson, Lea Thompson. A high school football player struggles to leave his future in the local steel mills for a future at college.

Cimino, M. (Director). (1978). *The deer hunter* [Motion picture]. USA: EMI Films. Cast: Christopher Walken, Robert DeNiro, Meryl Streep, John Savage. Examines the hellish worlds of the Vietnam War and an Ohio Valley steel town with some depth. Won the Academy Award for best picture.

Coen, J. (Director). (1996). *Fargo* [Motion picture]. USA: Polygram Filmed Entertainment. Cast: Frances McDormand, William H. Macy, Steve Buscemi. A car salesman's kidnapping plot goes awry and leads to murder. A female police detective investigates. Set in Fargo, North Dakota. Script by Joel and Ethan Coen.

Coles, J. D. (Director). (1990). *Rising son* [Motion picture]. USA: Sarabande Productions. Cast: Brian Dennehy, Piper Laurie, Matt Damon. A working class family struggles to survive the collapse of their Georgia factory town.

Dash, J. (Director). (2002). *The Rosa Parks story* [Motion picture]. USA: Chotzen/Jenner Productions. Angela Bassett plays Rosa Parks, who helped spark the civil rights movement in the United States.

Eastwood, C. (Director). (2004). *Million dollar baby* [Motion picture]. USA: Warner Brothers Pictures. Cast: Clint Eastwood, Hilary Swank, Morgan Freeman. A female prizefighter earns money and tries to help her family out of poverty.

Fincher, D. (Director). (1999). *Fight club* [Motion picture]. USA: Fox 2000 Pictures. Cast: Edward Norton, Brad Pitt, Helena Bonham Carter. A young office employee and a soap salesman build a global organization to help vent male aggression.

Fleischer, R. (Director). (1972). *The new centurions* [Motion picture]. USA: Chartoff-Winkler Productions. Cast: George C. Scott, Stacy Keach, Jane Alexander, Scott Wilson. A sensitive portrayal of rookie cops on the Los Angeles police force as they struggle with work and family life. Stirling Silliphant's script is based on Joseph Wambaugh's novel.

Ford, J. (Director). (1940). *The grapes of wrath* [Motion picture]. USA: Twentieth Century Fox. Cast: Henry Fonda, Jane Darwell, John Carradine. Adaptation of John Steinbeck's 1939 novel of Dust Bowl Okies headed west to the promised land of California where they find the American dream gone sour.

Forman, M. (Director). (1975). *One flew over the cuckoo's nest* [Motion picture]. USA: Fantasy Films. Cast: Jack Nicholson, Louise Fletcher, William Redfield, Brad Dourif, Danny DeVito. Film adaptation of Ken Kesey's novel of a social misfit committed to an insane asylum where he turns inmates into an organized rebellion against the system.

Freedman, J. (Director). (1986). *Native son* [Motion picture]. USA: American Playhouse. Cast: Carroll Baker, Matt Dillon, Victor Love, Elizabeth McGovern, Oprah Winfrey. A young black man struggles in racist 1930s Chicago. Richard Wright's novel is co-produced with PBS's American Playhouse series.

Gilbert, L. (Director). (1983). *Educating Rita* [Motion picture]. United Kingdom: Acorn Pictures. Cast: Michael Caine, Julie Walters. Adaptation of Willy Russell's play about a young working-class wife going to the university where she becomes entangled in the life of a boozing professor of literature.

Herek, S. (Director). (1995). *Mr. Holland's opus* [Motion picture]. USA: Hollywood Pictures. Cast: Richard Dreyfuss, Glenne Headly, Jay Thomas, Olympia Dukakis. Musician-composer resorts to teaching high school music and finds he loves it.

Higgins, C. (Director). (1980). *9 to 5* [Motion picture]. USA: IPC Films. Cast: Jane Fonda, Lily Tomlin, Dolly Parton, Dabney Coleman. Secretarial revolt against a harassing boss. This comedy is based on a story by screenwriter Patricia Resnick.

Hughes, J. (Director). (1985). *The breakfast club* [Motion picture]. USA: A&M Films. Teens from poor and middle-class backgrounds have conflicts with teachers and each other during Saturday detention.

James, S. (Director). (1994). *Hoop dreams* [Motion picture]. USA: KTCA Minneapolis. Documentary of two African American high school students who face the manipulative world of a career in basketball.

Kopple, B. (Director). (1977). *Harlan County, U.S.A.* [Motion picture]. USA: Cabin Creek. Academy Award-winning documentary of Kentucky mineworkers' strike against the Eastover Mining Company.

LaGravenese, R. (Director). (2007). *Freedom writers* [Motion picture]. USA: Paramount Pictures. A white teacher in an inner-city high school learns the rules and how to build relationships of mutual respect with students.

Lyne, A. (Director). (1983). *Flashdance* [Motion picture]. USA: Paramount Pictures. Cast: Jennifer Beals, Michael Nouri, Lilia Skala. A woman welder/stripper seeks romance and a career as a dancer.

Malle, L. (Director). (1985). *Alamo Bay* [Motion picture]. USA: Delphi IV. Cast: Ed Harris, Amy Madigan. Texas Gulf Coast fishing meets migration of Vietnamese immigrants.

Mandel, R. (Director). (1992). *School ties* [Motion picture]. USA: Paramount Pictures. Cast: Brendan Fraser, Chris O'Donnell, Matt Damon. A working-class Jewish student wins a football scholarship to a preparatory school, where he encounters anti-Semitism. Set in the 1950s.

Marshall, Garry. (1990). *Pretty woman* [Motion picture]. USA: Touchstone Pictures. Cast: Richard Gere, Julia Roberts, Jason Alexander. A "lost" executive gets directions from a prostitute, leading to intriguing relational dynamics that last more than one night. The movie bridges two classes—from poverty to wealth and the hidden rules of both.

Menéndez, R. (Director). (1988). *Stand and deliver* [Motion picture]. USA: American Playhouse. A teacher works with under-resourced students.

Nava, G. (Director). (1983). *El Norte* [Motion picture]. USA: American Playhouse. Cast: Trinidad Silva, Zaide Silvia Gutiérrez, Rodrigo Puebla. Saga of a brother and sister who come north from violence-torn Guatemala. Their struggle to migrate is followed by their struggle to survive in "El Norte"—the United States. Written and produced by Anna Thomas for the PBS American Playhouse series.

Nava, G. (Director). (1995). *My family, mi familia* [Motion picture]. USA: American Playhouse. Cast: Jimmy Smits, Esai Morales, Edward James Olmos. A Mexican American family's saga of coming to and surviving in Los Angeles.

Nichols, M. (Director). (1988). *Working girl* [Motion picture]. USA: Twentieth Century Fox. Cast: Harrison Ford, Melanie Griffith, Sigourney Weaver, Joan Cusack. Romantic comedy about a secretary with ambition and the struggle to rise up the corporate ladder.

Pearce, R. (Director). (1990). *The long walk home* [Motion picture]. USA: Dave Bell Associates. Cast: Sissy Spacek, Whoopi Goldberg, Dwight Schultz; narrated by Mary Steenburgen. Mid-1950s racial tensions in the segregated U.S. South as they affect a middle-class woman and her hard-working black housekeeper.

Peerce, L. (Director). (1969). *Goodbye, Columbus* [Motion picture]. USA: Willow Tree. Cast: Richard Benjamin, Ali MacGraw, Jack Klugman. Adaptation of Philip Roth's novel portraying urban and suburban Jewish families.

Petersen, W. (Director). (2000). *The perfect storm* [Motion picture]. USA: Baltimore Spring Creek Productions. Cast: George Clooney, Mark Wahlberg, Diane Lane, Mary Elizabeth Mastrantonio, John C. Reilly. A fishing crew and captain off Gloucester, Massachusetts, fight the threat of losing their ship and their lives in a storm.

Petrie, D. (Director). (1961). *A raisin in the sun* [Motion picture]. USA: Columbia Picture Corporation. Cast: Sidney Poitier, Claudia McNeil, Ruby Dee, Diana Sands. Adaptation of Lorraine Hansberry's play depicting a black Chicago family as it struggles to survive; Hansberry also wrote the screenplay.

Pollack, S. (Director). (1969). *They shoot horses, don't they?* [Motion picture]. USA: American Broadcasting Company. Cast: Jane Fonda, Michael Sarrazin, Gig Young. Based on the 1935 novel by Horace McCoy. Desperate attempts to win a marathon dance contest.

Rash, S. (Director). (1978). *The Buddy Holly story* [Motion picture]. USA: ECA. Cast: Gary Busey, Charles Martin Smith, Don Stroud, Maria Richwine. Biographical story of the teen rocker's rise from Lubbock, Texas, to national stardom, then early death.

Redford, R. (Director). (1988). *The Milagro beanfield war* [Motion picture]. USA: Esparza. Cast: Ruben Blades, Richard Bradford, Sonia Braga, Melanie Griffith, John Heard. Adaptation of John Nichols' novel of New Mexico struggle between landowners and rugged workers.

Reitman, J. (Director). (2007). *Juno* [Motion picture]. USA: Mandate Pictures. A teenage girl from a working-class background becomes pregnant and elects to allow a middle-class family to adopt the child.

Ritt, M. (Director). (1979). *Norma Rae* [Motion picture]. USA: Twentieth Century Fox. Cast: Sally Field, Beau Bridges, Ron Leibman, Pat Hingle, Barbara Baxley. Field plays a real-life southern textile worker who is won over to unionization by a northern labor organizer, then becomes a local champion. Field won an Academy Award for this role.

Roemer, M. (Director). (1964). *Nothing but a man* [Motion picture]. USA: DuArt. Cast: Ivan Dixon, Julius Harris, Abbey Lincoln. A young black man, with the help of a woman, struggles to survive in the repressive U.S. South of the 1960s.

Rydell, M. (Director). (1984). *The river* [Motion picture]. USA: Universal Pictures. Cast: Sissy Spacek, Mel Gibson, Scott Glenn. A family struggles to work and keep its farm despite threats from the bank and from a flooding river. Screenplay by Robert Dillon.

Schlesinger, J. (Director). (1969). *Midnight cowboy* [Motion picture]. USA: Florin Productions. Cast: Dustin Hoffman, Jon Voight, Sylvia Miles. A dishwashing cowboy comes to New York City to become a sexual stud, yet meets the cold reality of prostitution and homelessness shared with a city friend. Received Academy Awards for best picture, director, and screenplay. Based on a novel by James Leo Herlihy; the film was given an early X rating.

Schlöndorff, V. (Director). (1985). *Death of a salesman* [Motion picture]. USA: Bioskop film. Cast: Dustin Hoffman, John Malkovich, Charles Durning, Kate Reid. More recent version of Arthur Miller's Pulitzer Prize-winning drama of a middle-aged salesman facing age and business decline.

Scorsese, M. (Director). (1974). *Alice doesn't live here anymore* [Motion picture]. USA: Warner Brothers Pictures. Cast: Ellen Burstyn, Kris Kristofferson, Diane Ladd. A single mom's quest to find herself lands her in a western diner.

Scorsese, M. (Director). (2002). *Gangs of New York* [Motion picture]. USA: Miramax Films. Cast: Leonardo DiCaprio, Daniel Day-Lewis, Cameron Diaz. Set in early New York City where youth gangs battle.

Shankman, A. (Director). (2003). *Bringing down the house* [Motion picture]. USA: Touchstone Pictures. Depicts clashes based on the hidden rules of wealth and other classes at home and in the office.

Smith, J. N. (Director). (1995). *Dangerous minds* [Motion picture]. USA: Hollywood Pictures. Cast: Michelle Pfeiffer, George Dzundza, Courtney B. Vance. An inexperienced teacher (and ex-Marine) takes on a class of "unteachable" students in an inner-city school.

Spielberg, S. (Director). (1985). *The color purple* [Motion picture]. USA: Amblin Entertainment. Cast: Whoopi Goldberg, Danny Glover, Margaret Avery, Oprah Winfrey. Adaptation of Alice Walker's acclaimed novel of a poor black girl who gains self-esteem and control of her life.

Stack, J. (Director). (1995). *Harlem diary* [Motion picture]. USA: Discovery Channel Pictures. Documentary of nine Harlem youths who chronicle their life stories of trying to survive in the projects. Produced for the Discovery Channel but shown in theaters as well.

Stone, O. (Director). (1989). *Born on the fourth of July* [Motion picture]. USA: Ixtlan. Cast: Tom Cruise, Willem Dafoe, Caroline Kava. A wounded Vietnam veteran's questioning of the United States of America, based on the real-life saga of author Ron Kovic.

Stuart, M. (Director). (1979). *The Triangle factory fire scandal* [Motion picture]. USA: Alan Landsburg Productions. Cast: Tom Bosley, David Dukes, Tovah Feldshuh, Lauren Frost. A retelling of the Triangle Shirtwaist Factory abuse and fire of March 25, 1911.

Valdez, L. (Director). (1987). *La bamba* [Motion picture]. USA: Columbia Pictures. Cast: Lou Diamond Phillips, Esai Morales, Rosana De Soto. Story of Mexican American rock singer Ritchie Valens and his tragic death in a plane crash.

Van Sant, G. (Director). (1997). *Good will hunting* [Motion picture]. USA: Be Gentlemen Limited Partnership. Cast: Robin Williams, Matt Damon, Ben Affleck, Minnie Driver. A rough Boston youth with a genius for math shows up MIT academics, wins girl, and gains confidence with counselor. Written by Damon and Affleck, who received an Academy Award for the screenplay.

Van Sant, G. (Director). (2000). *Finding Forrester* [Motion picture]. USA: Columbia Pictures Corporation. An African American student struggles with hidden rules and social capital as he attends private school.

Wang, W. (Director). (2002). *Maid in Manhattan* [Motion picture]. USA: Revolution Studios. Cast: Jennifer Lopez, Ralph Fiennes, Natasha Richardson, Stanley Tucci. A single mom works as a maid uptown and meets a politician.

Wyler, W. (Director). (1946). *The best years of our lives* [Motion picture]. USA: Samuel Goldwyn Company. Cast: Dana Andrews, Harold Russell, Myrna Loy, Fredric March. Returning veterans from World War II reintegrate with hometown lives, yet struggle with war wounds; won seven Academy Awards.

Yates, P. (Director). (1979). *Breaking away* [Motion picture]. USA: Twentieth Century Fox. Cast: Dennis Christopher, Dennis Quaid, Daniel Stern. Reveals rivalry and class distinctions between college students and working class "cutters" (stonecutters) in Bloomington, Indiana.

Literature

Alexie, S. (1993). *The Lone Ranger and Tonto fistfight in heaven*. New York, NY: Atlantic Monthly Press.

Alexie, S. (2007). *The absolutely true diary of a part-time Indian*. New York, NY: Little, Brown.

Allison, D. (1988). *Trash: Stories*. Ann Arbor, MI: Firebrand Books.

Allison, D. (1993). *Bastard out of Carolina*. New York, NY: Plume.

Anderson, S. (1919). *Winesburg, Ohio*. New York, NY: B. W. Huebsch.

Arnow, H. (1954). *The dollmaker*. New York, NY: Macmillan.

Bell, T. (1941). *Out of this furnace*. New York, NY: Little, Brown.

Bellow, S. (1953). *The adventures of Augie Marsh*. New York, NY: Viking Press.

Berry, W. (1960). *Nathan Coulter*. Boston, MA: Houghton-Mifflin.

Berry, W. (1967). *A place on Earth*. San Francisco, CA: Harcourt, Brace.

Berry, W. (1974). *The memory of Old Jack*. Bellmawr, NJ: Harcourt, Brace, Jovanovich.

Bragg, R. (1998). *All over but the shoutin'*. New York, NY: Vintage Books.

Brooks, G. (1953). *Maud Martha*. New York, NY: AMS Press.

Cahan, A. (1917). *The rise of David Levinsky*. New York, NY: Harper.

Caldwell, E. (1932). *Tobacco road*. New York, NY: Charles Scribner's Sons.

Caldwell, E. (1933). *God's little acre*. New York, NY: Viking Press.

Carver, R. (1981). *What we talk about when we talk about love: Stories*. New York, NY: Vintage Books.

Carver, R. (1983). *Cathedral*. New York, NY: Vintage Books.

Chute, C. (1985). *The beans of Egypt, Maine*. New York, NY: Ticknor and Fields.

Chute, C. (1994). *Merry men*. Bellmawr, NJ: Houghton Mifflin Harcourt.

Cisneros, S. (1991). *Woman Hollering Creek: And other stories*. New York, NY: Random House.

Coles, N., & Oresick, P. (Eds.). (1995). *For a living: The poetry of work*. Urbana, IL: University of Illinois Press.

Coles, N., & Zandy, J. (Eds.). (2006). *American working class literature*. New York, NY: Oxford University Press.

Crane, S. (1984). Maggie: *A girl of the streets*. New York, NY: Random House.

Davis, R. H. (1993). *Life in the iron mills and other stories* (2nd ed.). New York, NY: The Feminist Press at CUNY.

DeMott, B. (Ed.). (1996). *Created equal: Reading and writing about class in America*. New York, NY: HarperCollins.

Doctorow, E. L. (1975). *Ragtime*. New York, NY: Random House.

Dybek, S. (1990). *The coast of Chicago: Stories.* New York, NY: Alfred A. Knopf.

Ehrlich, G. (1988). *Heart Mountain.* New York, NY: Viking Adult.

Ellison, R. (1952). *Invisible man.* New York, NY: Random House.

Erdrich, L. (1984). *Love medicine.* New York, NY: Holt, Rinehart, and Winston.

Evans, W. (1941). *Let us now praise famous men.* Boston, MA: Houghton-Mifflin.

Faulkner, W. (1926). *Soldier's pay.* New York, NY: Boni and Liveright.

Faulkner, W. (1932). *Light in August.* New York, NY: Smith and Haas.

Faulkner, W. (1940). *The hamlet.* New York, NY: Random House.

Faulkner, W. (1962). *The reivers.* New York, NY: Random House.

Ford, R. (1987). *Rock Springs: Stories.* Boston, MA: The Atlantic Monthly Press.

Henson, M. (1980). *Ransack.* New York, NY: West End Press.

Henson, M. (1983). *A small room with trouble on my mind.* New York, NY: West End Press.

Gold, H. (1966). *Fathers: A novel in the form of a memoir.* New York, NY: Random House.

Grey, Z. (1919). *Desert of wheat.* New York, NY: Grosset and Dunlap.

Hijuelos, O. (1993). *The fourteen sisters of Emilio Montez O'Brien.* London, England: Farrar Straus Giroux.

Kennedy, W. (1983). *Ironweed.* New York, NY: Viking Press.

Kerouac, J. (1950). *The town and the city.* New York, NY: Harcourt Brace.

Kerouac, J. (1957). *On the road.* New York, NY: Viking Press.

Kerouac, J. (1958). *The subterraneans.* New York, NY: Grove Press.

Kesey, K. (1962). *One flew over the cuckoo's nest.* New York, NY: Viking Press.

Kesey, K. (1964). *Sometimes a great notion.* New York, NY: Viking Press.

Kingsolver, B. (1993). *Pigs in heaven.* New York, NY: HarperCollins.

Kingsolver, B. (2000). *Prodigal summer.* New York, NY: Perennial.

Kingston, M. H. (1975). *The woman warrior: Memories of a girlhood among ghosts.* New York, NY: Vintage Books.

Le Sueur, M. (1990). *Harvest song: Collected essays and stories.* New York, NY: West End Press.

Lewis, S. (1920). *Main street.* New York, NY: Harcourt Brace.

Lewis, S. (1922). *Babbitt.* New York, NY: Harcourt Brace.

Linkon, S. L., & Russo, J. (2003). *Steeltown, USA: Work and memory in Youngstown.* Lawrence, KS: University Press of Kansas.

London, J. (1903). *The call of the wild.* New York, NY: Macmillan.

London, J. (1904). *The sea-wolf.* New York, NY: Macmillan.

Lopez, L. M. (Ed.). (2009). *An angle of vision: Women writers on their poor and working-class roots.* Ann Arbor, MI: University of Michigan Press.

Mann, H. (1904). *Adam Clarke: A story of the toilers.* New York, NY: Popular Book Company.

Martz, S. (Ed.). (1990). *If I had a hammer: Women's work in poetry, fiction, and photographs.* Watsonville, CA: Papier-Mache Press.

Mason, B. A. (1982). *Shiloh and other stories.* New York, NY: Harper & Row.

Mason, B. A. (1985). *In country: A novel.* New York, NY: Harper & Row.

Mason, B. A. (1988). *Spence and Lila.* New York, NY: Harper & Row.

McCall, N. (1995). *Makes me wanna holler.* New York, NY: Vintage Books.

McCourt, F. (1996). *Angela's ashes: A memoir.* New York, NY: Scribner.

McCrumb, S. (2001). *The songcatcher.* New York, NY: Dutton.

McCrumb, S. (2003). *Ghost riders.* New York, NY: Dutton.

Morrison, T. (1970). *The bluest eye.* New York, NY: Holt, Rinehart, and Winston.

Morrison, T. (1987). *Beloved.* New York, NY: Alfred A. Knopf.

Nekola, C., & Rabinowitz, P. (Eds.). (1987). *Writing red: An anthology of American women writers, 1930–1940.* New York, NY: The Feminist Press.

Nichols, J. (1974). *The Milagro beanfield war.* New York, NY: Holt, Rinehart, and Winston.

O'Brien, T. (1973). *If I die in a combat zone, box me up and ship me home.* New York, NY: Delacorte Press.

O'Brien, T. (1990). *The things they carried.* Boston, MA: Houghton-Mifflin Harcourt.

Olsen, T. (1961). *Tell me a riddle: Stories.* New York, NY: Lippincott.

Oresick, P., & Coles, N. (Eds.). (1990). *Working classics: Poems on industrial life.* Urbana, IL: University of Illinois Press.

Pancake, B. D. (1983). *The stories of Breece D'J Pancake.* New York, NY: Little, Brown.

Phillips, J. A. (1984). *Machine dreams.* New York, NY: Dutton.

Phillips, J. A. (2000). *Motherkind.* New York, NY: Alfred A. Knopf.

Pransky, J. (1998). *Modello: A story of hope for the inner city and beyond.* Cabot, VT: Northeast Health Realization Institute.

Sanders, D. (1993). *Her own place.* Chapel Hill, NC: Algonquin Books.

Sayles, J. (1991). *Los gusanos.* New York, NY: HarperCollins.

Shevin, D., & Smith, L. (Eds.). (1996). *Getting by: Stories of working lives.* Huron, OH: Bottom Dog Press.

Shevin, D., Smith, L., & Zandy, J.(Eds.). (1999). *Writing work: Writers on working-class writing.* Huron, OH: Bottom Dog Press.

Sinclair, U. (1906). *The jungle.* New York, NY: Doubleday.

Sinclair, U. (1917). *King coal.* New York, NY: Macmillan.

Steinbeck, J. (1932). *The pastures of heaven: Stories.* New York, NY: Covici-Friede.

Steinbeck, J. (1935). *Tortilla Flat.* New York, NY: Covici-Friede.

Steinbeck, J. (1936). *In dubious battle.* New York, NY: Covici-Friede.

Steinbeck, J. (1937). *Of mice and men.* New York, NY: Covici-Friede.

Steinbeck, J. (1938). *The long valley.* London, England: Penguin.

Steinbeck, J. (1939). *The grapes of wrath.* New York, NY: Viking Press.

Steinbeck, J. (1945). *Cannery Row.* New York, NY: Viking Press.

Steinbeck, J. (1952). *East of Eden.* New York, NY: Viking Press.

Stockett, K. (2009). *The help.* New York, NY: Penguin.

Twain, M. (1882). *The prince and the pauper.* Boston, MA: J. R. Osgood.

Twain, M. (1894). *Pudd'nhead Wilson.* New York, NY: Charles L. Webster.

Upchurch, C. (1996). *Convicted in the womb.* New York, NY: Bantam Books.

Vonnegut, K., Jr. (1979). *Jailbird.* New York, NY: Delacorte Press.

Walker, A. (1970). *The third life of Grange Copeland.* New York, NY: Harcourt Brace Jovanovich.

Walker, A. (1982). *The color purple.* New York, NY: Harcourt Brace Jovanovich.

Zandy, J. (Ed.). (1990). *Calling home: Working class women's writings.* New Brunswick, NJ: Rutgers University Press.

Poetry

Anderson, M. (2000). *Windfall: New and selected poems*. Pittsburgh, PA: University of Pittsburgh Press.

Angelou, M. (1994). *The complete collected poems of Maya Angelou*. New York, NY: Random House.

Antler. (1986). *Last words*. New York, NY: Ballantine Books.

Baraka, A. (1999). *The LeRoi Jones/Amiri Baraka reader* (2nd ed.). New York, NY: Basic Books.

Beatty, J. (1995). *Mad river*. Pittsburgh, PA: University of Pittsburgh Press.

Blair, P. (1999). *Last heat*. Washington, DC: Word Works.

Bryner, J. (1999). *Blind horse*. Huron, OH: Bottom Dog Press.

Coffman, L. (1996). *Likely*. Kent, OH: Kent State University Press.

Daniels, J. (1985). *Places/everyone*. Madison, WI: University of Wisconsin Press.

Daniels, J. (2003). *Show and tell: New and selected poems*. Madison, WI: University of Wisconsin Press.

Dobler, P. (2005). *Collected poems*. Pittsburgh, PA: Autumn House Press.

Knight, E. (1986). *The essential Etheridge Knight*. Pittsburgh, PA: University of Pittsburgh Press.

Kooser, T. (1980). *Sure signs: New and selected poems*. Pittsburgh, PA: University of Pittsburgh Press.

Laux, D. (1994). *What we carry*. Rochester, NY: BOA Editions.

Levine, P. (1991). *What work is: Poems*. New York, NY: Alfred A. Knopf.

Llewellyn, C. (1987). *Fragments from the fire*. New York, NY: Penguin.

McKinney, I. (1989). *Six o'clock mine report*. Pittsburgh, PA: University of Pittsburgh Press.

Paulenich, C. (2009). *Blood will tell*. Buffalo, NY: BlazeVOX Books.

Sandburg, C. (1920). *Smoke and steel*. New York, NY: Harcourt, Brace, and Howe.

Vollmer, J. (1998). *The door open to the fire*. Cleveland, OH: Cleveland State University Press.

APPENDIX I: Ten Core Bridges Constructs

1. Use the lens of economic class to understand and take responsibility for your own societal experience, while being open to the experience of others.

2. At the intersection of poverty with other social disparities (race, gender, physical ability, etc.), address inequalities in access to resources.

3. Define poverty as the extent to which a person, institution, or community does without resources.

4. Build relationships of mutual respect.

5. Base plans on the premise that people in all classes, races, sectors, and political persuasions are problem solvers and need to be at the decision-making table.

6. Base plans on accurate mental models of poverty, middle class, and wealth.

7. At the individual, institutional, and community/policy levels: Stabilize the environment, remove barriers to transition, and build resources.

8. Address all causes of poverty (four principal areas of research).

9. Build long-term support for individual, institutional, and community/policy transitions.

10. Build economically sustainable communities in which everyone can live well.

APPENDIX J: Websites

aha! Process, Inc.: *www.ahaprocess.com*

Bridges™ Out of Poverty: *www.bridgesoutofpoverty.com*

Schenectady Bridges: *schenectadybridges.com*

Stillwater CARES: *stillwatercares.org*

Community Action Duluth (MN): *www.communityactionduluth.org/*

Community Collaboration and Integration: *www.cciunites.org*

Getting Ahead™ Network: *www.gettingahead.com*

St. Joseph County (IN) Bridges Out of Poverty Initiative: *www.sjcbridges.org*

United for a Fair Economy: *www.faireconomy.org/*

Bibliography

Akerlof, G. A., & Kranton, R. E. (2010). *Identity economics: How our identities shape our work, wages, and well-being.* Princeton, NJ: Princeton University Press.

Albelda, R., Folbre, N., & Center for Popular Economics. (1996). *The war on the poor: A defense manual.* New York, NY: The New Press.

Alexander, Michelle. (2010). *The new Jim Crow: Mass incarceration in the age of colorblindness.* New York, NY: The New Press.

Alexie, S. (2007). *The absolutely true diary of a part-time Indian.* New York, NY: Little, Brown.

Andreas, S., & Faulkner, C. (Eds.). (1994). *NLP: The new technology of achievement.* New York, NY: Quill.

Anzaldúa, G. (2007). *Borderlands la frontera: The new mestiza* (3rd ed.). San Francisco, CA: Aunt Lute Books.

Barkai, J. (1996). Teaching negotiation and ADR: The savvy samurai meets the devil. *Nebraska Law Review, 75,* 704–751.

Becker, K. A., Krodel, K. M., & Tucker, B. H. (2009). *Understanding and engaging under-resourced college students: A fresh look at the influence of economic class on teaching and learning in higher education.* Highlands, TX: aha! Process.

Biggs, J. B. (1986). *Enhancing learning skills: The role of metacognition.* In J. A. Bowden (Ed.), Student learning: Research into practice (pp. 131–148). Melbourne, Australia: University of Melbourne Press.

Block, P. (2009). *Community: The structure of belonging.* San Francisco, CA: Berrett-Koehler Publishers.

Brookfield, S. D. (1990). *The skillful teacher: On technique, trust, and responsiveness in the classroom.* San Francisco, CA: Jossey-Bass.

Brouwer, S. (1998). *Sharing the pie: A citizen's guide to wealth and power in America.* New York, NY: Henry Holt.

Brown, J. S., Collins, A., & Duguid, P. (1989). Situated cognition and the culture of learning. *Educational Researcher, 18*(1), 32–42.

Burd-Sharps, S., Lewis, K., & Martins, E. B. (2008). *The measure of America: American human development report 2008–2009.* New York, NY: Columbia University Press.

Chapman, K. J. (2001). Measuring intent: There's nothing 'mere' about mere measurement effects. *Psychology and Marketing, 18*(8), 811–841.

Chinni, D., & Gimpel, J. (2010). *Our patchwork nation: The surprising truth about the 'real' America.* New York, NY: Penguin Group.

Coles, W. E. (1992, November). *Keynote address.* Paper presented at Composition Coordinators' Retreat, Kent State University Regional Campus System, Newbury, OH.

Covey, S. R. (1989). *The 7 habits of highly effective people: Powerful lessons in personal change.* New York, NY: Simon & Schuster.

Crum, T. F. (1998). *The magic of conflict: Turning a life of work into a work of art.* New York, NY: Simon & Schuster.

Daniels, C. (2007). *Ghettonation: A journey into the land of bling and the home of the shameless.* New York, NY: Doubleday.

Davidson, R. J., & Begley, S. (2012). *The emotional life of your brain: How its unique patterns affect the way you think, feel, and live—and how you can change them.* New York, NY: Hudson Street Press.

DeParle, J. (2004). *American dream: Three women, ten kids, and a nation's drive to end welfare.* New York, NY: Viking Penguin.

de Soto, H. (2000). *The mystery of capital: Why capitalism triumphs in the West and fails everywhere else.* New York, NY: Basic Books.

DeVol, P. E. (2010). *Bridges to sustainable communities: A systemwide, cradle-to-grave approach to ending poverty in America.* Highlands, TX: aha! Process.

DeVol, P. E., & Krodel, K. M. (2010). *Facilitator notes for investigations into economic class in America.* Highlands, TX: aha! Process.

DeVol, P. E., & Krodel, K. M. (2010). *Investigations into economic class in America.* Highlands, TX: aha! Process.

DiClemente, C. C., & Velasquez, M. M. (2002). Motivational interviewing and the stages of change. In W. R. Miller & S. Rollnick (Eds.). *Motivational interviewing: Preparing people for change* (2nd ed., pp. 201–216). New York, NY: Guilford Press.

Diller, Jerry V. (1999). *Cultural diversity: A primer for the human services.* Belmont, CA: Wadsworth Publishing Company.

Donnelly, J. (Ed.). (1997). *Who are the question-makers? A participatory evaluation handbook.* New York, NY: Office of Evaluation and Strategic Planning, United Nations Development Program.

Doran, G. T. (1981). There's a S.M.A.R.T. way to write management's goals and objectives. *Management Review, 70*(11), 35–36.

Dowst, K. (1980). The epistemic approach: Writing, knowing, and learning. In T. R. Donovan & B. W. McClelland (Eds.), *Eight approaches to teaching composition* (pp. 65–85). Urbana, IL: National Council of Teachers of English.

Drill down. (2010). Retrieved from http://www.mindtools.com/pages/article/newTMC_02.htm

Fairbanks, M. (2000). Changing the mind of a nation: Elements in a process for creating prosperity. In L. E. Harrison & S. P. Huntington (Eds.), *Culture matters: How values shape human progress* (pp. 268–281). New York, NY: Basic Books.

Farson, R. (1997). *Management of the absurd: Paradoxes in leadership.* New York, NY: Touchstone.

Feuerstein, R. (1985). Structural cognitive modifiability and Native Americans. In S. Unger (Ed.), *To sing our own songs: Cognition and culture in Indian education* (pp. 21–36). New York, NY: Association on American Indian Affairs.

Fisher, R., & Ury, W. (1983). *Getting to YES: Negotiating agreement without giving in.* New York, NY: Penguin.

Freedman, J., & Combs, G. (1996). *Narrative therapy: The social construction of preferred realities.* New York, NY: Norton.

Friedman, B. M. (2006). *The moral consequences of economic growth.* New York, NY: Vintage Books.

Freire, P. (1999). *Pedagogy of the oppressed.* New York, NY: Continuum.

Fuller, R, W. (2004) *Somebodies and nobodies: Overcoming the abuse of rank.* Gabriola Island, BC: New Society Publishers.

Fussell, P. (1983). *Class: A guide through the American status system.* New York, NY: Touchstone.

Galbraith, J. K. (2008). *The Predator state: How conservatives abandoned the free market and why liberals should too.* New York, NY: Free Press.

Galeano, E. (1998). *Upside down: A primer for the looking-glass world.* New York, NY: Metropolitan Books.

Gans, H. J. (1995). *The war against the poor.* New York, NY: Basic Books.

Gee, J. P. (1987). What is literacy? Teaching and learning: *The Journal of Natural Inquiry, 2*(1), 3–11.

Glasmeier, A. K. (2006). *An atlas of poverty in America: One nation, pulling apart, 1960–2003.* New York, NY: Routledge.

Goleman, D. (1995). *Emotional intelligence.* New York, NY: Bantam Books.

Goleman, D. (2006). *Social intelligence: The new science of human relationships.* New York. NY: Bantam.

The growing divide: Inequality and the roots of economic insecurity [Trainer manual]. (2009). Boston, MA: United for a Fair Economy.

Haque, U. (2011). *The new capitalist manifesto: Building a disruptively better business.* Boston, MA: Harvard Business Review Press.

Harrison, L. E., & Huntington, S. P. (Eds.). (2000). *Culture matters: How values shape human progress.* New York, NY: Basic Books.

Hart, B., & Risley, T. R. (1995). *Meaningful differences in the everyday experience of young American children.* Baltimore, MD: Paul H. Brookes.

Henderson, N. (1996). *Resiliency in schools: Making it happen for students and educators.* Thousand Oaks, CA: Corwin Press.

hooks, bell. (2000). *Where we stand: Class matters.* New York, NY: Routledge.

Horstman, M. (n.d.). How to give feedback. Retrieved from http://www.manager-tools.com/podcasts/Manager_Tools_Feedback_Model.pdf

Jaworski, J. (1996). *Synchronicity: The inner path of leadership.* San Francisco, CA: Berrett-Koehler.

Jenkins, L. (2004). *Permission to forget: And nine other root causes of America's frustration with education.* Milwaukee, WI: ASQ Quality Press.

Johnson, A. G. (2006). *Privilege, power, and difference* (2nd ed.). New York, NY: McGraw-Hill.

Joos, M. (1967). The styles of the five clocks. In R. D. Abraham & R. C. Troike (Eds.). *Language and cultural diversity in American education* (pp. 145–149). Englewood Cliffs, NJ: Prentice Hall.

Kelly, M. (2001). *The divine right of capital: Dethroning the corporate aristocracy.* San Francisco, CA: Berrett-Koehler.

Kelly, T. L. (2004). The theme of transformation in the work of Carl Upchurch. *The new tomorrow: A voice for blacks and Latinos.* Retrieved from http://web.pdx.edu/~psu17799/upchurch.htm

Kimmel, M. S., & Ferber, A. L. (Eds.). (2010). *Privilege: A reader.* Boulder, CO: Westview Press.

Kiyosaki, R. T., & Lechter, S. L. (1998). *Rich dad, poor dad.* Paradise Valley, AZ: TechPress.

Klein, N. (2007). *The shock doctrine: The rise of disaster capitalism.* New York, NY: Metropolitan Books.

Kretzmann, J. P., & McKnight, J. L. (1993). *Building communities from the inside out: A path toward finding and mobilizing a community's assets.* Chicago, IL: ACTA.

Kretzmann, J. P., & McKnight, J. L. (with Dobrowolski, S., & Puntenney, D.). (2005). Discovering community power: A guide to mobilizing local assets and your organization's capacity. Evanston, IL: Asset-Based Community Development Institute. Retrieved from http://www.abcdinstitute.org/docs/kelloggabcd.pdf

Krodel, K., Becker, K., Ingle, H., & Jakes, S. (2008). Helping under-resourced learners succeed at the college and university level: What works, what doesn't, and why. Retrieved from http://www.ahaprocess.com

Lareau, A. (2003). *Unequal childhoods: Class, race, and family life.* Berkeley, CA: University of California Press.

Lave, J., & Wenger, E. (1991). *Situated learning: Legitimate peripheral participation.* New York, NY: Cambridge University Press.

Leondar-Wright, B. (2005). *Class matters: Cross-class alliance building for middle-class activists.* Gabriola Island, Canada: New Society Publishers.

Lind, M. (2004). Are we still a middle-class nation? *The Atlantic, 293*(1), 120–128. Retrieved from ahaprocess.com/fi les/HelpingURLSucceed_whitepaper05152009.pdf

Lobovits, D., & Prowell, J. (1996). Unexpected journey: Invitations to diversity. Retrieved from http://www.narrativeapproaches.com/narrative%20papers%20folder/journey_chart.htm

Lopez, L. M. (Ed.). (2009). *An angle of vision: Women writers on their poor and working-class roots.* Ann Arbor, MI: University of Michigan Press.

Lui, M., Robles, B., Leondar-Wright, B., Brewer, R., & Adamson, R. (2006). *The color of wealth: The story behind the U.S. racial wealth divide.* New York, NY: The New Press.

Lupton, R. D., (2011). *Toxic charity: How churches and charities hurt those they help (and how to reverse it).* New York, NY: HarperCollins Publishers.

Marzano, R. J. (2007). *The art and science of teaching: A comprehensive framework for effective instruction.* Alexandria, VA: Association for Supervision and Curriculum Development.

Martinot, S. (2003). *The rule of racialization: Class, identity, governance.* Philadelphia, PA: Temple University Press.

McKnight, J. (1995). The careless society: Community and its counterfeits. New York, NY: Basic Books.

Mehrabian, A. (1981). *Silent messages: Implicit communications of emotions and attitudes.* Belmont, CA: Wadsworth.

MGTC24: Detailed outline of weekly activities. (n.d.). Retrieved from http://www.utsc.utoronto. ca/~phanira/WebSkills/fall09-course-outline-skills.htm

Michaels, W. B. (2006). *The trouble with diversity: How we learned to love identity and ignore inequality.* New York, NY: Metropolitan Books.

Miller, M. (2009). *The tyranny of dead ideas: Letting go of the old ways of thinking to unleash a new prosperity.* New York, NY: Times Books.

Miller, W. R., & Rollnick, S. (2002). *Motivational interviewing: Preparing people for change* (2nd ed.). New York, NY: Guilford Press.

Miringoff, M., & Miringoff, M-L. (1999). *The social health of the nation: How America is really doing.* New York, NY: Oxford University Press.

Montano-Harmon, M. R. (1991). Discourse features of written Mexican Spanish: Current research in contrastive rhetoric and its implications. *Hispania, 74*(2), 417–425.

Moustakas, C. E. (1966). *The authentic teacher: Sensitivity and awareness in the classroom.* Cambridge, MA: Howard A. Doyle.

Murray, C. (2012). *Coming apart: The state of white America, 1960–2010.* New York, NY: Crown Forum.

National College Transition Network. (2009). College for adults. Retrieved from http://www.collegeforadults.org

O'Connor, A. (2001). *Poverty knowledge: Social science, social policy, and the poor in twentieth century U.S. history.* Princeton, NJ: Princeton University Press.

Palmer, P. J. (1998). *The courage to teach: Exploring the inner landscape of a teacher's life.* San Francisco, CA: Jossey-Bass.

Payne, R. K. (2005). *A framework for understanding poverty* (4th rev. ed.). Highlands, TX: aha! Process.

Payne, R. K. (2012). *A framework for understanding poverty: 10 actions to educate students.* Highlands, TX: aha! Process.

Payne, R. K. (2008). *Under-resourced learners: 8 strategies to boost student achievement.* Highlands, TX: aha! Process.

Payne, R. K., DeVol, P. E., & Smith, T. D. (2006). *Bridges out of poverty: Strategies for professionals and communities* (3rd rev. ed.). Highlands, TX: aha! Process.

Pfarr, J. R. (2009). *Tactical communication: Law enforcement tools for successful encounters with people from poverty, middle class, and wealth.* Highlands, TX: aha! Process.

Phillips, K. (2002). *Wealth and democracy: A political history of the American rich.* New York, NY: Broadway Books.

Pimpare, S. (2008). *A people's history of poverty in America.* New York, NY: The New Press.

Pransky, J. (1998). *Modello: A story of hope for the inner city and beyond.* Cabot, VT: Northeast Health Realization Institute.

Putnam, R. D. (2000). *Bowling alone: The collapse and revival of American community.* New York, NY: Simon & Schuster.

Rivlin, G. (2010). *Broke, USA: From pawnshops to Poverty, Inc.—How the working poor became big business.* New York, NY: HarperCollins Publishers.

Robinson, E. (2010). *Disintegration: The splintering of black America.* New York, NY: Doubleday.

Rose, M. (1989). *Lives on the boundary: The struggles and achievements of America's underprepared.* New York, NY: Free Press.

Roseland, M. (2005). *Toward sustainable communities: Resources for citizens and their governments.* Gabriola Island, Canada: New Society Publishers.

Rothenberg, P. S. (2005). *White privilege: Essential readings on the other side of racism* (2nd ed.). New York: NY: Worth Publishers.

Sapolsky, R. M. (1998). *Why zebras don't get ulcers: An updated guide to stress, stress-related diseases, and coping.* New York, NY: W. H. Freeman.

Sawyer, D. (Anchor). (1991). True colors [Television series episode segment]. In M. Lukasiewicz (Producer), *PrimeTime Live.* New York, NY: American Broadcasting Corporation.

Senge, P. M. (1990). *The fifth discipline: The art and practice of the learning organization.* New York, NY: Currency Doubleday.

Senge, P., Smith, B., Kruschwitz, N., Laur, J., & Schley, S. (2010). *The necessary revolution: Working together to create a sustainable world.* New York, NY: Broadway Books.

Sharron, H., & Coulter, M. (2004). *Changing children's minds: Feuerstein's revolution in the teaching of intelligence.* Highlands, TX: aha! Process.

Shaughnessy, M. P. (1977). *Errors and expectations: A guide for the teacher of basic writing.* New York, NY: Oxford University Press.

Shebat, G. (2009). *Fundamentals of college writing* [Course assignments]. Youngstown, OH: Youngstown State University.

Shipler, D. K. (2004). *The working poor: Invisible in America.* New York, NY: Alfred A. Knopf.

Shuman, M. H. (2007). *The small-mart revolution: How local businesses are beating the global competition.* San Francisco, CA: Berrett-Koehler Publishers.

Smith, A. (1994). *An inquiry into the nature and causes of the wealth of nations.* New York, NY: The Modern Library.

Smith, L. (2010). *Psychology, poverty, and the end of social exclusion: Putting our practice to work.* New York, NY: Teachers College Press.

Smith, H. (1994). *The illustrated world's religions: A guide to our wisdom traditions.* New York, NY: HarperCollins.

Sowell, T. (1997). *Migrations and cultures: A world view.* New York, NY: HarperCollins.

Sowell, T. (1998, October 5). Race, culture, and equality. *Forbes,* 144–149.

Stout, L. (2011). *Collective visioning: How groups can work together for a just and sustainable future.* San Francisco, CA: Berrett-Koehler Publishers.

Surowiecki, J. (2005). *The wisdom of crowds.* New York, NY: Anchor.

Taylor-Ide, D., & Taylor, C. E. (2002). *Just and lasting change: When communities own their futures.* Baltimore, MD: Johns Hopkins University Press.

Tett, G. (2010). *Fool's gold: The inside story of J.P. Morgan and how Wall Street greed corrupted its bold dream and created a financial catastrophe.* New York, NY: Free Press.

Twin Cities RISE! (2009). *Empowerment: A course in personal empowerment.* Minneapolis; MN: Author.

Tuckman, B. W. (1965). Developmental sequence in small groups. *Psychological Bulletin, 63*(6), 384–399.

Upchurch, C. (1996). *Convicted in the womb.* New York, NY: Bantam Books.

Valenzuela, C., & Addington, J. (2006a). *Four features of racism* [Available from Minnesota Collaborative Anti-Racism Initiative, 1671 Summit Ave., St. Paul, MN 55105].

Valenzuela, C., & Addington, J. (2006b). *Systemic racism: Daily strategies for survival and beyond* [Available from Minnesota Collaborative Anti-Racism Initiative, 1671 Summit Ave., St. Paul, MN 55105].

Vella, J. (2002). *Learning to listen, learning to teach: The power of dialogue in educating adults* (rev. ed.). San Francisco, CA: Jossey-Bass.

Washburne, C. (1958). Conflicts between educational theory and structure. *Educational Theory, 8*(2), 87–94.

Wenger, E., McDermott, R., & Snyder, W. M. (2002). *Cultivating communities of practice: A guide to managing knowledge.* Boston, MA. Harvard Business School Publishing.

WETA. (2010). Home. Retrieved from http://www.ldonline.org/index.php

Wheeler, R. S. (2008). Becoming adept at code-switching. *Educational Leadership, 65*(7), 54–58.

Wheeler, R. S., & Swords, R. (2006). *Code-switching: Teaching Standard English in urban classrooms.* Urbana, IL: National Council of Teachers of English.

Wheeler, R. S., & Swords, R. (2010). *Code-switching lessons: Grammar strategies for linguistically diverse writers.* Portsmouth, NH: Heinemann.

Wilkinson, R. G., & Pickett, K. (2009). *The spirit level: Why more equal societies almost always do better.* London, England: Penguin.

Wilson, W. J. (1990). *The truly disadvantaged: The inner city, the underclass, and public policy.* Chicago, IL: The University of Chicago Press.

World Bank. (2005). *World development report 2006: Equity and development.* New York, NY: Oxford University Press.

Zull, J. (2002). *The art of changing the brain: Enriching the practice of teaching by exploring the biology of learning.* Sterling, VA: Stylus.

About the Author

Philip E. DeVol, president and CEO of DeVol & Associates, LLC, has been training and consulting on poverty issues since 1997. He co-authored *Bridges Out of Poverty: Strategies for Professionals and Communities* (1999) with Ruby K. Payne, Ph.D., and Terie Dreussi Smith, and in 2004 he wrote the first edition of *Getting Ahead in a Just-Gettin'-By World: Building Your Resources for a Better Life* to help people in poverty investigate the impact of poverty on their communities and themselves.

He works in North America and internationally with communities that apply Bridges constructs—including sites in Canada, Australia, and Slovakia—where Bridges Communities have been awarded two European Union grants to further the work there. Bridges Communities bring people together from all classes, political persuasions, and sectors to address all causes of poverty in a systemic way. The many Bridges Communities using Getting Ahead led to this new edition of *Getting Ahead in a Just-Gettin'-By World.*

DeVol consults with Bridges Communities on a variety of topics to assist knowledge transfer among the many individuals, organizations, and communities that are adopting Bridges principles in their settings, as well as developing new levels of expertise. In addition to writing and consulting, DeVol works with aha! Process's collaborations with other organizations to implement innovative, high-impact strategies for ending poverty and building sustainable communities where everyone can do well.

His 2010 book *Investigations into Economic Class in America,* co-authored with Karla M. Krodel, applies the Getting Ahead concepts to college life for under-resourced postsecondary students. That book was honored in 2011 by the Association of Educational Publishers, winning its Distinguished Achievement Award for Adult Curriculum (Life Skills); the book was also a 2011 Innovation Award finalist. Finally, a collection of DeVol's essays and articles was published in 2010 under the title *Bridges to Sustainable Communities: A Systemwide, Cradle-to-Grave Approach to Ending Poverty in America,* describes how communities, organizations, and businesses across the U.S. have applied Bridges concepts.

In his current work DeVol builds on his 19 years as director of an Ohio outpatient substance abuse treatment facility in which he designed treatment programs and collaborative systems for school-based prevention, community-based intervention, and Ohio's first alternative school for recovering young people. During this time he also co-authored *The Complete Guide to Elementary Student Assistance Programs* with Linda Christensen.

He and his wife, Susan, live in the country near Marengo, Ohio, just a few miles from his two children and their three grandchildren.

Notes

Notes

Notes

Notes

WE'D LIKE TO HEAR FROM YOU!

Join our Network:

www.GettingAhead.com

Share with us on Facebook:

www.facebook.com/BridgesOutofPoverty

Respond to our blog:

www.ahaprocess.com/blog

Subscribe to our YouTube channel:

www.yourtube.com/ahaprocess

Visit us on the web:

www.BridgesOutofPoverty.com

Visit our online store for related titles by Philip DeVol

www.ahaprocess.com

aha! Process, Inc.
P.O. Box 727
Highlands, Texas 77562

Local: +1 (281) 426-5300
Toll-Free: +1 (800) 424-9484
Fax: +1 (281) 426-8598